GOLF
ROAD

GOLF ROAD

My Time with
The Masters of the Game

LAWRENCE MALESTIC

FOREWORD BY
GARY PLAYER

Printed in the United States of America.
First paperback edition May 2022.

Cover and layout design by G Sharp Design, LLC.
www.gsharpmajor.com

ISBN 978-0-578-28606-8 (paperback)

Library of Congress Control Number: 2022909243

For the true loves of my life, Lynne & Lauren.

TABLE OF CONTENTS

FOREWORD
by Gary Player

HAVING COMPETED IN just about every corner of the globe, and on some of golf's grandest stages, it's pretty safe to say that I absolutely adore the game. It's in my blood. That is precisely why I chose many decades ago to make it my livelihood.

There have been countless books written about the game of golf, from instruction manuals, to narratives about the biggest tournaments in its illustrious history, to anecdotal tales about everyday occurrences on the course. I've written several on the subject myself. But, there have been very few written from the perspective of one who aids a professional golfer in his elusive quest for victory—a tour caddie.

Larry Malestic was my caddie in the early 90's when I was competing regularly on what was then the Senior PGA Tour. Our relationship was a dichotomy; part employer/employee, and another part father/son. Golf just happened to be the avenue that would lead to our friendship.

What you are about to read is the extraordinary tale of his caddie evolution from novice, to seasoned professional, during a glorious period of the sport. I'm proud to say that I stood on the fairway beside him during part of that transformation. I will never forget the look on his face sitting next to me as we drove up Magnolia Lane at Augusta National, his first trip up the fabled drive.

So, enjoy your journey down ***Golf Road: My Time with The Masters of the Game***. My sincere wish is that you enjoy reading these stories at least half as much as we enjoyed living them.

Gary Player

INTRODUCTION

IN ONE OF his renowned monologues, the legendary comedian Jerry Seinfeld quipped, "Did ya' ever notice that all butlers are named Jeeves? If your parents name you Jeeves, they've pretty much mapped out your life for you."

Oddly enough, it was very likely my destiny to live a large portion of my life as a professional tour caddie, because my parents raised me on a street called *Golf Road*. My father still owns that house in Glenview, Illinois, and although he never stood on the front lawn when I was a baby and proclaimed, "My boy was born on Golf Road and he's going to be a big success in the golf business," it turned out that I would, in many ways, live on Golf Road until the end of my days.

During the years between 1984 and 1997, I had the unique privilege of working for, and mingling with the likes of Lee Trevino, Chi Chi Rodriguez, Jack Nicklaus, Arnold Palmer and dozens of other players whose names are vital to the history of the game. As a professional caddie to the superstars of golf, I had a backstage pass to the inner sanctum of the game, and a career that would take me to 18 countries and the top courses on earth, including the hallowed grounds of Augusta National, the Old Course at St. Andrews, Royal Melbourne and other fabled venues. During those golden years I packed the bag for more than 20 winners, and in the process, got an insider's view of what goes in the world of professional golf.

My intention for this book was not to produce a Hollywood tell-all that would knock these stellar celebrities off their pedestals by exposing their peculiar personalities, private exploits and financial excesses. But it's impossible to write about them without revealing at least *a few* of those details, so although I have tried to maintain the utmost respect, I will admit that some of the golf legends were difficult, demanding, eccentric and downright abusive. Some of what I'm sharing in these pages will probably get me into hot water with my former employers, but my intention was to paint a fair and accurate picture of life on the road, and on the links with the emperors of the golf universe.

I did not intend to write an instruction manual on golf, though I do provide some detailed narratives about how certain tournaments were played and won (or lost), and the specific struggles that some of my players had in their quests for victory. One of the many perks of rubbing elbows with the legends of the game was polling them on their swing and putting philosophies. For example, I'd ask them if they felt like they putted mostly with their left hand or right hand, or a combination of the two, and the answers were as different as their styles. Gary Player's putting was anchored by his left hand, and more specifically, the absence of breakdown of the left wrist. But watch Jack Nicklaus and it's evident that he was hitting it with his right hand, using the left strictly for support. I asked Lee Trevino which hand he putted with, and he broke into a lengthy tale about how he took it back with his right and through with his left. He even had a doctor friend make a cast for his left wrist to prohibit it from breaking down through impact when he practiced. The cast had a zipper in it so he could take it on and off.

What you'll find in these pages in an affectionate overview of my days on the professional circuit as not only a caddie, but as a trusted confidant to my employers. I knew their secrets, their habits and their inner demons. I also knew the members of their entourages and their intimate circles of friends and family, from their wives and children, to the pilots who flew their private jets.

I've read other books written from a caddie's perspective, but almost every one of the authors was a writer who *became* a caddie for the sole purpose of writing a book. My saga expresses the flip-side of that scenario…I am a caddie who became a writer for the sole purpose of telling my story.

I had the good fortune to play a small role in the game during an exquisite era of its history. I look back and yearn for those bygone days, just the way many do for the golden years of Hollywood. But they're both gone forever, and all I can do now is describe this extraordinary epoch in the history of golf so that you can savor it for yourself and hopefully understand what a grand time it was.

THE SENIOR SKINS
GAME, 1991

THE FIRST TEE announcer's voice belted out over the loud-speaker system, "Now on the tee, the winner of 18 major championships, including six Masters…"

Standing on that tee with Jack Nicklaus, Arnold Palmer, Gary Player, Lee Trevino and my boss, Chi Chi Rodriguez, my ass was so tight you couldn't get a pin up there with a jackhammer. My heart felt like it was going to explode any second. Even after eight years as a professional caddie to some of the biggest names in the business, I still had trouble getting enough oxygen. This was five-minutes-to-midnight-on-execution-night pressure.

The men in this fivesome harbored enough silver in their trophy cases to provide prestigious tableware for half the country, and the pressure was on.

Tee balls were all struck, and we were off down the first fairway. For a moment I reminisced about how many times over the years I'd walked a golf course packing a bag (or two, or three). But this wasn't the same as looping for Mr. and Mrs. Dwyer on a Sunday afternoon at North Shore Country Club. This time I was surrounded by golf's *Chosen Ones.*

I made yet another mental note to check and double-check all yardages. This was no time for a mathematical error. When reading putts, I needed to get a look from as many angles as possible, and most importantly, I had to do it with my best poker face. I couldn't let anyone see me sweat. If Chi Chi sensed even a whisper of anxiety from me, I'd be of no use to him.

All approach shots were resting safely on the first green when the ramification of having five players (instead of the traditional four), hit me. Tending the pins was going to be interesting.

Golf etiquette dictates that it is not proper to step on a golfer's line, and while this may seem trivial to a non-golfer, anyone in the industry knows to obey this sacred golf commandment. Every professional golfer at some point in his career has muttered the words, "Did you see that? He stepped right in my line!"

Unfortunately, I was the first one to cross the minefield. Did I mention they had this thing surrounded? They were coming at it from every direction. We lined up Chi Chi's putt, decided on line and speed, and I embarked upon my mission to grab the flag. I took a deep breath and assessed the situation.

How the #$@& am I going to get in there?

Chi Chi was waiting. I decided on the best route to the hole, and timidly crept my way toward the flag. I probably looked like I had sore feet, taking tiny steps forward, edging closer and closer until I was almost there, with my arm outstretched.

And then, finally, I got it. Mission accomplished!

With flag in hand, I was filled with a combination of elation and relief. And then it happened...a professional caddie's worst nightmare. In front of golf's elite and millions of television viewers,

Lee Buck Trevino shouted out not once, but twice, "LARRY, YOU'RE STANDING IN PALMER'S LINE!"

Mortification doesn't even begin to hint at what I was feeling at that moment. I felt as if I had been stripped publicly and was standing naked in front of the entire golf world. Everyone in the group looked at me like I had just told the Pope a hooker joke. But it was far worse than that. *I'd stood in the King's line.* In medieval times I would have been drawn and quartered for this offense. If the Golfing Gods allowed every tour caddie one instance where he could snap his fingers and disappear instantly, I would have used mine right there.

I jumped away from the pin and meekly made my way back, this time more successfully. Chi Chi two-putted for par, and after everyone else holed out, we moved on. But for the next six months I said to myself a thousand times, *"Nice way to start your first Senior Skins Game, moron!"*

The funniest thing about it was that Arnold was oblivious to the whole incident. I think he was too busy checking out a blonde that he spotted in the gallery.

The Senior Skins Game train rolled along. Putts were made, holes were halved, and skins were made here and there. But in this format, the last six holes were the most valuable, and the big money was still out there for the taking.

We stepped on the 18th tee with a four-hole carryover. The pressure had been mounting, and by this time even the normally gregarious Lee Trevino was as quiet as a mime. The winner of this hole would be the champion of Senior Skins '91.

A peculiar aspect of the Skins Game format is that it is the only time you will ever witness professional golfers genuinely pulling for one another. Such was the case on the 18th green that day. Jack had made tap-in birdie and someone needed to make a putt on top of him to force a playoff. It was Jack vs. the world.

Gary Player was first to putt and missed from the cheap seats, but Arnold was in there tight and rolled his in.

Bunkered at the Senior Skins Game.

The tournament officials informed the group that sudden death would commence on the tenth hole. Chi Chi quipped, "Why do they have to call it sudden death? We are seniors, you know!"

We began our lengthy trek over to number 10 when something happened that I will never forget. Allow me to preface this story with a little insider morsel. Lee Trevino was the only guy who ever got inside Jack Nicklaus' steel trap of a mind. He never missed an opportunity to psychologically spar with Jack, and he was brilliant at it. A perfect example was The U.S. Open at Merion. This story is legendary in the golf world, and it bears repeating here.

Back in 1971, Nicklaus and Trevino paired off against each other in an 18-hole playoff for the U.S. Open trophy. They were on the first tee preparing to commence play when Lee pulled a large rubber snake out of his bag and threw it at Jack. I was only nine years old at the time and wasn't even close to beginning my journey into golf, but I've seen the now-famous footage of the event, and it appeared to startle Jack, even though he claims it didn't. For the casual observer, this appeared to be just an amusing prank, but it was far more serious that, because it was well known in the circle that Jack was deathly afraid of snakes. Maybe Lee wanted to find out if it was true, and if it wasn't, we'd all get a big laugh out of it. Whether it actually had any bearing on Jack's play, we'll never know. His name is on the U.S. Open trophy several times, but was conspicuously absent that year.

With that story in mind, you can begin to understand the way Lee liked to mess with Jack and the Senior Skins Game 20 years later was no exception when, as we were all walking over to the 10th, a man drove by in a golf cart and Jack called out to him.

"Yes, Mr. Nicklaus?" the driver responded, stopping his cart. "Could you give me a lift over to the clubhouse? I have to take a leak." Jack asked.

"Sure, Mr. Nicklaus! Hop on in!"

Before the man could even think of hitting the gas, Lee yelled out, "Hold on a minute, Jack!" By this time I figured he had to go too and wanted to ride along. But Lee didn't have to use the bathroom. Instead, he went into a detailed pitch (that he'd obviously planned in advance, which is the beauty of his sharp wit) about how it was unfair for Jack to ride to the bathroom when everybody else had to walk.

"Jack, the way I see it, you're gonna get a lift all the way over to that clubhouse, take a leak and get a lift back to the tenth tee. You'll show up there fresh, cool and rested, but the rest of us gotta' trudge over there in the hot sun. It ain't fair. If we gotta' walk, you gotta' walk!"

The rest of us were thinking, *he's kidding...right?* But he wasn't kidding, and Jack knew it. He leapt off the cart and stormed off in the direction of the clubhouse.

We continued on our trek to the tenth tee. The group was completely silent now, and tension filled the air like the Hawaiian humidity. I figured this must have been what it was like on the Bataan Death March.

Chi Chi was walking beside me.

"Pards, can you believe Lee just did that?"

"Hell yeah, he's been doing it for years. Why stop now?" I countered.

At that moment Lee sidled up to me and said gleefully, "Hey Larry. You think I got Jack's chili hot?" The question dripped with conniving pleasure.

"Yeah. He looked pretty pissed off," I replied.

Lee continued to walk beside me, a spring in his step, looking genuinely pleased with himself. I think he considered Jack's mind a place only he could sneak into. Everyone else got stopped at the door.

Needless to say, when Jack finally joined us at the 10th tee after his bathroom break, there wasn't a lot of chatter going on, and the notion that Lee was off Jack's Christmas list was palpable. Jack was wearing a stone-faced stare that I'm sure every player who has ever finished second to him has seen before. Basically, we were sitting at a stoplight in a Volkswagen waiting to race a guy in a Lamborghini. We were about to get *smoked*.

The tenth at Mauna Lani is a long par 5, not reachable in two—unless you're Jack Nicklaus and Lee Trevino has just gotten under your skin. After all the mere mortals hit their lay-up shots, we took the second-longest walk of the past 30 minutes. The trek to Jack's drive took so long, my clothes went out of style. He absolutely nuked it. The 3 iron that followed was a Nicklaus work of art...a high, cutting beauty that I thought might burn up on re-entry. It landed softly on the green somewhere around 25 feet from the hole. Clearly, one of the others would have to stuff a wedge in there tight *and* make the putt.

No one scared the hole with his approach, and Jack routinely cozied his putt up there for easy birdie. The rest of the participants grinded over their putts, but it just wasn't meant to be.

The writing was on the wall, and Jack was not going to be denied. After no other birdie was made, it was anti-climactic. The cameras swarmed Jack as he was designated Senior Skins Game Champion of 1991. The rest of the group separated for our respective sojourns back to the clubhouse, our tails between our legs.

As Chi Chi and I walked, he let off some steam.

"I don't know why Lee does that crap, pissing Jack off like that. If you're gonna go bear hunting, you better make sure you got enough bullets."

I wondered how many times Lee's ploys blew up in his face and everyone else was left in Jack's wake. I wondered if the other players were griping to their caddies about how they wished Lee would just keep his mouth shut. I even wondered what Lee himself was thinking on the way back. Would he do it again? Remembering the giddiness in his voice during our brief chat, it's more than safe to say that he wouldn't have been able to resist.

And so, Chi Chi got shut out at Skins '91. Not one. Nada. Zilch. Zippo. We traveled all that way for a shot at the brass ring and came home with nothing but a deep tan; all of that effort in vain. The week wasn't a total write-off though. I got a chance to peek into one of the craftiest minds in golf, and Chi Chi, being the class act that he is, still paid me a couple of thousand for my efforts.

I'M ALRIGHT, NO NEED TO WORRY 'BOUT ME!

"NORTH SHORE COUNTRY Club is looking for boys to caddie this summer," Sister Agnes announced, her scratchy voice emanating from the P.A. system of Room 8 at St. Isaac Jogues Catholic School. "Anyone interested should come to my office at 3:00 p.m. today."

She was a large, intimidating woman, and the thought of going to her office was less appealing than having a cavity filled, but I had a burning desire to make some money, and decided that this deserved further investigation. It was impossible for me to know at the time how that one announcement would shape my life in such a deep and profound way.

I retrieved the phone number to the club and a few other minor details provided by Sister Agnes. Despite the fact that I knew nothing about golf and was a scrawny 11 year-old, the thought of making money over the summer appealed to the Warren Buffett in me.

I raced home and excitedly told my mother about my plan to get into the caddie business. She pretended to be interested as I made my call to the club. I was informed that I had to be 13 years old, and was required to sign up as soon as possible. This posed two problems. The first and most obvious was that I wasn't old enough, and the second and more difficult to overcome, was that I would need a ride to the club. You see, I was one of seven children, and to say Mom wasn't too enthusiastic about driving us around would be an understatement. I would have rather trekked across the Himalayas barefoot than ask my mom for a ride anywhere. But this was a special case, and I proceeded to beg my mother to take me to a place called North Shore Country Club. She begrudgingly agreed, but immediately went into a rant about how this wouldn't be a regular occurrence.

We made the left-hand turn from Glenview Road onto the majestic driveway leading up to the opulent clubhouse, and I knew I was in a different world. The place had a different aura about it. It reeked of wealth, and I had never seen wealth before.

We pulled into the parking lot and I tried to put on an air like I was meant to be there, but my façade failed miserably. I meandered up to an opening in the building with a large, shiny ledge in what appeared to be some kind of storeroom, which I later learned was the bag room window. This was an area in which I would be soon spending more time than I could possibly fathom.

A boy of about 18 appeared in the window and stood looking down at me.

"I'm here to become a caddie," I proclaimed.

"That's great," he sneered. "Now could you please get out of the window?"

He said this with great authority while pointing down at a line painted on the ground. I backed up and noticed what looked like a goalie crease in front of a hockey net, and that was my introduction to one of the 10 caddie commandments of North Shore Country Club…stay out of the bag room window or there'll be hell to pay.

"Sorry," I muttered quietly.

"Jay, we got a kid out here who wants to be a looper," he yelled behind him.

What the hell is he talking about? I don't want to become a looper, whatever that is. I want to become a caddie.

"Be right there," a deep voice resonated from a back office.

I waited patiently, making sure not to venture anywhere near the sacred line protecting the almighty bag room window. I scanned the finely manicured grounds of the golf course and two words came to mind…*clean* and *green*. Then I heard a voice that would have an impact on my life for years to come.

"I'm Jay, the caddie master."

Jay Moorehead was a Redwood of a man, standing 6'5". He was tall, but the most notable feature of his physique was a bulbous, pot-belly that made him look like he was smuggling a bowling ball under his sweater. He had salt-and-pepper hair swept toward the front of his weathered face, a mustache, and a hearing aid in each ear.

He had a speech impediment that made him sound like Bill Murray's character Carl Spackler in the movie Caddyshack. As a matter of fact, it was rumored that at some point in his life, Bill Murray crossed paths with Jay and modeled Spackler's dialect after him. Murray was from the immediate area, leaving it as a distinct possibility, but deep down everyone knew this was just caddie lore.

"So you want to become a looper," he said.

"Yes," I replied. "I'm here to become a caddie."

"You have to be 13 to caddie. Are you 13?" he asked.

"Yes, I am," I responded. Caddie commandment number two is *lie if the benefit is great enough.*

"You're kinda small for 13. Are you sure you're 13?" he quizzed me a second time.

"Yeah, I'm 13," I said confidently.

"Okay, be back here tomorrow at 3:30 for caddie lessons."

As I made my way back to the car where my mom was waiting, I was formulating my good news/bad news pitch for her. The good news was that I had talked my way past the underage issue and needed to return for caddie lessons the following day. The bad news was that I'd need another ride.

The next day at school, time dragged on endlessly as I eagerly anticipated my 3:30 appointment and the beginning of my tutelage. Mom emitted only a minimum amount of static on the drive to the club, much to my pleasant surprise.

Donnie Perkowitz was the assistant caddie master and my instructor for my first caddie lesson. He showed me how to pick up the golf bag properly, and once upon my shoulder, swing it around so that the weight of it was carried on my lower back. We made our way to the first hole where he proceeded to tee up a driver and hit it down the fairway.

"Where'd it go? he asked me.

"Where did what go? I stupidly inquired.

"THE BALL!"

"Oh. Uh, it went that way," I sheepishly answered, pointing in the general vicinity of the first fairway.

"Good," he said. "Remember to keep quiet and keep your eye on the ball."

I thought I was doing a pretty good job until we arrived at the first green and I set the golf bag down right in the middle of it.

"No, no, no! What are you doing? You leave the bag on the side of the green, not on it," he snapped.

"Sorry," I replied meekly.

I told you I didn't know squat about the silly game, except that it was played by old men wearing really ugly pants. What I really learned that day was one of the most important caddie commandments of all. It is of paramount importance, no matter what level of caddying you're at. You gotta' have a chrome-plated heart. There's no room for softies in this business. This truth stuck with me for decades.

A couple more days of caddie basics, such as replacing divots, cleaning clubs and tending the flag, and I was officially ready for my inaugural loop.

The term loop originated in Scotland, the home of golf, and also the home of the famous St. Andrews golf courses, which are set up in such a way that the front nine goes out away from the clubhouse and the back nine comes back in, forming a "loop." Thus, caddies were called "loopers." This word would become a staple in my lexicon for years to come. I can still to this day hear Jay's voice saying, "C'mon Maletnick, got a loop for ya'." I'll probably hear that on my deathbed.

Even though I was now a legitimate looper, I didn't quite have the nerve to catch my first loop on a weekend, so I came up with a plethora of excuses. The most convenient was that mom wouldn't drive me anymore and I would have to bike the three miles to the club. I had several other good excuses, but the bottom line was, I was scared. But eventually I mustered up the courage, saddled up the old Schwinn and made my way to NSCC It was show time! As I entered the caddie yard through the gate in the chain link fence, Jay saw me and said, "There he is. I didn't think we were ever going to see you again."

I found a vacant spot on a bench in the caddie yard trying as hard as I could to emit the vibe that I was supposed to be there, but in truth, I felt like the new kid in school. I sat quietly and took in the sights and sounds of all things looper (gambling, cussing, spitting and other debauchery are some of the first activities that come to mind). What was really evident to me was that everyone seemed to have a nickname. Yoohoo derived his from the fact that he walked in the caddie yard every day with a bottle of the chocolate drink in hand. Yoda had the misfortune of resembling the *Star Wars* character, and Motormouth never shut up. There was Sport, Curly, Cookie and a host of others. I wondered what moniker I would get stuck with.

I also noticed Jay's modus operandi as he assigned the loops. He'd sit on the bag room window looking down at the pairing sheet. Then he would start walking slowly, perusing the yard like a shark hunting tuna. His eyes would fix on someone and he'd move a little faster in their direction. Then he'd go in for the kill, ending with those magic words, "C'mon, gotta' loop for ya'. You take…"

I watched this process for quite a while and began to wonder if I would ever get picked. I was learning another vital caddie commandment. Hurry up and wait.

After a couple of hours, devoid of any hope that I'd finally get assigned a bag, I noticed Jay leering in my direction. Could it be? He strolled over, pointed at me like he was picking me out of a criminal lineup and announced, "C'mon, gotta' loop for ya'!"

My heart raced as he escorted me past the bag rack to two carts facing the first tee. Then he sprang the wonderful news on me that I would be "popping my cherry with a cart job." Cart caddying was mentioned during my training, but not in depth, and the deer in the headlights expression on my face probably told Jay that I wasn't too excited about this scenario.

"It's the same as carrying a single, only you're not packing the bag. Just run behind the cart, replace their divots, rake their traps, wash their balls on the green and tend the flag for them." Jay instructed.

That's great, my first loop and instead of caddying for one person, I'm working for a foursome. It wouldn't be so bad if I knew what the hell I was doing.

I made my way to the first tee where the foursome I was assigned to was prepping for their round, their heads buried in their golf bags as they searched for gloves, balls, tees and other necessities. I stood quietly waiting for someone to notice me. Finally, one looked up and said, "Hi, Son. What's your name?"

"I'm Larry, and I'll be your caddie for today."

"Great, Larry. I'm Mr. Zanoni, that's Mr. Twist, Mr. Seng, and that gentleman over there is Mr. Lorenz."

They acknowledged me half-heartedly as they went about their pre-game activities. Then Mr. Lorenz bellowed out in a gruff voice, "Now get on out there and keep your eye on the balls. That's what we have you for!"

That one statement was a harbinger of my first day as a caddie, because Mr. Lorenz was all over me like a pit bull on a poodle. He yelled at me on the 2nd for moving while he was playing his shot, the 4th for losing his ball in the trees (even though I didn't hit it there), and the 7th for raking his footprints in the bunker before he played his shot (he was kind enough to lecture me on the rules of the game after that faux pas). Then he bitched me out on the 9th for standing too close to him. I was waiting to get reamed for breathing his air.

I was seriously considering making a run for freedom when we made the turn, but decided to stick it out for the back nine and then put an end to the shortest career in the history of looping.

Then something happened that would shape my future. Mr. Zanoni, having witnessed the depth of my abuse on the front nine, decided to intercede on my behalf.

"Son, come on over here," he beckoned.

I made my way across the 10th tee and he slung his arm around my shoulder and said, "I want you to stay by me the rest of the round. Okay?"

"Yes, sir," I replied.

Mario Zanoni became my bodyguard for the final nine holes of that round. He shielded me from Bob Lorenz like a Secret Service agent guarding the president, and even helped me with my caddie duties. If Mr. Lorenz barked at me about where his ball was, Mr. Zanoni would answer for me. He grabbed the flag for me when I was raking a sand trap, and replaced a couple of divots when I was across the fairway. Most importantly, he kept Mr. Lorenz off my ass. I think he would have taken a bullet for me if Mr. Lorenz tried to pick me off.

By the grace of God and with some enormous help from a kind man, I made it through that first round unscathed. I've thought about how differently things may have turned out if Mario Zanoni hadn't come to my rescue the way he did. I can guarantee you that if I was man-handled that whole round, I probably wouldn't have ever stepped foot onto North Shore Country Club again.

Recently I was compelled to share this story with someone I knew deserved to hear it. Mario Zanoni passed away some time ago but I knew that his son, Bill, was a member at North Shore. I tracked him down, gave him a call and introduced myself. He remembered me, and we shared some small talk before I began to give him the highlights of my career as a professional tour caddie. I told him about how I had been to 18 countries, caddied for 26 winners, worked the Masters twice and the British Open three times, and lost to Jack Nicklaus in an 18-hole playoff for the U.S. Senior Open while caddying for Chi Chi Rodriguez. After finishing my verbal resume, I told him the story about the kindness of his father and the immeasurable impact it had on the course of my life. There was a long silence on the other end of the phone and then he told me he really appreciated my sharing the story with him. I'm sure it conjured up wonderful memories of his father, and I am so glad that I called him.

I did make it back to NSCC several more times that summer, but it was a couple of years before I really immersed myself and became a fixture at the club. After a couple of my friends discovered caddying and became part of the scene, I felt much more comfortable there.

I've already made it quite clear that my mom's wardrobe did not include a chauffeur's cap; thus my travels to and from the club were of the two-wheel variety. Mornings in Chicago could be beyond brisk, even in the summer, which made the first leg of the journey almost unbearable. I also made the daily mistake of under-dressing, which didn't help. Wrapping my hands in my caddie towel to ward off the bitter cold made the three miles a little more tolerable. Finally arriving at the club meant the end of the pain, and I don't believe I've ever appreciated the warmth of the sun as much as I did on those mornings in the caddie yard after getting off that bicycle. After going once or twice around the course, I would despise that very planet by the end of the day.

The pre-loop shenanigans were always something to look forward to. It was almost a bummer to catch an early loop because you knew more fun was to be had in the caddie yard than on the golf course. As I've said, gambling was a ubiquitous vice in the yard, as caddies could be very creative in coming up with activities to bet on, whether it was rolling balls into the holes on the practice green (or the slots in the sewer cover) or putting money on your golfer's score against another in your foursome. The only thing that I don't recall betting on was whether another looper would pick his nose and eat it, like they did in the movie *Caddyshack*, but that's only because no one thought of it.

Anytime I refer to the caddie yard I'm compelled to think of a prison yard, and frankly, they're very similar in that you see groups or cliques mulling about and bullshitting. You definitely wanted to be associated with the cool guys, not the dweebs or the nerds. I can guarantee you that the act of bullying originated in a caddie yard. The worst was being targeted as the lone dork of the yard, which could make life really difficult. Caddies could be brutal to the timid and meek, subjecting them to physical and psychological torture that rivals anything they dished out at Guantanamo.

There was one kid in particular that I remember, who got beat up, wedgied and taunted by everyone in the yard. Thank God there wasn't access to tar and feathers. The apex of abuse occurred when he got "pantsed" by the yard bullies, which means they removed, by force, all garments covering his southern hemisphere. I can still see that kid running down the front drive bare-ass naked from the waist down. I laughed so freakin' hard I thought my appendix was going to burst. In an ironic twist of fate, I heard that kid graduated from Harvard Law School, spoke before Congress and is ultra-successful. They say the ultimate revenge is living well, but I still can't get the vision of that poor kid running with no britches out of my head.

To understand the inner workings of the caddie yard, you must understand the caddie hierarchy system. There were four rungs on the caddie ladder—B caddies, A caddies, honor caddies and high honor caddies. The B caddies, also referred to as B jocks, were the youngest and smallest of all. They carried singles or cart-caddied, and needless to say, got the shittiest loops. I started out as a B jock.

The A caddies were a little bigger and were transitioning from carrying a single to the big step of packing doubles. Think of them as the sophomores of the yard.

Honor caddies were next, and the term was the epitome of an oxymoron. Honors were the bigger and older kids who packed doubles and got the good loops. The crème-de-la-crème were the high honor caddies. Looking back, the term is amusing because many of them did show up in altered states. These were the oldest and best loopers the club had to offer. To become a high honor caddie, one had to prove himself on the course, and kissing Jay's ass a little bit didn't hurt. High honors got the primo big money loops.

What you have to also understand is that Jay had a vested interest in the matchmaking process between caddie and loop, as his tip from the club member was directly related to the service the caddie provided. I've witnessed Jay getting slipped many nice tips from happy club members. Conversely, I've also seen Jay get stiffed and receive a lecture because of a caddie's perceived on-course insufficiencies.

To simmer it down, here's the way it worked. If you were in good with Jay you'd get the best loops of the rung that you were on. But, if you found yourself on Jay's shit list, you were in for lengthy periods on the course, looping for crabby, nasty people, for very little money. Some of the violations that would place you in the latter group were: showing up late, not showing up at all (especially for a tournament), underperforming on the course (thus subjecting Jay to a lecture depriving him of a tip), being disruptive in the caddie yard, or being unhelpful in the yard. I learned quickly that running clubs down to the driving range or sweeping the yard without being asked was a great way to win favor with the Master of the caddie universe.

Schadenfreude is a German word that translates to taking pleasure in the misery of others. Over the course of time, I learned that this activity was on every caddie's hobby list, especially at the country club level. There was a pathetic enjoyment derived from the knowledge that someone else just got into a heap of dung. Plus, there was the added bonus that, if you were on the above mentioned list, it also meant that you just dropped a space or two from the top. If you were the culprit of an event that was beyond the normal malfeasance, you subjected yourself to a combination of the worst loops with the added bonus of having to clean the caddie bathroom. The second half of this punishment is banned under the 8th Amendment, which prohibits cruel and unusual punishment, and I can honestly tell you that I would rather kiss Hillary Clinton on the mouth than ever have to clean that bathroom again. And if a caddie ever committed an extremely high-level crime, banishment from North Shore Country Club was deemed being sent down the road.

Despite the *Schadenfreude*, at age 13 I realized that caddying was a great way to make money, prompting me to dive head first into the venture. What other job can a 13 year-old get? I was an up-and-coming B jock, and was subjected to all the standard abuse from my superiors. I got wedgied frequently, but thankfully not atomic wedgied, which meant they pulled your underwear all the way over your head. I was also stuffed head-first in a garbage can and locked in the caddie bathroom while my loop waited on the first tee.

After my caddie initiation was over and I became a familiar face in the yard, the older loopers left me alone in search of more vulnerable prey. I was also making a name for myself as a decent B jock.

Part of my reputation enhancement stemmed from an incident with a member who was at the top of the shitty loop list named Dr. Zurfli, a grouchy little man who was hell to caddie for. Heaven help you if you were stuck caddying for this guy and lost his ball. Not many NSCC members were given nicknames but we called this guy The Fly. Sometimes a little caddie recon was necessary to see which loops were coming up for assignment, which meant entering the sacred confines of the bag room window to catch a glimpse of the day's pairing sheet. This was a clear violation of the rules, but was worth the risk, because if a loop like The Fly was coming up, word spread through the caddie yard like a wildfire…"Oh shit! The Fly's going out!" followed by every caddie scrambling for cover like a mortar round was coming in.

You definitely didn't want to make direct eye contact with Jay if you thought The Fly was the loop in the chamber. Most of the time it didn't matter that everyone disappeared when The Fly was getting assigned, because Jay usually had someone picked out from the top of his doo-doo chart, and they could hide all they wanted; Jay would find them. As luck would have it, yours truly was at the top of the aforementioned list in this instance. I earned this distinction because I'd made an executive decision to take a Saturday off, only to find out that it was a tournament day and Jay was short of loopers. As they say, don't do the crime if you can't do the time.

Jay approached me and said, "C'mon Maletnick. gotta' loop for ya'. You take The Fly!" He laughed and flapped his arms, which made him look more like an albatross than a fly. He did this every time he assigned The Fly, and it was funnier than hell to witness, especially if you were taking pleasure in the misery of the poor kid who got the assignment. Even if you were the recipient of this hideous loop, you'd chuckle until you realized that the next five hours of your life were going to be spent with this miserable s.o.b. gnawing on you the whole time. If you complained to Jay about it, he'd chime in with his favorite and most common Jay-ism: "My philophosy is [no, I didn't misspell philosophy…Jay pronounced it that way] if you're looking for sympaty [he mispronounced sympathy too], you'll find it in the dictionary, between shit and syphilis."

I met Dr. Zurfli—The Fly—on the first tee, and he was lukewarm to me at best. He grumbled about me keeping quiet and most important, to keep my eye on the ball, which, he reminded me, was the reason I was there. *Where is Mr. Zanoni when you need him?* Surprisingly, my first round with The Fly went better than expected. I didn't lose a ball and managed to stay out of his cross-hairs. I would live to caddie another day.

We eventually made our way to the clubhouse where Dr. Zurfli paid me (underpaid me), and then walked over to Jay and announced that I was the best caddie he'd ever had, sliding a tip in Jay's hand as he said it. Jay told him he was glad it worked out and gave me a wink. I was feeling pretty good about myself until I realized that I had just positioned myself in a place I didn't want to be. I might as well have just scored a job in the boiler room of the Titanic. Some of the members had their favorite caddies, and certain members became your regular loops. Once this golf marriage occurred, every time your loop showed up, you knew he was yours, and the other caddies knew it too. It was generally good to have such arrangements, but only if you had a primo loop. The Fly was definitely not the loop you wanted to claim ownership of, and now I had done just that. I would get stuck with him every time he played, even though his bark was far worse than his bite. I wouldn't have done such a stellar job if I had known it would turn out this way. I should have been smart enough to butch the loop on purpose. In caddie lingo, butching a loop meant doing a crappy job, which would prompt Jay to say on your next loop, "C'mon, gotta' loop for ya'…Don't butch it." There was one looper who butched so many loops he adopted the nickname Ginsu, as in the knife. One of the few nicknames worse than that was given to a kid who got caught with his finger in his nose, up to the first knuckle. Booger is not what you want to be called in the yard.

As it turned out, my days with Dr. Zurfli turned out to be painless. Call it my first lesson in human nature. I realized that he was a no-nonsense man who expected his money's worth, and there's nothing wrong with that. I actually grew to like that old man, but I couldn't let it be known, because it wouldn't be cool if everyone found out that I liked The Fly. I also curried big favor with Jay for handling him, and I got many good loops in return.

In the middle of that summer, something happened that affected all of us. Greg Bettina was an older boy who was one of the lucky recipients of the prestigious Evan's Scholarship given out to caddies in the Midwest. He was out on a round during a freak thunderstorm that came out of nowhere, which was pretty common for the area, and before he could find shelter, a bolt of lightning caromed off a tree, and struck him. He was rushed to the hospital in critical condition where he remained in a coma for several months before finally passing away. I can still remember vividly the sight of his footprints burned in the grass at the base of that tree. We all learned the hard way that Mother Nature was not to be messed with, and the rules regarding inclement weather were completely changed as a result of Greg's death.

Jay's actual name was Roger, but the first thing you learned was to NEVER call him Roger or you'd be packing for crappiest loops the club had to offer. He preferred to be called Jay or Jaybird, though the origin of that moniker was a mystery. Jay grew up on the Monterey Peninsula, and the second thing one learned about him was that he shot 65 at Pebble when he was 17.

Jay took some getting used to at first, but once embedded in the NSCC caddie system, you realized that he was captain of the ship and they broke the mold after he was created, because he was one-in-a-zillion. Any boy who has ever cashed a caddie ticket at North Shore does some sort of Jaybird impersonation. Combine all the other illicit activities perpetrated in the caddie yard, and it doesn't come close to how much time was spent doing Jay impersonations. If it's true that the best way to show affection is to imitate someone, then we must have been infatuated with Jay. It wasn't just his speech patterns, but his sayings that were the most amusing. These are some more of my all-time favorites: Rain or shine, we'll be on time (his mantra when you were trying to explain to him why you didn't show up to caddie because it was raining). It doesn't cost any more to go first class. You just can't stay as long. And one of his favorites, "That place has the best steak in the world...maybe even in the country." He used this statement all the time, just insert whatever subject he was pontificating about. Then there was the classic, "De only club I'll ever belong to is Canadian Club."

Although his speech was entertaining, his golf swing won the prize. If anyone's golf swing ever looked like a cow giving birth to a roll of barbed wire, it was Jaybird's, and imitating it was second only to mimicking him vocally. His move was about as unique as Miller Barber's. He'd bend over at the waist almost like he was swinging under a tree, with his toes pointed out and his knees together. His arms hung from his body like a couple of salamis in a deli. He'd drag the club back along the ground more than anyone I've ever seen on his take-away, ending with the old-school, helicopter finish. It was really a sight to behold, but the guy could really play, and I personally never questioned the validity of his career round at Pebble. He, like millions of others, had aspirations of taking his game somewhere big, but it wasn't to be, and he ended up at The Shore. He had a pretty cozy gig there with the salary he was paid by the club, which included free room and board above the curling lodge and tips from the members. The last leg of his financial bonanza was the concessions in the caddie room. If you really cared about staying in good standing with the man, you'd patronize that establishment whether you were hungry/thirsty or not. Frugality was not an attribute that sat well with Jay. As I got older, I learned the hard way that dining out with him could really diminish one's financial state, as leaving a 100% tip was not out of the norm. We took a cab to a restaurant once and he slipped the valet 20 bucks for opening the car door. As someone once said, a fool and his money should never have gotten together in the first place.

The members paid us after a round by signing a ticket, which we then brought to Jay who gave us the cash. I can still remember that moment of truth after spending 4-5 hours with a loop and wondering what the payment for my services would be. If things didn't run so smoothly out there it was more of a morbid curiosity, kind of like catching your first glimpse of a new wound you acquired. Upon handing the ticket to Jay, he'd pull a wad of cash from his pocket that would literally choke a horse, peel off the allotted amount and make a comment that reflected the job you did. "Oh my word...did you butch that!" Or "Oh my word, you brought him up!" (from what he normally pays).

There was a tear-off portion of the caddie ticket for grading purposes. The grades ranged from excellent to poor, with a comment section just in case you really screwed up. A point system was in place for each grade and a running tally was kept in the caddie room. Prizes were awarded at the end of the year for the top three places in each caddie category. Needless to say, every caddie strove to be the top gun in his group. I knew of at least one crafty looper who would sneak in the box and make his ticket go "Jimmy Hoffa" if he knew he was getting a 'poor,' which subtracted points from your total.

I spent more time at NSCC that summer than I had ever spent away from home up to that point in my short life. Like most dreadful things, the journey to the club became less miserable the more I did it, and the return home never bothered me, solely because I had cash in my pocket. The Shore was a second home, and my fellow caddies were unfortunately, a second family, dysfunction and all. The caddie yard was a cacophony of enough caddie bullshit to fertilize a large farm. The B jocks would sit around and yak about every flippin' shot of their last loop. The A caddies would wonder who their next loop was going to be, and how much they'd make. The honor caddies would sit around and contemplate which one of them was going to be the next to graduate to high honor status, and the high honors would spin their yarns about someone bigger than themselves that they beat up at some point in their lives, or a *Penthouse Forum* type of sexual conquest they were involved in. It's funny how no caddie would EVER admit that someone kicked the crap out of him or worse, that he was a virgin.

There's a scene in the movie *Forrest Gump* where Forrest and Bubba first arrive in Viet Nam and Lt. Dan gives them a speech about basic survival tips. He tells them not to do anything stupid, and lectures them on the importance of taking care of one's feet, specifically, maintaining dry socks. These rules also applied to looping. Sometimes avoiding stupidity was impossible, but caring for one's dogs was akin to maintaining the tires on your car. If you neglected them, you'd find yourself walking very gingerly as you made your way around the course and unfortunately, there was no roadside assistance to call in the event of a blowout. Walking around a dew-covered golf course made this a monumental task unless you were up for wearing galoshes, which then placed you atop the caddie ridicule list. Most chose to deal with pruney, blistered feet rather than a bunch of smart-ass caddies.

The yard was not the place for those who wished to maintain a healthy diet. The kids today use Red Bull, Monster or Starbucks as the propellant for their bodily motors. Unfortunately, these weren't available in my early years, so we used good old-fashioned sugar. Nothing got you buzzing early in the morning like the combination of Dr. Pepper and Starburst. Most loopers passed on breakfast and showed up at the club empty. Needless to say, it was very common to see a kid chowing down on a pizza or hot dog with a candy bar chaser from Chez Jay at 7:30 in the morning. If you were lucky, your loop would provide you with a Rudy Dog when they stopped at the halfway house between the 6th and 13th holes. Rudy, who ran the place, was a greasy, pock-faced German, and these nitrate-packed little puppies were called Rudy Dogs. Man, did they hit the spot, though it might have had something to do with the fact that we were hauling someone's luggage miles around a golf course, which really cranks up an appetite. Hell, Rudy could have given us a turd in a bun and we would have been happy. As I got older, I chummed up to Rudy and became his lottery errand boy, running his tickets to the pharmacy down the street from the club. For this, I was rewarded with Rudy's special chicken salad which was the best in the world…maybe even in the country.

Wondering whether your group was going to stop at the halfway house was second only to wondering how much you were going make after the round. About the 11th hole, your boiler would start grumbling and the thought of wolfing down a Rudy Dog crept into your hungry mind. By the 12th, it consumed you, as starvation took precedence over the task at hand. The 13th was a par three and after tee shots were executed came the moment of truth. You'd be packing the bag and staring lovingly in the direction of the halfway house, almost willing the group toward it. Then cruelly, you'd catch a whiff of the fantastic aromas emanating from that little shack. It almost made you want to cry out, "Please, please STOP!"

Sometimes the group headed directly over and it was evident that was the plan. Other times, one of the members would say to another, "You wanna stop?" "Sure, why not." Hopefully followed by, "You boys get what you want." Then we'd go around the back of the halfway house where there was a small pass-through window. Rudy would serve us our fare after he was done taking care of those footing the bill, followed by the 13 milliseconds it took us to eat. I can still hear the sound of dice being rolled by the members to see who would be the lucky recipient of our tab. We used to joke that we were camels, the golf course was the desert, and the halfway house was the oasis. Grabbing a dog and a coke there made the home stretch that much more bearable, especially if you were on your second trip around.

The horrendous flip-side was walking right past the halfway house or, even worse, having one member ask another, "You wanna stop?" "Ummmm…No, let's wait until we get in and then grab something." I sure as hell wished someone asked me my opinion on the matter. Without a Rudy Dog break, we really had to man-up for the final holes. I wish I had five bucks for every time I forecaddied the 14th and bitched about the stiffs that didn't stop at the halfway house.

All told, it's about five miles around North Shore Country once, unless your loop was hitting it sideways, in which case it felt like twice that length. The Shore is a classic design similar to hundreds of courses you'll find scattered throughout the Midwest. Designed by Colt, Mackenzie and Allison around 1920, its signature feature was the abundance of large trees of all types lining the pristine fairways. North Shore was host of the 1933 U.S. Open, where an amateur named Johnny Goodman edged the rest of the field and took home the trophy, a feat that has not been accomplished since.

The course was relatively flat but required controlled driving of one's ball to set up the approach shot to the green. The putting surfaces varied in size, but perfectly matched the hole they accompanied. Only a few possessed large swails, but these accentuated the prescribed hole. Comprised of bent grass, they were as pure and true as any you'll find anywhere, and lacked much in the way of grain.

What was really special about the course was the way it started and ended. The 1st was a long, dog-leg right, par 4 that demanded precision right out of the gate, and the closing 17th and 18th ended many a good round if one fell asleep. You'll often hear someone describe a course by saying that it's one where you hit every club in your bag. This applied to NSCC, due to the varying lengths of the holes. Some of the members sucked at the game so bad that this adage held true several times over. You could spot the extraordinarily bad ones from a mile away. You don't get a tan when you're in the trees all day.

As a caddie, there was intense mental preparation and evolution of thought over the course of a round, especially if you were packing for a hack. The first stage was realizing that you were in for a lengthy period of mental cruelty and trying desperately to latch on to some coping mechanism that might ease the pain. After a couple of holes you'd start to accept the discomfort, much the way you would with a hemorrhoid flare-up. By the 5th you'd be fantasizing about your member buying you a Rudy Dog when you got to the 6th, but you had more of a chance of getting elected president of the United States.

With the 8th came the realization that you were closing in on the halfway point. Making the turn, the ludicrous notion that maybe the group would only play 9 holes crept into your thoughts, but you had about as much chance of this happening as you did of getting fed on the 6th. The 10th conjured up the feeling that if God was ever going to strike you dead and put you out of your misery, it might as well be now. The 11th through the 13th encompassed the halfway house dilemma I described earlier. By the 16th you came to the conclusion that you might actually survive, much the way you'd feel after being lost at sea, and spotting a freighter off in the distance. If it was your first time around for the day, 17 brought about the question of whether or not you were going to have to go around again. 18 was a happy hole because payday had arrived unless, as you approached the green, you saw Jay sitting on a golf cart behind it. Then your elation turned to deflation because this meant only one thing and it wasn't that Jaybird needed some air. It meant he was out of caddies and your next loop was on the 1st tee already. He'd whisk you over out of the goodness of his heart, sometimes without your even being able to grab some sustenance. Then the whole gruesome experience would commence all over again. You knew not to complain either, because of Jay's theory on sympathy and more specifically, where to find it. We didn't go 36 every day but during the busy summer months, we averaged about three-four times per week, and there were runs where you might go around twice five days in a row. These weeks were back breakers, and after emerging from one, you slept like you were in a coma.

At the end of my first full summer of caddying, I had cut my teeth as a bag toter, and a decent one at that; so much so, that I was in the running for top B jock honors. It came down to the wire, and at the year-end caddie banquet, a tie was announced, giving me a choice between a new set of Ben Hogan irons or a 13" black and white Panasonic television. Oddly enough, I hadn't personally sparked an interest in the silly game, so I opted for the tv. This turned out to be a poor choice because I would eventually take a stab at golf, but more importantly, I got into the habit of staying up, watching late-night movies on that Panasonic, which made rising early the next morning that much more difficult. Looking back, a coffee maker would have been a more appropriate choice.

The next couple of summers were spent scratching and clawing my way up through the caddie ranks, enduring the trials and tribulations I have described. I jockeyed my way into A caddie status, which entailed packing a double and the physical toll it took on my thin frame. If we were indeed camels, then packing a double 36 holes was like crossing the Sahara. At this point in my caddiedom it occurred to me that for the first time in my life, someone actually cared about my opinion and followed my instructions. Plus, these were people of means and power. In no other situation would a bigwig for the McDonalds Corporation give a crap about the opinion of a 16 year-old smart-ass, but the golf course was my office, not theirs. If I was reputed to be a top looper, then he'd hit the shot standing on his head if I so told him to. Frankly, it was a bit of a thrill to be able to influence those of such a high socioeconomic level with my expertise. I'm not implying that I ever thought I was better than anyone else. Quite the contrary —when one becomes a caddie, it's made crystal clear that you're not better than *anyone* else.

About this time in my life I began to dabble in the game just a bit. So much of my existence was spent watching someone else play, I figured I might as well give it a shot. My aunt gave me a set of clubs that resembled those Old Tom Morris used to win the 1895 British Open, and Jay showed me the proper grip. I'd grab some old balls I had collected and run to a field down the street from my house and start slashing at it. It wasn't pretty at first, but after a while I'd start to get it airborne. Then, just when I thought I had it figured out, I'd shank it into one of the adjacent houses or blade it into traffic on the busy street. Welcome to golf.

The Glenview public golf course, aptly nicknamed 'The Weed' and situated half-way between my home and North Shore, was the place that my fellow loopers and I adopted as our club. It wasn't comparable in any way, shape, or form, to The Shore but it was cheap and close. The biggest drawback to playing there was the amount and pace of play. Pick the wrong time and you'd be out there so long, you wished you had brought a change of underwear with you. There was another public course named after Chick Evans, but it was a goat track operated by the Forest Preserve District and, to put it into perspective, if North Shore was Marilyn Monroe, then Chick Evans was Marilyn Manson. Thus, we only played there as a last resort.

After making my bones as an A caddie, I was promoted to the rung of honor caddie, and it's worth noting again that those two words just don't belong in the same sentence, much less side by side. It was at this point that NSCC became the axis of my universe instead of just someplace I worked, even though the novelty of looping had vanished long ago. I had adopted some illicit habits, so besides caddying there by day, my hoodlum friends and I would return at night to imbibe alcoholic beverages, burn the wacky tobacki and roam the countryside. One would think that given the vast amount of time we spent there during daylight hours, it would be the last place we'd want to hang out, but for some reason we loved it there, and claimed it as our turf.

It was at this point that I honed a couple of skills that would serve me well. The first was caddying with a hangover (this would come in especially handy when I turned pro). The second was a skill that was specific to club caddying. When Jay assigned a loop, he'd walk you over to the bag rack along with the other loopers he was putting you out with. It could be two of us each packing a double, or me and two B jocks packing singles. Whatever the case, some of the time he wasn't specific on who carried which bags. He'd tell you to take that foursome, so you had to assess the golfers' abilities in microseconds just by looking at their equipment. I can't convey strongly enough the importance of this skill, because the next five hours of your life depended on it. Choose wisely and you might have a front row seat to a good round of golf and more importantly, you'd be walking the shortest distance between tee and pin, straight down the fairway all day. Make the wrong choice and you'd be hating life while you searched for your player's ball in the trees, raked the equivalent of the Gobi Desert in bunkers, replaced a football field full of divots, and wished you were the other looper.

Your first indicator was the general look of the whole ensemble. If the golf bag was one of those 1920s leather deals with Sam Snead Signature golf clubs the guy bought at K Mart, you knew he couldn't play a lick. No offense to Sam; I'm sure he was compensated handsomely to put his name on those turds. A ball retriever in the bag was also a red flag, especially if the grip was worn. If there were covers on the irons or tubes in the golf bag, you were sure the owner of the equipment sucked at the game. I have never, ever caddied for someone who had one of these items and could break 120. If both were in the bag, run for the hills. If you saw one of those little chipping clubs that the guy obviously ordered from a discount golf magazine, pass. If the putter looked like one they give you when you go miniature golfing, just walk on by. Lastly, if there was a Power Pod in the bag, this was not the loop for you. For those of you unfamiliar with this club, it was a driver sold years ago that looked more like a prosthetic leg than a golf implement.

Items that gave a good indication that the owner had some game included a Ben Hogan Sun Jet golf bag with any set of forged irons, i.e. Wilson Staff Tour Blades, an Acushnet Bullseye putter, or a Wilson 8802, MacGregor Eye-O-Matic woods, or more than one sand wedge. But the number one indicator of a good stick was a 1 iron. If you saw a knife in the bag, grab that puppy quick. I'm not inferring that these rules applied 100% of the time of course. A few times, after doing my equipment analysis, I got out on the course only to realize that I had been duped. The golfer that I thought could play had the best game that money could buy, or he borrowed the sticks from someone else.

Ron Santo, who played 3rd base for the Chicago Cubs and was a member of the '69 team that was infamous for blowing a huge lead in the final stretch of the season, became a member at The Shore right around the time I was promoted to high honor caddie. There were a number of top quality people that you wanted to claim as your loop, but Santo was in a league of his own. Ron was cool. He caused a stir at the club from the beginning for several reasons. First, he didn't look like any member I had seen before. This man was a former professional athlete and was built like one; no spare tire around this guy's middle. He also wore the tightest fitting polyester golf pants, which I'm sure the female membership didn't mind at all. To top it off, he paid caddies like a slot machine, which didn't set well with some of the cheapo's at the club.

Jay put me out with Santo for one of his mid-week money games. His guests were always heavy-hitters who played for high stakes. We meshed well on the course, and Santo told Jay he wanted me to loop for him whenever he played. I now possessed the premier member as *my* loop, and rightfully so, as I had put in more than my fair share of time becoming top jock in the yard. One unique aspect of caddying for Santo was that he paid according to how he fared; if he won big, he paid big. A good indicator of the on-course wagering was the wad of C-notes in the top pocket of his golf bag. I checked it out when I forecaddied, and it was usually tens of thousands.

Equipment analysis didn't apply to this loop, because I packed for Ron and his partner for the day, while another high honor would handle the other two. No butches caddying in this group, as this was no place for the weak, timid or inexperienced. Santo greased Jay big time and expected the best of the best, even if they were aiding his adversaries.

I wasn't aware at the time, but working in this group would prove to be my training ground for the future. Poor advice given to a "regular" member might have been the difference between breaking 90 or not. A wrong call made in this group could mean the exchange of serious moolah, and Santo wasn't one to mince words; he'd rip me a new one if he were displeased. So I learned to really focus on all aspects of the task at hand when assessing a shot, i.e. wind direction, lie of the ball, elevation and physiological condition of the player. The most important thing I learned was to lay my neck on the chopping block and commit to the advice I was giving. If it worked out, I'd be rewarded handsomely; if not, I would get an earful. There was no way of knowing at the time how much this experience would serve me in the future.

I couldn't begin to guess what the median handicap was at North Shore, but I will tell you that the majority of the members would've been standing in a soup line if the game was how they made a living. That's not to say there weren't any good players. Actually, there were some exceptional players, and Roger Hurd was one of them. He stands out in my mind as the man with the prettiest, most fluid golf swing at the club. A quiet, unassuming man, he dominated the club championship year after year. Unfortunately, what he possessed in golf ability, he lacked in the disbursement of cash department. He wasn't cheap, but he wasn't what loopers would consider a "paymaster." I didn't mind caddying for him because I really loved watching his action, but that only went so far. Another life lesson learned: *go where the money is.* Watching a sweet golf swing wasn't going to pay my way into a Ted Nugent concert.

I was now in my early 20s and beginning to realize that I had blown a huge opportunity by dropping out of college and caddying full time at North Shore. I was a lost boy in tall grass. Put another way, if I were a fish, I would have been flounder. One aspect of caddying full time is that when all the other kids were in school during the early and late part of the season, Jay needed to utilize his available caddie force to the maximum. This meant packing a triple on Tuesday and Thursday mornings for the ladies. This isn't a fish story...we would pack three smaller bags, two on one shoulder, one on the other (I'd usually switch the double bag shoulder at the turn). Then we'd pack another double in the afternoon for the men. I can't tell you how many times I'd be on the 17th hole of my second loop, questioning my brilliant decision to drop out of school. They say that you have to use your brain or your brawn in life, and during this period, I was in the latter category. I was so whipped after one of these days that I would be asleep long before my head hit the pillow. Things weren't looking too rosy, but my luck was about to change in the form of a chubby little man from across the pond.

If wanting to know how a professional caddie gets paid is the most frequently asked question, then how I got into professional caddying is a very close second. When I was educating you on the different rungs of the caddie ladder, I failed to tell you about one more rung, the Holy Grail of loopdom: pro jock. Jay was a pro jock before he took the job at North Shore, and over the course of his tenure on the tour, he befriended Scotty Gilmour, a.k.a. Scotty from Scotland. I had heard so many stories from Jay over the years about his pro caddie friend Scotty that I felt like I knew him before I met him.

Scotty Gilmour was born and raised in the Gorbols, one of the roughest areas of Glasgow, Scotland. A carpenter by trade, he discovered golf, and more specifically caddying, in his early years, and it turned out to be his ticket out of hell. Scotty was one of the true pioneers of professional caddying, coming to America in the late 1950s and forging his way onto the scene. In those early days, African Americans dominated the ranks, making him persona non grata, but over time he embedded himself in the system. He was one of the first white caddies to loop at The Masters, and he had packed for almost every big name in the game. But his claim to fame was working for

Tony Jacklin (though not when he won the U.S. and British Opens. They say timing is everything, and as you'll see, Scotty's stopwatch must have been defective).

My mentor Scotty Gilmour & Greg Norman at The Masters.

When passing through Chicago, Scotty would stop at The Shore, see his old buddy Jay and catch a loop or two. One August he happened to be in the area and dropped in. He was packing for the Shark at the time, but this was when he was on his way up and was just known as Greg Norman. Jay put us out on a loop together.

I didn't know any pro jocks other than Jaybird, but Scotty wasn't what I expected one to look like. He reminded me of an old relic you might see in a caddie museum, or every painting I'd ever seen of a St. Andrews looper. He was short and pudgy, with thinning grey hair pulled back and a deep tan enveloping a very lived-in face. Besides a Scottish accent that had begun to fade, the most notable aspect of him was his teeth, or lack thereof. They resembled a row of bombed-out houses.

We exchanged a brief introduction on the first tee, but didn't have much time to chat as we readied for our loop. We made our way around the track that day, tending to our caddie duties as we went. It wasn't until the 14th, when we forecaddied, that we had time to talk. Out of the blue, Scotty piped up and asked me, "So Larry, did you get laid last night?" It wasn't really what I was expecting out of him, but I chuckled and answered, "Well, as a matter of fact…"

That one question was the icebreaker, and I got to know Scotty a little more each day over the next few weeks. He was an interesting and animated character who had a real zest for life. He had just married a British gal who had a couple of sons, and they were coming over soon. Having never been to America, he asked me if I would show the boys around when they arrived, and I agreed.

The first time I laid eyes on Wayne and Gary Edwards, I wanted to die laughing. They were both skinny, had massive unkempt coifs, whiter-than-snow complexions, tight-fitting jeans that ended mid ankle, and really big feet. The combination of the pants and shoes made them look like circus clowns. It was obvious they weren't from the area. It immediately occurred to me that the loopers were going to have a blast messing with these guys. Then they opened their mouths, and when I heard their British accents, I knew that wasn't going to help the situation.

When I learned they were from Liverpool, England I jokingly asked them if they knew the Beatles. They politely chuckled, and I believe I heard one of them called me a wanker, but I wasn't sure.

Wayne, a.k.a. Wiz, Wizzie, or the Wizard, and Gary, a.k.a. Gaz, Gazard or the Gizzard, knew absolutely squat about the game of golf. Liverpool is a tough town and you won't find many posh country clubs there. They were streetwise kids whose lives were changed forever when their Mum married the Scotsman. He got them into caddying and they would be packing at North Shore for a couple of months until they left to go to the California Desert, and then off to Europe to work professionally on the European Tour.

Gary (Gaz) was a nice kid, but Wayne (Wiz) and I took to each other like we were brothers from another mother. He was, and remains, one of the funniest, most clever people I have ever come across. Case in point, I asked him early on, "Wiz, how old is Scotty?" "Well, I'm not quite sure but I do know that he caddied for Barabbas in the Nazareth Open. They lost to Judas Iscariot in a playoff and Barabbas stiffed him. Only gave him three pieces of silver."

We caddied by day, and then, if we had enough energy, we went out at night. I showed Wiz and Gaz around Chicago and introduced them to some of the girls I knew, who upon hearing their accents would get all gushy and say, "Oh my gosh. They sound like the Beatles!" I teased Wiz about it later on and he said, "I've go' a three-inch dick and a nine-inch accent."

By early November the club had officially closed, and Scotty, Barbara and the Liverpudlians had moved on to the sunny, southern California. I was in the state of depression. They say the winters in Chicago are so cold the politicians have their hands in their own pockets, and I can vouch for that. It didn't help that I'd get calls from Wiz telling me that he was sunburned, or that he and Gaz got into a fight over who was going to turn the Jacuzzi back on.

I had never really been anywhere except for the yearly, family trot down to Florida, and that was by car. Flying on an airplane was an alien concept to me. All I knew about California was that The Beach Boys were from there, the girls were all blonde babes, and the weather was perfect all the time. Scotty asked me on more than one occasion to come out with them, and I toyed with the idea, but for some reason, Chi-town was a ball and chain affixed to my leg.

In mid-December a combination of events would alter the course of my life. First, we had a solid week of sub-zero temperatures. It was so cold, I saw a team of sled dogs mushing down the middle of Michigan Avenue. Second, and most motivating, I was hanging out with some friends, participating in our normal naughtiness, when I mentioned that I was thinking about going out to California and possibly to Europe to try my hand caddying professionally. An antagonistic friend of mine chimed in, thinking he was calling my bluff, "Who the #$@& are you kidding? You ain't goin' to California, and you sure as shit ain't goin' to Europe!"

His challenging tone helped me make up my mind right then and there. I purchased a ticket, hopped a flight and went to California.

He went to prison.

MOMMAS, DON'T LET YOUR BABIES GROW UP TO BE CADDIES

I MIGHT AS well have been on the moon. The California desert reminded me of every lunar landscape I had ever seen.

Freed from the frigid Chicago cold, I started peeling garments off like layers of an onion the moment I disembarked from the jet. It was amazing to me that two places on the same continent could be so vastly different. The snowcapped mountains framing the desert floor were the first I had ever seen. It's no secret the Midwest is as flat as a board.

Scotty picked me up at the Palm Springs Airport and brought me back to the family digs in Palm Desert, where Mum and the boys were basking in the glorious sunshine. It was evident they were half-lit as Wiz handed me a cold one and told me I had some catching up to do. I jumped into a bathing suit, went out to the pool, and the rest of that first night was a blur. And so, the next chapter of my life commenced. To quote a line from the classic *Wizard of Oz*, "You're not in Kansas anymore, Dorothy."

The Palm Springs area in the early 1980s still possessed a small town feel and hadn't been contaminated by the coastal masses migrating east from Orange County. Traffic was light, and you didn't have to wait in line for anything. The streets were named after Hope, Ford and Sinatra, and there was a reason for that. These guys could have hung their hats anywhere, but they chose this place because, during the winter months, it was like stealing. I really felt it was unfair, almost illegal, that while most of the country endured miserable weather, Southern Cal was blessed with ideal meteorological conditions day after day after day. Being a good Catholic boy, I almost felt a little guilty about it, but I got over it.

The boys and I went on daily jaunts to discover all we could about this magical place. If I was shocked coming from Chicago, the boys must have been electrocuted coming from Liverpool. A favorite spot of ours was up Highway 74, a winding mountain road toward San Diego, that Wizzie donned, 'mental mountain road.' The vantage point from there was breathtaking, with Mt. San Jacinto and San Gorgonio to the west, the Salton Sea to the east and the desert floor lying quietly beneath us. We'd bring a cooler full of bevies and a BBQ to a viewing area at the top called Vista Point. With our bellies full and the alcohol level peaking, we'd hit drivers off the mountain with total disregard for the road and vehicles below. It was irresponsible of us, but at the time, irresponsibility wasn't just a habit, it was a passion.

Another favorite was the Aerial Tramway to the highest peak on Mt. San Jacinto, overlooking the whole of the desert. We'd have several pops at the restaurant at the top and then go hiking, totally ill-equipped for the activity. We could have easily ended up one as of those stories in the news about idiots who go hiking without the proper gear or knowledge and have to be saved by the local search & rescue team.

At night we visited numerous watering holes, where we'd partake of libations and chat up the local femininas. For strictly comedic purposes, we went to The Nest, a Desert institution that's been around forever and was popular with the older crowd. It was affectionately known as Grab-A-Granny, *because* the average age in the place was 88 (there's nothing funnier to a bunch of young guys than watching octogenarians hookin' up). At the time, the Desert was still known as 'God's little waiting room' because the wealthy folks from the coast came to spend their waning years until they were called to that big country club in the sky.

After a couple weeks of illegal fun under the sun, the realization came that finances were diminishing rapidly. Luckily, Scotty had a connection at a new club called The Vintage and was in the process of getting a caddie program off the ground. I use the term caddie program very loosely, as the four of us would be it. In the wealth category, North Shore had some members with serious spondoolies, but The Vintage Club was in a different strata. The cart paths were paved in gold. It was rumored that a few of the members there made $1,000,000…a day! The place just reeked of power and affluence, and I loved being anywhere near it. If I hadn't needed the cash as much as I did, I would have worked there for nothing.

We put in our dues waiting to get loops at The Vintage, and after a while, word spread amongst the membership that we were on hand. We started getting jobs just in the nick of time, because the cash situation was just this side of broke.

With some air under our financial wings, the talk turned to the coming end of the season in the Desert. The ultra-wealthy don't like to sweat, so before the thermostat got cranked up to broil, they loaded up their Gulfstreams and jetted off to their other homes in exotic and tony destinations. Scotty, Barbara and the boys were planning a sojourn to jolly old England to work the PGA European Tour, but unfortunately, a G-4 was nowhere in the equation. Once again, Scotty enticed me to join them, and given the choice between jetting to Europe, or heading back to the s.o.s. (same ole shit) of Chicago, it was a no-brainer.

Scotty, Barb and Gazzie made their way over, while my brother-in-arms, Wizzie, stayed behind with me. Up until now, a passport wasn't a high priority but now was a necessity, so a trip to Los Angeles to expedite the process was in order. We rented a car, drove to the 'City of Angels' and filed the paperwork at the U.S. Customs Office. It would take two days, so we made the most of it, visiting Venice Beach, Hollyweird and other sightseeing venues during the day. We slept in the Chrysler rental at night to conserve what funds we had; this would also prove to be valuable training for our future. It's worth noting that if you plan on sleeping with a buddy in very close quarters, do not let him eat a late-night chili-dog.

With passport in hand, I was soon to be abroad for the first time, as we boarded a flight at LAX bound for London. Like a gang plotting to knock over a 7-11, we planned our attack for the upcoming season on the PGA European Tour. Wiz had a flat in Liverpool—right on the Mersey River—that would serve as our base of operations. I was giddy with excitement just looking at some of the countries we'd be traveling to. I'm sure the half dozen in-flight cocktails had a little something to do with my euphoria.

At the time, I had no idea that something that big could stay airborne for that long, but we finally touched down at Gatwick Airport, both feeling a bit rough around the edges. A quick trip through customs and I'd be on foreign soil, bound for the home of the legendary Beatles.

SEE THE WORLD:
BE A LOOPER

MY ARRIVAL IN Europe was heralded by a series of comical mishaps that began with me stupidly bragging to the customs inspector at the airport that I was coming to the United Kingdom to caddie on the European Tour. Apparently they considered caddying a form of employment, as opposed to my belief that it was just a way to see the world. Their opinion on the issue trumped mine, and I was informed that I had to return to the U.S. Fortunately, Wiz worked some diplomatic magic and coaxed the powers-that-be into a detour to France, where we found accommodations at a Parisian brothel, and spent a glorious week trying our best to get into, and stay out of trouble before returning to England on a cross-channel ferry. I finally made it into the United Kingdom, and this time, when the customs official asked what my business was in the U.K., my response was, "I'm on holiday." With that, I took my first step onto British soil. A quick leg to London and then a segmented train journey north to Liverpool, and we were in the hamlet of Rock Ferry by late afternoon.

Wizzie's flat was right on the River Mersey, and it lived up to its reputation. It was on the second floor with a lounge, kitchen, one bedroom and a bath. A nifty feature of the place was a large window in the kitchen, cut into the angled wall, which opened up and made roof access possible. It was a perch where we would spend plenty of time, watching vessels of all types navigating their way up and down the waterway, Liverpool City Centre in the backdrop.

A not-so-nifty feature was that, even though it was a government-subsidized unit that cost Wiz all of $12 per month, he failed to pay the gas and electric bills. This was a small inconvenience that he sidestepped by wiring a cord from a hallway light outside the flat into his abode. With so many appliances on one plug, the cord got so hot you could toast bread on it. We also discovered what a pain in the ass it was to fill up a bathtub with hot water from an electric kettle. But this would be our headquarters for the upcoming summer months as we planned our assault on the PGA European Tour, and it was home.

Wiz showed me around his town and introduced me to his friends. I loved being there, but if I had to describe the place in two words, they would be harsh and bleak. If I thought meeting Scotty had a big impact on my life, I shudder to think where Wiz and Gaz might have been if he hadn't married their mother. The two most obvious guesses were in prison, or in the ground.

One of the real bonuses of being there was our ability to cut way back on our funds. Wiz knew the cheapest places for consumables, most notably a fish 'n chips shop near the flat where we could get a tin of chicken fried rice that would last 3 days for 1.5 pounds. With his vast knowledge of the local pub network, it was possible to go out with a five pound note in your pocket, and wake up the next morning with a hangover and one pound left. It's also worth mentioning that when taking the ferry across the Mersey, it is impossible not to sing, or at least think of the words to the song made famous by Gerry and the Pacemakers.

One of the things I loved best about being at Wiz's was meeting all the 'birds' he had bragged about back in the States. Now I was the one with the 3" dick and the 9" accent.

At the time, there was a tournament in Tunisia just before Madrid, but most caddies picked up the tour in Spain for the Cepsa Madrid Open. We made the trek from Liverpool and showed up at Puerto De Hierro Golf Club in Madrid. In my mind I could hear Jay preaching to the loopers back in the caddie yard at North Shore, "Maletnick's in Spain popping his cherry as a pro jock."

I felt confident that I had a fairly good handle on caddying as a whole, but I was graduating from AAA ball to the big leagues, and I knew there would be a learning curve. The first item on our caddie agenda was getting a bag for me (Wiz was already hooked up with a player he worked with the prior season). A close second on our list of priorities was getting yardage for the course. Back at The Shore there were Sunburst Locust trees that were a marked distance to the middle of the green on each hole. That was the depth of yardage documentation needed to caddie for a 20 handicap. Frankly, when a guy's shanking and topping it around the course, it really doesn't matter how far he is to the pin. Now that I was in the biggies, I'd have to know the exact distance to the front of the green, and then implement a daily pin sheet to attain the yardage to the flag.

I'm fully aware that in today's game the caddies go out and measure the distance from all sprinkler heads using lasers that are accurate within 1/1000 of an inch and other high tech gadgetry to aid them in their job. These gizmos divulge a myriad of information, including yardage to the front of the green and to the hole, wind velocity and direction, barometric pressure, elevation, and phase of the moon. Their yardage books are bibles that contain more information than a Chilton's Automotive Repair Manual. Back in my early days on the European Tour, the golf courses didn't even have irrigation systems, so there were no sprinkler heads to document. The tour officials spray-painted red and yellow circles in various locations on each hole, which served as yardage monumentation. Thus, it was common to hear one caddie ask another, "Hey, what do you have for the red mark on 14?"

There were two ways of gleaning yardage information for a course back then. The first was simply to get your ass out on the track and pace the yardage from the painted circles and then note them on something that you were pretty sure you wouldn't lose. The caddie biz at that time hadn't even advanced enough to have anything closely resembling a formal yardage book. A blank notepad would usually suffice, but I remember seeing one looper scribble his yardage on a sandwich wrapper. Notice that I used the term 'pace the yardage' in calculating the distance. Calibrating your stride to an exact yard was a science, and only half the battle. Some of the *high-tech* caddies sprang for a yardage wheel, which was worth its weight in gold, but a pain-in-the-ass to travel with.

The second and obviously easier way to obtain yardage for the tournament course was to just ask someone for theirs and copy it. It was grammar school all over again. We referred to this as car park yardages, as that's where the exchange of this information usually took place. Under Wizzie's direction, this was how we got our yardage for my inaugural attempt at professional caddying. In hindsight, one needs to be fairly selective as to whom they retrieve this vital info from.

Standing in the parking lot with a bunch of caddies I didn't know reminded me of my first day at North Shore. There was plenty of competition and you had to be ready to pounce on a prospective bag as soon as a player emerged from the cab or courtesy car dropping him off at the course. I was at a big disadvantage because I was unfamiliar with the players. That explains why I propositioned two tournament officials, and the locker room attendant, before I finally struck gold and found a golfer who was looperless. We consummated our employment arrangement, after which he gave me his golf bag, along with a smaller matching bag, and instructed me to meet him at the range.

They say you always remember your first time, but I beg to differ. The only thing I remember about my first pro job was that he hailed from Australia, spoke with an accent, and could keep up with a truck driver in the profanity department. The week would prove to be the equivalent of a sexless one-night stand.

His bag felt like it was packed with bricks, and for the life of me, I couldn't figure out what the little one contained, but that secret would be revealed in due time. When I luckily stumbled upon the driving range, the first thing I noticed was caddies standing out in the landing area. *What the hell were they doing out there?* Welcome to the era of shagging balls. The European Tour was so primitive back in those days, the players brought their own practice balls to hit. Because of this antiquated fact, it wasn't even called a driving range but instead, a "practice pitch." We caddies were the unfortunate recipients of those shots. If you think it was brutal to caddie hung over, imagine shagging balls while nursing one.

What's-his-name showed up at the range and told me, "Go out about 65 to 70 yards. I'll start with some soft wedges and work my way through the set, ending with the driver."

"Okay," I replied, as I turned to make my way out.

"Hey!" Don't forget this. You'll need it," he called out, holding out the now-empty shag bag.

"Oh, right." I took it and commenced my trip into harm's way.

I had never before had golf balls whizzing dangerously close to my cranium, and frankly, I wasn't too thrilled about it. I hadn't seen this written anywhere in the job description, and had I known there was the threat of serious bodily injury caddying professionally, I might have been more diligent about college.

I learned very quickly that paying attention was the key to shagging balls successfully. The only thing more difficult than watching incoming projectiles was trying to pick them up mid-flight. I almost discovered this the hard way when I was distracted for a split second, heard the distant crack of my player's shot and tried feverishly to track the flight of the ball as it reached its apex in the sky. The clock was ticking, as the shot was en route directly to yours truly. Unable to locate it, and in a fit of desperation, I resorted to turning away at the last second, curling my body up in a protective ball to cushion the blow. The shot landed with a thud, three feet in front of me.

"*This is #$@&ing crazy*," I said to myself. "*What the hell did I get myself into?*"

I'm pretty sure I saw my golfer chuckling after the escapade, which made me sincerely happy that he was entertained, even if it was at my expense.

After an hour of practice, he waved me in. I grabbed the now full shag bag and started making my way toward the firing line. This was the beginning of my education in how to gauge which players were the biggest assholes on the tour. They were the guys who would bean a caddie, and it wouldn't even faze them. They'd continue hitting balls like nothing happened, while a looper was in a prone position 260 yards away with a Maxfli logo imprinted on his skull.

We made our way to the first tee for a practice round where a couple of my player's mates were waiting for him. They were burdened with the same accent and swore as much as my man. I was intrigued by the way they pronounced the word *fock*, instead of *#$@&*. Talk to any Australian for any length of time, and you'll hear, "Everything in Australia is the best in the focking world, mate!"

The foursome hit their tee shots, and we ventured down the first fairway. If North Shore was the penthouse, then this course was the shithouse. It reminded me of The Weed back in Glenview.

Upon reaching my player's ball, I pulled out my yardage notepad and looked for one of the painted circles. I spotted a yellow one up ahead and paced to it, being extra careful in my pacing and calculation. According to my car park yardage, the yellow spot was 115 yards to the front edge. I paced 8 steps to it and the green was 30 deep.

My employer asked, "All roight mate, what've we got?'

"You have 138 yards to the center of the green," I answered.

"Always give me the focking distance to the front of the green, and then to the focking hole, mate," he shot back.

"Oh sorry. You have 123 to the front and 138 to the middle."

"Can't focking be. Ya sure? It looks a lot focking further than that," he said.

"Lemme check it. 115 plus 8 paces equals 123 to the front, plus 15, makes it 138 to the center," I reiterated.

"Well, all roight, but it sure looks focking further," he said as he pulled a 9 iron out of the bag.

He went through his pre-shot routine and proceeded to flush it, dead at the pin. "Be as good as you focking look, mate," he said. The shot completed its journey, landing 30 yards short of the green.

"What the fock is that?" he asked sharply.

He walked abruptly over to the yellow mark in the fairway and started pacing toward the green. Any time you see a professional golfer do this after a shot, it's a good indicator that he believes he's been on the receiving end of an Agatha, as in Christie, as in mystery yardage.

I followed meekly behind him hauling his two-ton golf bag on my shoulder. When I finally arrived at the green, he was standing there holding the 9 iron.

"Whatta' ya' focking got from the focking yellow mark to the front?" he asked.

"115 yards to the front edge of the green," I answered, trying my best to stick to my guns.

"It's not 115 yards, it's 151 focking yards, mate," he snapped.

"Oh, right, sorry. I'll make a note of that," I retorted as I whipped out my yardage notepad and began scribbling. I'm embarrassed to admit that, at the time, my eye wasn't trained enough to tell the difference between 115 and 151 yards.

This was a recurring event during the course of the practice round, which was not reinforcing my golfer's faith in my abilities as a caddie. I was extremely fortunate he didn't sack my ass before the tournament even began.

After finishing the round, I went in search of Wiz to have a word with him regarding the yardage issue. I found him yakking with some of the caddies in the car park and before I could even get a word out, he said, "Shit-can the yardage that you have."

"Yeah, I know. It's all #$@&ing wrong. What's the problem?"

"The guy we got it from has a bit of a problem. He's dyslexic."
"Oh really, is that right? Thanks for telling me, now that my player thinks I'm a #$@&ing moron."

Professional caddie commandment number one: Don't ever mention caddying when entering any foreign country. Number two: If you're too lazy to walk the course for yardage and choose to obtain the information from another caddie, be absolutely sure he's not dyslexic.

My first stab at professional caddying started out poorly and ended on the same note. My man missed the cut, I had the weekend off, and he also didn't express any interest in furthering our employment bond, which came as no big revelation to me. I did make my base pay for the week, a nominal amount that barely covered my expenses, and I learned a very valuable lesson.

On our expedition to the next stop in Milan for the Italian Open, we befriended several of the other caddies who followed the tour. They were a colorful bunch that hailed from a myriad of countries. Having never traveled abroad, I was taking a crash course in currency exchange, and wisely invested in a Casio wristwatch calculator to aid in my monetary calculations. Truth be told, I got freaked out when I was told our room would be 120,000 Italian Lira per man, per night, and there were four of us. I was relieved when I discovered that was only $4.92. Incidentally, sleeping head-to-toe in a bed with three other caddies was the closest I've ever felt to being a canned sardine, smell and all.

The golf course in Monza was close enough to the famous racetrack, you could see the cars off in the distance and hear the whine of their high performance engines. Lady Luck shined down on me as one of the Australian caddies we befriended set me up for the week with American golfer Chip Beck. Taking the position more seriously and remembering the events of Madrid, I paced the yardage myself, being extra careful in my notations. He's an easy-going man, and even though my inexperience must have been as plain as the nose on my face, we got along well. He made the cut finishing tied for 21st, and I actually made a little money, though I must stress the word *little*.

We were back on British soil for the next event at Moortown in Leeds. Once again, I was fortunate to hook up with a player from New Zealand in what would turn out to be my first regular gig.

I was introduced to Stuart Reese by the same Australian caddie who'd set me up with Chip Beck the prior week. After hearing his accent, I assumed he too was Australian, and went so far as to ask where in Aussieland he was from. I learned right quick that the best way to piss off a Kiwi was to call him an Aussie, and vice versa. Each believes they're more metropolitan than the other. Funny thing is, they're both from countries where the sheep outnumber the people by 120,000,000 to 1.

A smallish Robert Redford look-a-like, Reesie, as he liked to be called, was a bit of an aging hippie, which was fairly evident in his casual stroll down the fairway, hands in his pockets, whistling a Moody Blues tune. He wasn't long, but a straight driver of the ball, and putting was his strong suit. The most impressive aspect of his game was that he was a mudder; he excelled in poor weather conditions, which was basically all the time on the European Tour. He exhibited this trait later in the week when we were subjected to Arctic weather during a round. I couldn't figure out how he was playing the game when it was so cold I was having trouble packing the bag.

We scored digs at a local bed and breakfast fairly near the golf course. The price was right and the typical English breakfast of bangers, eggs, pork and beans and toast fueled us properly for the lengthy days. It also helped our hangovers.

No matter what tour one caddies on, a routine of finding and frequenting a local eating and drinking establishment occurs over the course of the week. Once you've worked a tour for more than a season, you remember the hot spots, especially the ones that the best-looking females patronize. Incidentally, if you ever happen to be fortunate enough to be chatting up such a lass and nature calls, by the time you return from relieving yourself you might find another caddie sitting in your seat making a move on your behalf, This means he is putting the cock block on you. Thus, it was very common to hear a caddie griping, "That wanker is trying to cock block me! You can't even take a leak around these #$@&ing guys."

This particular week the pub of choice was a place called The Kings Arms. When I heard that's where the lads were, I asked, "Hey Wiz, where's The Kings Arms?" Exhibiting his uncanny timing and with a look that would have made any stand-up comedian green with envy, he replied, "Around the Queen's ass."

When we found the aforementioned tavern, our crew was there and already half in the bag. Wizzie was working full-time for an Irishman named Philip Walton, and for some odd reason, made the crucial mistake of bringing his shag bag to the pub. In the midst of our 3rd pint, one of the other patrons approached him and asked, "Have ya' go' golf balls in there?" pointing down at it.

Wiz refrained from making his usual sarcastic comment and simply answered, "Yes, I do."

"Would ya' be interested in selling any of 'em?" he followed.

"No. I couldn't do that. These are my player's practice balls!" he answered emphatically.

"Okay, I was just asking. Don't get your bloody knickers in a twist," he countered as he made his way back to his seat.

After several more pints with the lads, Wiz realized the sad state of his economy and began biting his lower lip, the lead indicator that his wheels were turning. I had known him long enough to know what he was up to. He grabbed the shag bag and made his way across the pub, returning several minutes later, a dirty grin decorating his tanned face.

"Wiz, you didn't just do what I think you did," I queried.

"He'll never miss 'em. It was just a dozen of them," he said as he made a gesture to the barkeep for another round.

A couple of more pints down our gullets, and Wizzie went missing for a second time. I thought he might be shaking hands with the unemployed, but noticed the shag bag was also MIA, verification that he wasn't in the men's room. When he reappeared a few minutes later, I asked him, "Wiz, what are you doing, man? Those are your player's practice balls. What are you going to tell him?"

"I dunno'," he answered, and then yelled out, "Bartender, my good man, a round of grogs for the lads," followed by cheers and back-patting from all the boys. About this time, he was as popular as a warden with a fist full of pardons.

As the night wore on, Wiz didn't have to leave his seat to make a sale. He was a golf ball vending machine, doling them out to anyone who ponied up the dough. By closing time, he had managed to sell every one of his player's practice balls and the shag bag! We were drunker than skid row bums at an open-bar wedding and staggered back to our digs, laughing like crazy. In a few hours, one of us was going to have difficulty seeing the humor in it all.

We awoke the next morning with our heads throbbing. Once again I posed the question to my friend, this time without the influence of alcohol, "Well Wiz, what are you going to do?"

"I dunno', I really don't know," he answered, with a look on his face like he was on a plane going down. On the trip to the course I was knee deep in schadenfreude. Even though Wiz was my best mate and traveling companion, I was giddy that he was in such a pickle, and voiced my pleasure.

"Hey Wiz, you're seriously #$@&ed right now. Looks like you'll be in the car park looking for a bag next week. Seriously, what are you going to tell Philip?"

"I'll just have to tell him the truth." he answered.

"Oh, that'll go over real nice, I'm sure. 'Uhh, Philip, I sold all your practice balls, and your shag bag, so my idiot friends and I could get ripped last night.' You'll be up for *Caddie of the Year* for that one," I rejoiced.

As we arrived at the golf course and approached the bag room, the moment of truth was upon him. Wiz prepared to throw himself on the mercy of the court when his man came busting out of the bag room and excitedly announced in his high pitched Irish accent, "Oh fer #$@&'s sake, Wiz, somebody's stole me #$@&ing practice balls!" obviously unaware that Wiz had taken them with him. Thinking quickly, even though he was coping with a gigantic hangover, Wiz chimed in, "Are you serious? Man, that's terrible. What is this world coming to?"

Wiz dodged a big one there. Had he 'fessed up, he would have not only gotten sacked, but word would have spread amongst the players about the incident and Wiz would have been a marked man. Lucky son-of-a-bitch didn't have to shag balls that week, either.

In those days on the European Tour, the total purse, per event, averaged between $200,000 and $300,000. Today, players on the PGA Tour make that much for finishing 10th. As caddies, our base wage for the week was around $140, plus what meager percentage we'd make if our man made the cut. If inexpensive digs were not available and the overall cost of staying was high, we'd be fortunate if the week was a break-even proposition. Our consumer price index for each venue became a pint of lager. The cost of a brew was the barometer of the cost of going to a tournament. That being said, a typical conversation between caddies went something like this:

"Hey, are you going to Copenhagen next week?"
"I'm not sure. I heard it's really expensive there."
"Sure is, a pint is about 6.5 Pounds ($10)."
"No, I won't be making that trip. I'm due for a week off."

Or it might also go something like this:

"Will we be able to find cheap digs next week in Jersey?"
"Should do, a pint is only 59 Pence (under $1) there."

The practice pitch at St. Cloud Golf Club in Paris was not spacious by any measure, so shagging balls that week possessed a real element of danger. We caddies were in such close proximity to each other that we had to keep your eyes peeled for any golfer's shot coming our way. Inevitably, I failed to see an incoming ball and got nailed dead in the center of my forehead, knocking me to my knees. My mother always told me I had a hard head, and I now had proof of it. I got back on my feet and tried to locate the assassin but to no avail.

Getting beaned on the practice pitch was a caddie rite-of-passage back in those days.

Another golf-related wrong occurred that week when Reesie got paired with Sam Torrance for the first round. On one hole, I left Stuart's bag standing up while I went to retrieve yardage and of course, it fell over right in Sam's downswing, causing him to hit it sideways. He was one of the cooler players but because of my blunder, was more pissed off than Leona Helmsley after receiving a tax bill.

I added two more caddie commandments to my tablets after that week. The first: Never, ever leave a golf bag standing up because the Golfing Gods have a sense of humor and will topple it at the exact opportune moment. Number two: When all else fails, duck.

For the European PGA Championship the next week at Wentworth in Surrey, England, we made a corporate decision to address the logistic/fiscal issue of staying in hotels and each purchased pup tents to stay in at the golf course. The most obvious benefit of this was the enhancement of our profit margin, but I use the term profit very loosely. The other benefit was that we'd be at the tournament, negating the transportation issue. The only real drawback was the personal hygiene issue; that and a few others we didn't consider.

We found a spot in the woods at the club that we deemed suitable and without asking permission, set up a tented village. Our motto at the time was: act first and beg for forgiveness later.

We built a cozy little neighborhood, our tents in a circle, with a place for a campfire in the center, all in the midst of a thicket of large trees and lush foliage. We attempted to infiltrate the clubhouse for showering purposes, but Wentworth is a high-end joint and they weren't having any of it. We got lucky and found a bathroom on the course that was left open and did our best to cleanse ourselves using the sink and faucet. From week to week, this would prove to be the biggest challenge when camping at an event.

Unhappy Campers

One of the premier aspects of roughing it was the camaraderie that developed between the camping caddies, as we became known. We were the United Nations of loopers, and even though there were 16 of us from half as many countries, we were all brothers-in-arms, and a strong bond was formed. In the spirit of all things caddie, a good nickname was in order, so we put our heads together and came up with The Sod Hogs, derived from the fact that the earth was our bed. Little did we know at the time, after many weeks of this living arrangement, our odoriferous nature would resemble that of swine.

It is difficult to convey to you how awesome it was to come back to the campsite, after imbibing several pints at the local pub, to find a bonfire roaring in the middle of our temporary housing tract. One of our crew, Rockin' Robin, was decent on the guitar and provided background music for effect. We sat around the fire, glassy eyed, until one by one, we adjourned to our private dwellings. Some nights, we didn't even go out, choosing to stay 'home' and eat in, which entailed throwing canned goods into the fire and then fishing them out after a couple of minutes, devouring the contents straight from the can. We got resourceful and fashioned the rebar gallery rope holders lining the golf course into a spit for cooking chicken and other delectables. It was the caddie version of the Showtime Rotisserie, and even though it wasn't fancy, it sure was tasty. Refrigeration was an unobtainable luxury; needless to say, we drank our fair share of warm ale, which seemed to get us even more plastered. We discovered that a hidden bonus of staying in nylon tents was that you could enjoy the auditory nature of another's flatulence without having to endure the odor.

Next stop on the tour schedule was the event on the isle of Jersey, one of the Channel Islands in the English Channel. The two choices for transport to Jersey were either a long, puke-infested ferry ride, or by air. I'll give you one guess which one I pushed for. Plymouth was the departure point to fly to Jersey, so we packed up our gear on Sunday after the final round at Wentworth and hopped a train in that direction.

The isle of Jersey is a tax haven for the rich and playground for the young. It was said that if you couldn't get any action there, you couldn't get any in a whorehouse with a fist full of fifties. We found a camping ground near the golf course where there were oodles of young ladies staying. Plus, our choice for watering hole o' the week was a place called La Buvette, located a short distance away in St. Helier. A pint of lager was under $1, they absolutely would not accept a tip, and the joint was chock full of attractive ladies. It was looper Xanadu. The golf course was a seaside links course with a view of the water from almost every hole. Reesie played okay, finishing tied for 33rd, but that week was more about fun than money and we were all just trying to cover our nut and make it to the next event.

We went back to the bigger island for The Tournament Players Championship at St. Mellion the following week. Upon arrival there, we went in search of a suitable camp site and found an abandoned house off the 10th hole that we promptly claimed as our digs and named Theresa Greenfield's. The place was in shambles but the upper floor could accommodate us all and we figured it would be a nice break from the cramped quarters of our usual three-sided dwellings. We immediately went to work unrolling our sleeping bags, and in no time the place resembled a Turkish refugee camp. You would have thought we had been staying there for a month.

Basil Von Rooyen, part of the South African contingent of The Sod Hogs, was nicknamed Thirsty, due to his voracious appetite for alcoholic beverages. He had a friend named Roger Fairbairn from back home who joined up with us to follow the tour, and we learned that he was on the run from the South African government because he skipped out on his mandatory Army service, which was required of every young man. He was basically AWOL, and figured this was the perfect way to hide. Now that I think about it, following any tour was the perfect witness protection program. I wondered how many of my colleagues were on the run from someone or something. I realized that I was out there because I was on the run too…from myself.

Boris Janjic was another member of our gang. He hailed from down under, and in typical Aussie fashion, was quick to tell you how much better everything was there. It made everyone wonder why he ever left Australia. His catchphrase was, "Is that any focking good, Sonny?" which he blurted out whether it was a golf shot to his liking or a hot looking female.

Boris wasn't a bad guy, but he was a human toothache—a gnawing pain that really bothered you after a while. We implemented a caddie rule that one could not talk about any happenings from the day's round, unless it was something totally extraordinary, like your man making two holes-in-one. This came about because we'd be in the pub enjoying post-round bevies and someone would make the mistake of asking Boris, "How'd your man do today?"

That's all he needed to open the flood gates. "Well, he hit his drive left off the first tee and when we got to the ball, it was sitting in a focking divot, so he took an extra club and blew it over the focking green and…Then, on the second I told him it was a focking 8 iron…" The man had no internal editor.

One time Boris started this crap with Wiz, who quickly cut him off, "Boris, hold on a minute. Gimme 50 pounds."

"Give you 50 pounds. Why would I focking give you 50 pounds, mate?"

"If I'm going to have to go through this round with you, I'm gonna get #$@&ing paid for it! It's either that or shut the #$@& up!"

Another time, we were letting off some steam in the pub and Boris announced, "It's been a focking while, I'm gonna get laid," as he perused the place for his next unlucky victim.

Wiz put his pint glass down on the bar and declared, "Boris, the only chance you have of getting laid is if you crawl up a chicken's ass and wait!"

Once, when Boris pulled up to the bar and announced to us, "Well, I saved my man four fockin' shots out there today" Wiz chimed in with, "What, you didn't show up until the 5th tee?"

We wrapped up our week at Theresa Greenfield's and decided to skip the next two weeks in Biarritz and Monte Carlo. You probably think we were nuts to pass up the chance to visit ground zero of the Lifestyles of the Rich & Famous, but we were coming off seven events in a row that included some brutal travel and living conditions. Plus, the CPI (caddie pint index) spiked at both of these venues. There were no tournaments on the tour that were more expensive than these two.

Liverpool was a stone's throw from Plymouth, and we made it back to our base camp, a.k.a. Wiz's flat, on Sunday night. We were exhausted and beyond happy to be there and recharge our batteries. I can't say the same for Mr. and Mrs. Robinson, the tenants who lived in the flat below. They greeted us when we entered the building. "Oh… Hello, Wayne," with plastic smiles, their disdain for our presence impossible to conceal.

"Hello, Mr. and Mrs. Robinson," Wiz replied, followed by an uncomfortable few seconds of silence.

"So when will you be leaving?" they asked.

"A couple of weeks," he answered.

"Oh…really…well, that's great. Bye," as they scurried into their flat.

They were horrible liars and we could hear them griping almost before the door was closed. Now that I think about it, with all the noise we generated and with our night owl lifestyle, I wouldn't have wanted us as neighbors either.

After a couple more weeks of staying out all night and sleeping all day at Wiz's, we made our way to Glasgow for the tournament at Hagg's Castle. The camping arrangement there was more than sufficient, as we set up at the far end of the practice pitch. There was a rugby club which contained showers we could use and best of all, there was a pub on-site. Our nomadic band expanded when Rick and Sheila parked their caravan adjacent to our tents. This was a blessing and a curse because Sheila ran a little canteen business out of the trailer, making us tea and toast in the morning, sandwiches during the day and a meal at night. The bitter end of the bargain was having to endure Rick's constant babbling on about every subject under the sun, but it was a small price to pay for the culinary trade off. Overall, they were nice folks and we would catch lifts with them in the near future, an activity we dubbed "sweating it out with Rick and Sheila."

The only negative facet of our campsite was the lack of burnable material, which was rectified when a couple of the boys found several enormous truck tires. Burning them created smoke equal to a volcanic eruption, but the fires burned hot and long, which helped if the urine disposal issue arose during the night. I'm pretty sure those fires were visible from outer space and unbelievably toxic.

Davey Kirk, a.k.a. Captain Kirk, Kirkie or Cap'n, was a native Glaswegian caddie who followed the tour on a regular basis. He was the quintessential Scot; a thick little man with a pinkish complexion, red hair and a large scar traversing his left cheek, the result of a good old fashioned glassing. His brogue was thicker than peanut butter, making his speech almost incomprehensible. I learned to do a lot of nodding around Kirkie.

At the time, he was working for a quirky Welshman named Philip Parkin, whose cheese was slipping off his cracker. Seriously, this guy was one brick short of a load. He had a ton of talent but always seemed to get in his own way on the course. During one of the tournament rounds, Philip accused Kirkie of supplying him with a defective distance to the flag. As unintelligible as Cap'n was, I don't know how Philip could have come to the conclusion that a yardage was wrong. The disagreement started out small and blossomed into a full on yelling-match, culminating in Kirkie dropping the bag and walking off the course. The situation has to get pretty hairy for this to occur, and usually, when it does, a volunteer will come forth out of the gallery and tote the bag to finish the round. Not in this case though. Parkin picked up Kirkie's discarded caddie bib (which he had actually thrown at Parkin), and put it on to pack his own bag. When he arrived at his ball, he figured out the yardage, took off the bib, played his shot, put the bib back on, replaced the divot, tended to the other caddie duties and continued packing the bag. This sequence of events was replayed over the course of the last 8 holes. We all rushed to the 18th green to catch a glimpse of the whacko caddying for himself.

After the round, Kirkie confronted him to demand his base wage for the week, but Parkin wasn't amenable to it. The embers were rekindled, ending with the Cap'n confiscating Philips' sticks, vowing to hold them hostage until he was paid what he believed was owed him. Parkin then took the matter into his own hands and called the police, who gave the clubs back to Parkin and told him to pay up. The incident was covered in the sports section of the paper the following day, and actually received more press than the leader of the tournament.

Kirkie wasn't a Sod Hog, but he wasn't a member of our opposing clique, The Supercads, either. They were a band of caddies who basically thought they were better than us, constantly peering down their noses when looking in our direction. When we were still staying in regular digs, we'd ask them where they were staying and all we'd get out of them was gibberish and sideways talk, as if disclosing that information was a security breach. Truth be told, they were aware of our party habits and looking back, I wouldn't have wanted to stay where we were staying, either. Kirkie swayed in our direction and butted heads with several of the Supercads on a regular basis, going so far as to give one a Glasgow kiss (head butt) a couple of times.

Sadly, several years later, Davey Kirk was traveling with four other caddies when the driver fell asleep at the wheel and the vehicle plunged off a cliff. Miraculously, two of the occupants survived but Kirkie wasn't one of them, and he perished in the crash.

The famous Stevie Williams was a card-carrying member of the Supercads back in those days on the European Tour, but you wouldn't have recognized him. He had wavy shoulder length hair and was a pretty buff dude. It was rumored that he wrestled crocodiles at some point in his past, and he had a reputation for his ability to handle himself, mano-a-mano. He was a cross between Crocodile Dundee and a WWF wrestler. I don't recall Kirkie ever giving him a Glaswegian smooch, but that would have been one hell of a cage fight. Even back then, Steve had an air about him like he was on a mission to fulfill some kind of destiny. Unlike us, he was out there to make money, not just to party and get laid.

Luminous Eyebrows and 15 Club Duncan were a couple of other reigning members of The Supercads. The former was so-called by his moniker because he was fair-haired and possessed eyebrows that seemed to glow, even in bright light. Even worse, the latter attained his unfortunate nickname because he let his man tee off not one, but two days in a row with an extra implement in his bag. Not exactly the way you want to be addressed if you are a professional tour caddie.

But the Tiger Woods of characters caddying on the European Tour was an Englishman who went by the moniker of Silly Billy. The Brit's proper name is still a mystery, but he always showed up at the course in a tattered suit and carrying a briefcase, like he was there to complete a business merger. The façade toppled when you noticed the remnants of straw in his hair from the barn he slept in the night before. I got a look inside his briefcase once and saw the contents, which included a notepad containing poetry he had written, a yo-yo, a pack of chewing gum, a toothbrush and a girlie picture.

Billy had curly black hair with grey accents, a pointy nose, beady steel blue eyes and teeth like a jack-o-lantern. His most notable facial feature was a deep cleft in his chin that must have been difficult to shave, judging by the stubble that always seemed to elude the razor.

Billy was the king of caddie one-liners, including:

"You couldn't club a cave man."

"The last time you gave the right club, the Pope was an altar boy."

"You're about as much help on the golf course as a snooker table on a high-speed yacht."

"If I was as ugly as you, I'd walk on my hands and teach my ass how to chew gum."

Billy's on-course escapades were second only to his one-liners. It was European Tour lore that he was working for the great Severiano Ballesteros in an event years ago, when they stepped on the 14th tee leading by a couple of shots on Sunday. Seve was weighing his club options and asked Billy, "How far to carry the trap on the left?"

Billy flipped open his yardage notepad, quickly perused it, and announced, "235 yards."

Seve looked perplexed and asked a second time, "How far?"

"235," Bill answered, this time more authoritatively.

Seve stood glaring at the bunker and asked, "Billy, are you sure?"

"I'm positive," he retorted.

"Let me see the yardage book," Seve continued. Billy ignored him as if he had just asked him in Spanish.

"Billy, let me see your yardage book!" this time more firmly.

Billy slowly and reluctantly surrendered it to the Spaniard, who promptly rifled through it, searching for the data. What he found was that every page was dead blank. Billy had been eyeballing the yardage the entire tournament, his ploy discovered late in the final round. Even though he had been duped, Seve the Great managed to hold it together and go on to win the event. Most golfers would have unraveled like a cheap sweater. For his efforts, Billy was given his pay for the week, along with his walking papers.

Another legend has it that Billy was working for an up-and-coming British golfer at The Open when they reached a par 3 of 190 yards. After receiving this information, the young man asked Billy, "What do you like here?"

Billy's response was, "I like a nice 5 iron here." "

Billy, I feel a little bit of a breeze hurtin' here. I was thinking 3 iron."

"It's a 5 iron," Billy responded, with resolve.

"I don't know Billy…"

And Billy replied, "Look, I was caddying for Gary Player at this tournament years ago and from this exact tee and this exact distance he hit a 5 iron."

"All right, Billy, I'll hit 5," the player reluctantly surrendered.

He went through his routine and proceeded to hit that 5 iron as flush as he possibly could, the ball on a direct path to the flag. He was holding his pose and drooling, waiting in anticipation to see where the ball would eventually finish, and it landed 20 yards short of the green. He raced to his bag to commence the discussion on the obvious miscue.

"Goddammit it Billy, that was the wrong #$@&ing club. Whadda' got to say for yourself?"

Without skipping a beat, Billy yanked his cigar out of his mouth and calmly said, "Gary Player came up short, too."

Billy was caddying for another Spaniard, Manuel Pinero, when there was another club-related discussion in the middle of a fairway. In this instance, Pinero liked a 7 iron, but Billy talked him into hitting 6. Pinero blew it over the green and Billy blurted out, "Great shot… wrong club!" followed by his maniacal laugh.

A young British golfer Billy was working for asked him, after receiving the yardage to the hole, "Billy, do you think I can get an 8 iron there?" Billy's quick response, "Eventually!"

My all-time favorite happened during a rain delay at the Irish Open in Dublin. Players and caddies were crammed in the men's locker room, chatting and waiting for the skies to clear. There was a brief period of silence as conversational topics started to dwindle, and Billy piped in with, "I had a date last night and I told her, 'Hey Lovey, yu'r knickers (underwear) are coming down.' And she said, 'How do you know?' And I told her, 'I'VE JUST DECIDED!' "

Wiz and I had the pleasure of traveling to an event with Billy once. It was a crash course in the art of going from one place to another for free. Billy's self-acknowledged claim to fame was that he had traveled more miles without paying than anyone in the history of travel. He enlightened us on the proper way to board a train without a ticket and avoid the conductor. He also taught us how to sneak on a ferry without purchasing a ticket by getting a lorry (truck) driver to let us hide in the sleeper of his cab.

After Kirkie and the others were killed in that tragedy, a collection was taken up for their loved ones. Players and caddies gave generously, but unfortunately, someone made the enormous blunder of trusting Billy with the proceeds, which is like trusting the government with your money. He permanently borrowed one of the courtesy cars and pulled a Jimmy Hoffa on us. They found the car abandoned in an airport in Spain months later, but Billy hasn't been seen or heard from since.

The next event after Glasgow was in Stockholm, where the CPI peaked again. We hadn't yet made up our minds if we were going, and decided to see how we felt after Hagg's Castle. By Monday morning our tent village was reduced to two, as the rest of the lads had gone, and the only evidence that a once vibrant community had existed there were the remains of a tire still smoldering in the makeshift fire pit. I awoke that morning and yelled over in the direction of Wiz's tent, "Hey Wiz, are you awake?"

"Yeah, I'm awake," the conversation now occurring from tent to tent.

"Wiz, wanna go to Sweden?" I asked.

"Nah. Do you?"

"Not really. So, where do you want to go?" I asked.

"I don't care, where do you want to go?" he countered.

"I dunno—wanna go to back to the flat?"

"Nah," he answered.

"How about Paris?" I inquired.

"Nah."

"I heard Barcelona is nice."

"Nah," he answered empathetically.

"How about Brussels, Wiz?"

After a long pause came his response, "Okay. All right, Brussels it is."

We packed our gear and for no apparent reason, went to Belgium to see what was going on there. Sometimes I really miss the carefree days of being a Sod Hog.

After our week of rebel rousing in Brussels, we joined back up with the Sod Hogs at The Belfry in Sutton Coldfield, England. They already had Sod Hog Central set up, which the tour officials made us relocate on the back of the practice pitch. It's a tony resort and I guess they didn't think our tents added to the panache of the place. There was a killer nightclub at the facility called The Chalet, so needless to say, there was plenty of shagging balls and lugging the clubs around with a big hangovers that week.

I decided to give it a rest one night and just take it easy in my Prince Michael of Kent (tent) after grabbing a bite to eat. As I listened to some music, I felt the earth tremble and then stop abruptly. I whipped off my headphones and stuck my head out of my tent and discovered that Gaz and his player had driven the player's Jaguar onto the range and decided to do a power slide on the wet grass, the car coming to rest about one foot from my head! They were absolutely torched and carrying on like mad men, totally oblivious to the fact that they nearly parked the car on top of me. That's something you don't have to worry about when you're staying in a hotel.

The tournament at The Belfry concluded, and The Sod Hogs were on the move again to St. Andrews (one of the most spectacular venues in the game), but I decided to stay behind to spend a few extra days with Debra, a lovely lass I'd met. Wiz gave me guff about it, stressing that we were going to the outdoor cathedral of golf, but given the choice between going there and hanging out with Debra, I stuck to my guns, telling him, "St. Andrews isn't going anywhere. I'll see you there."

After a couple of glorious days with Debra, I went north for the 113th Open Championship. The idea of going to the home of golf, The Royal and Ancient Golf Club at St. Andrews was exhilarating beyond words.

Upon arriving there, I saw or felt what all the fuss is about. The atmosphere of St. Andrews envelopes you like a warm sweater. Even though the course, from a manicure standpoint, is dare I say, a goat track, the rich tradition and history of the game is palpable. One can peer out onto the course and imagine Old Tom Morris swinging away at it with a wooden shafted club, wearing a plaid jacket and tie. The feeling I got when I looked from the 18th tee over the Swilcan Bridge and down the fairway with the R & A Clubhouse in the background, was the same thing I felt the first time I laid my eyes on the Eiffel Tower. I have a painting of that exact view hanging in my office and as I write this, I am still able to conjure up these emotions.

I wandered around searching for a Sod Hog, when I bumped into Johann, a South African member, who informed me that Wiz was at the putting green by the 1st tee. It was as if I hadn't seen him in years and I was ecstatic to hook back up with him, but he had an added bonus…Scotty was with him! If it felt like I hadn't seen Wiz in years, it felt like I hadn't seen the Scotsman in decades. With the greetings behind us, we spun our adventures for Scotty. When I arrived at the part where I was turned away from the London airport because of my lack of a work permit, he laughed and said, "Oh fer #$@&'s sake, Larry, I told you not to say anything about caddying."

"Really, Scotty, when exactly did you inform me of this little detail? When we were pissed out of our minds at a bar in the Desert?"

"Oh #$@&, yeah, maybe," he declared with a laugh.

At St. Andrews, Wiz and I were in the same boat, as he didn't have a bag either, but Scotty had a connection at ABC and got us jobs as spotters for the telecast. We were assigned to follow a group around the course and report on scores and other issues via radio headsets. The pay was nominal but it was better than nothing and helped offset some of the cost of being there while allowing us to be on the golf course instead of behind the ropes like everyone else. Camping was out of the question at St. Andrews, so we rented a house in the quaint hamlet of Craigrothie, some miles away, which added the expense of taxi fare to and from the golf course. We minimized this by packing as many of us as we could into a cab, reminding me of the old college tradition of seeing how many students would fit in a phone booth.

The '84 Open was the coming-out party for Aussie Ian Baker-Finch, who was a mainstay on the leader board for much of the tournament, but came down 18 on Sunday with two broken wings and an engine on fire, eventually finishing tied for 9th. I was disappointed for him, but not for his caddie Wobbly, who was a reigning member of The Supercads and a complete wanker.

The tournament became a three-way showdown between Balles-teros, Langer and Tom Watson, vying to win this record-setting 6th British Open. Wiz and I were assigned to follow the Fred Couples/Lanny Wadkins pairing, and after the completion of their round, we ventured back out on the course to shadow Ballesteros playing his final hole. We crossed the Swilcan Bridge right behind him, and I can tell you that I will never, ever forget the sound of that raucous crowd surrounding the 18th. We managed to sneak past the R&A Gestapo manning the clubhouse and made it out onto the rear steps to witness one of the greatest finishes in Open history. The explosion of applause when Seve snuck that final birdie in the side door, and the maniacal grinning and fist pumping that followed, is forever etched in my memory. He used a silhouette of the image from that moment in time as his logo. I happened to be standing a mere 75 feet from him when it happened.

Wiz and I, to keep from burning ourselves out, took another week off after The Open, which we spent at the flat. I considered going back to see Debra but ultimately decided on some rest and relaxation in Liverpool. We would meet up with that traveling band known as the Sod Hogs in Dublin the following week.

Today's game has become so technical with all the advances in metallurgy and composite materials that it's hard to keep up. If you watch a golf telecast, you'll hear commentators refer to launch angles and ball spin rates. The lofts and lies of the players' equipment are measured to the most stringent specifications, using equipment developed by NASA. If they choose to tweak a club to maximize performance, a technician is available to set it to an exact degree.

At the '84 Irish Open, I was in the locker room waiting for my most recent job acquisition when I witnessed the reigning Open

Champ Seve Ballesteros performing some club recalibrating himself, with no high-tech gear to aid him. He had every one of his irons out of his bag, propped up against the lockers. He grabbed one, and holding the grip of the club like it was a cane, began banging the toe on the tile floor. He then gripped it properly, set up in an address position and stared at it intently. He grabbed it once again, began banging the toe and again took an address stance with it. When he got it where he wanted it, he looked at me, his audience of one and proclaimed, "Perfect." Then he took the next in line and started the process all over again. Some of them he would just grip and address and utter the same single word, "Perfect." I saw him take one and wedge it under the row of lockers and push down on the grip in a repeating motion. It looked like he was pumping water from a well. Obviously trying to flatten the lie, it ended with the same result, "Perfect."

Like so many of the early greats in the game, Seve was a former caddie. He taught himself the game, learning through trial and error. He also learned to use his eye to properly set his lofts and lies of his sticks. If today's technology had been available then, of course, he would have utilized it, but at the time, he used what he had and trusted: his eye, a tile floor and a row of wooden lockers. I believe he had it dialed in as I watched him hoist the Claret jug two weeks before and he finished 2nd that week at the Irish Open.

We sweated it out with Rick and Sheila, catching a lift with them to Galway for the Celtic International. The price we paid for the free ride was having to endure Rick's constant blather about everything from how he taught his rabbit to smile when he was a kid, to the refining process of petroleum, from start to finish. We just did a lot of nodding and pretended we were interested, hoping that he wasn't going to spring a pop quiz on any of his amazing subjects. We leapt out of the car before it came to a complete stop at the tournament.

Earlier, I was being a bit of a Pollyanna regarding the camping situation. It was wonderful in ways and there were benefits, but over time, the harsh realities were beginning to set in and erode my caddie longevity. Most of it was weather-related. The meteorological conditions in Europe are so capricious that you can experience all four seasons in one day, but rain is a staple of the weather there. Caddying in the rain really sucked, making you sincerely wish that you were an octopus. That was the only possible way to hold an umbrella, the yardage book and pin sheet, golf bag, dry golf glove and a dry towel at the same time. Then, when your miserable round was over, instead of going back to your digs and catching a hot shower like the rest of the caddies, we got to go back to our tents and deal with our saturated clothing as best we could in a wet, confined space. A hot shower to defrost was a fantasy unless the locker room was accessible, and even if it was, afterwards, the only place to hunker down was in our triangular boudoirs. You could forget about kicking back and watching some television.

Heaven forbid it was raining when it was time to pack up and move on to the next tourney. Once, we made the huge mistake of packing up our tents when they were still wet. They were ravaged by more mold than a post-Katrina house, and no matter how hard we tried to sanitize them, we couldn't rid them of their plague. Under the environmental laws of today, a hazmat crew would have declared those tents uninhabitable.

If it was difficult to care for our feet while a club looper at North Shore Country Club, it was a monumental chore while caddying on the European Tour and living in a tent. Our bodies were abused by the caddying, our minds abused by the golfers, our livers from the nightlife, and our feet bore the brunt of the wear-and-tear. Keeping them dry and healthy was a lesson in futility. Clean, dry socks were a precious commodity, and it wasn't uncommon to see a Sod Hog tent decorated with an array of moldy, filthy socks in an attempt to dry them out. Most of the time, we engaged in a sartorial triage, wearing the pair that was the least disgusting. But even worse than the mold and the rest of the disgustingness was the fact that living in tents did not help the romantic prospects of a single, young man travelling through Europe. Even Rudolph Valentino would have had a hard time enticing a woman to accompany him to a tent.

The European Tour chugged along and my caddie battery was starting to run low. Sleeping in tents, phone booths, on train station benches and anything else that would hold us was beginning to wear on my nerves. I was tired of being lost all the time and having to ask directions from someone who didn't speak English or wasn't interested in helping us reach our destination. I was sick of hauling a golf bag in freezing weather. To semi-paraphrase Mr. Twain, the coldest winter I ever spent, was the summer I caddied on the European Tour. The travel and experiences were worth their weight in gold, but I was missing the comforts of home. The thought of returning to the motherland was beginning to seep through the crevices of my war-torn mind. I decided to stick it out through the Panasonic European Open at Sunningdale and then take it on home. That meant a trip to Switzerland for the Ebel European Masters at Crans-Sur-Sierre. Frankfurt, Germany was the stop prior, which left us a quick hop to the birthplace of neutrality.

The golf course at Crans-Sur-Sierre is located on a plateau at 5,000 feet above sea level in the Swiss Alps. With unbelievable views of Mont Blanc and the Matterhorn, it was an idyllic venue for a golf tournament, and even though I was burned out, I didn't mind hauling a golfer's luggage around a golf course that week. The CPI spiked at this tournament also, but it was a place you had to see at least once in your life. Staying in a hotel was out of the question, so we found a suitable camping location near a lake, which was not only aesthetically pleasing, but also satisfied our hygienic needs.

The Sod Hogs on top of the world.

One of the many highlights of being in Crans was taking the cable car up to the top of the mountain. There were actually two cable cars to get to the top; the first was a large one that held about 30 people, and then everyone transferred to smaller ones that held four. It was on the second one that Wiz discovered how to unlock the door and hang out of the car, dangling precariously several hundred feet above the valley below. I had no sooner coaxed him back in, when he and Gaz began rocking side to side, making the car swing violently as it ascended. That really made my ass pucker and I pleaded with them to stop.

After several libations in the mountaintop bar, the detachment of Sod Hogs was feeling on top of the world, and it wasn't just the altitude. We ventured out of the bar and hiked up the final 100 yards to the very top of the mountain. Normally, crossing the length of a football field was a piece of cake, but at that elevation, in our inebriated state, it was barely negotiable. We panted and wheezed as we lay on the ground, feeling like we had just summited Kilimanjaro.

Finally catching our breath, we rose one-by-one and took in the spectacular vistas afforded us at that altitude. There was an enormous, sprawling glacier resting quietly and peacefully in the valley below us. One of the lads committed the crucial mistake of getting too close to the edge of the precipice we were atop, which gave Wiz the opportunity to push him over, yelling, "#$@& OFF!" as he did. Simon happened to be wearing his slick waterproofs, causing him to rocket down the steep slope like he was on a waterslide. We had just discovered how we would spend the next three hours, as we hurtled ourselves down the face of that glacier and then trudged up it, only to throw ourselves down again.

Back in those days, our travel schedule was predicated on one issue—whether or not we possessed the dough to get to a certain destination. It was nearing the end of the season and I was getting homesick. And I now had the money to get back stateside. I had done a pretty good job of saving enough to purchase an airline ticket, which I carried with my passport on my person at all times, just in case I had to flee. Looking back, I guess we were the war criminals of the golf world, except the U.S. was my intended safe-haven rather than Argentina.

We worked the final round at Crans, had a couple of pre-travel libations, and began our pilgrimage to Mother England. The effects of the long day and the alcohol took their toll, and we were absolutely knackered as we rode the train. Once we crossed the border into France and neared Paris, we transferred to a commuter train, which negated the option of stretching out and sleeping. Wiz bypassed this slight problem by climbing up onto the luggage rack above the seats that ran the length of the car. We all followed suit shortly thereafter when we realized it was the only game in town. It wasn't a claustrophobic's ideal sleeping location but it worked. I dozed off thinking the situation would make an awesome country tune, "*I'm half-in-the-bag on the luggage rack of life.*"

We happened to reach Paris right at rush hour the following morning, and one-by-one we began climbing down from our perches. The commuters on that train had no idea we were up there, and the French aren't the most happy-go-lucky bunch in the world. Try putting your foot on the top of someone's head at 6:30 in the morning and see what kind of reaction you get. We got an earful of French expletives.

The camping scenario at Sunningdale was satisfactory, as we found a suitable locale for our tent village, equipped with plenty of wood for campfires. They say the epitome of mixed emotions is your mother-in-law going over a cliff in your new Mercedes. I was experiencing my own, knowing that these might be my last days as a Sod Hog.

GOLF IS FLOG SPELLED BACKWARDS FOR A REASON: LIFE WITH THE AUSSIE

THIS IS A difficult chapter to write, based on the fact that having Bruce Crampton as my employer was bittersweet, to say the least. A large portion of the time I was content and making a good living; the remainder, I was contemplating taking a swing at him. I am torn between my loyalties to Bruce, even after all these years, and my duty to portray the way it really was. All that being said, here goes.

The metamorphosis of the Senior Tour from one event to a full-blown tour is an interesting one. The Legends of Golf was the embryo that would grow and become the Senior PGA. Tour, and a ton of the credit has to be given to Fred Raphael, one of the masterminds of the Shell's Wonderful World of Golf series. He recognized that there was a market still interested in watching old golf relics compete. There were no complaints from the players, as most believed their days of glory had passed and had resigned themselves to living out their years on what little money they didn't make. It was no secret that the Senile Tour was the biggest mulligan they would ever be granted.

The Senior PGA Tour wasn't just the greatest sporting venture of the 80s and early 90s, it was a sociological experiment measuring the long-term effects of the pressure on the human psyche of playing professional golf. This wasn't the main objective of the endeavor, but it turned out to be a byproduct, and the results were unnerving. Some of the players and caddies had been in the sun way too long. Chi Chi was the only player I ever heard admit that we were all getting a little goofy.

It was April of 1987 and I was familiar with Bruce Crampton because he paired with my boss, Orville Moody in The Legends of Golf played in Austin, Texas. Bruce was called The Ironman because he played every event and had amassed seven victories. He was one of the dominators on the Senior PGA Tour at the time, and Orville was one of a select few who gelled well with him both on and off the course. Bruce didn't possess an overabundance of friends, and the fact that Orville was one of them was a paradox. They were complete opposites in many ways.

To begin with, they played the game differently. Bruce hit it strictly left-to-right; Orville hit it any way he chose to. Bruce was a solid putter; Orville wished he was. Bruce was pretty dour on the course; Orville didn't get too worked up about anything. But their biggest dissimilarity was in their physical statures. Bruce was a fitness fanatic and wouldn't consume anything detrimental to his health. Orville was rotund and had his own space at the Sonic Drive Thru back in Sulphur Springs, Texas where he lived. Thus, I described Bruce's swing was "poetry in motion." Orville's was 'poultry in motion.'

Bruce and Orv had it dialed in the first round of The Legends, shooting 59 in the best-ball event. This was before the days of high-fives, but they had their own form of celebration. Any time Orville made birdie, Bruce rubbed his barrel-like belly. NBC televised the tournament, and this ritual got a lot of airtime

The second round was more of the same until Bruce's caddie distracted Bob Goalby, one of the other competitors in the group, while he was playing his shot. Bob was a bit of a hot head and got in Bruce's face.

"You keep your #$@&ing caddie outta' my way when I'm hitting my shot!" This sabre rattling was poorly timed, as Orville was out of the hole, leaving Bruce alone to fend for the team. The wind was stolen from our sails when he made the first team bogey of the event.

I was really pissed off, and standing on the next tee, decided to take matters into my own hands by giving Bob the daggers. We stared each other down like a couple of boxers at a pre-fight weigh-in, and I'd like to tell you that I intimidated him, but he was a pretty big guy, besting me in height by about a foot. Make no mistake about it, I was barking up the wrong tree. He probably could have stuffed me into one of my shoes if given the chance. Our eyes locked for an uncomfortable second, neither saying a word, and then he broke the ice by leaning in toward me and saying in a Clint Eastwood tone, "Same to you, son."

We weathered that little hiccup, and the team of Moody and Crampton went on to win the event. It was my first trip to victory lane as a professional tour caddie, even though it was an unofficial event. I could imagine Jaybird back at North Shore telling all the loopers in the caddie yard, "Maletnick finally popped his cherry as a pro jock. Won da' Legends of Golf with da' Sarge" (Sarge was Orville Moody's nickname).

A short month after the Legends win, Orville informed me that Bruce was looking for a new caddie. He wanted someone who could provide more assistance on the course, and Orville thought I'd be a perfect candidate. I loved working for Sarge, but the chance to go work for a top player was right up my alley. He took me straight over to Bruce and set it up. It was a selfless thing to do, but that's what kind of man Orville Moody was. I thanked him for everything he had done for me and asked, "Orv, who's going to pack for you?" "I think my daughter Michelle," he replied.

I was now packing for one of the top guns on the Senior PGA. Tour, and I felt like a 16-year-old kid who just got handed the keys to a Ferrari. It was time to hit the open road and see what this guy could do. The first observation I made when I picked up Bruce's bag was that he ran his golf operation like a military outfit, and that meant it was time for boot camp. He laid out the guidelines and expectations that he had for me, which included being prompt and ready to work, showing up in proper attire, clean and shaven. We also discussed the compensation package which did not include 10% of wins, but a small bonus. It was a non-negotiable offer. He also informed me of what he expected of me on the golf course, which included proper club maintenance and yardage duties. Anything above and beyond that, he would let me know as it arose. Practice rounds were played at 8:30 every Tuesday morning, no exceptions. Bottom line was, I was working for a top player and had to conduct myself like a top caddie. I felt confident in my abilities as a professional caddie and was up for the challenge before me. It was time to stop acting like a Sod Hog and become a Super Cad.

The first event working for Bruce was the Silver Pages Classic played in Oklahoma City. I showed up at the course and ran into Dennis, one of the caddies on the tour. Before I could even say hello, he asked me, "Did you hear? Little Joe shot and killed John last night."

Initially, I thought he was talking about John Lynch, Chi Chi's caddie, but I was quickly informed that it was John Gerski, who packed for Dale Douglass. He and one of the other caddies got into an altercation, culminating in his murder. I knew a lot of these guys were carrying knives, but was disturbed to find out how many were packing heat. For self-preservation purposes, I made a mental note in upper case letters to avoid mouthing off to any of these Saturday-night-special-equipped thugs who wouldn't think twice about sending me on a one-way trip to the glorious Ever After. Better a live caddying chicken than a dead hero.

That inaugural event with the name Crampton on my caddie bib was a harbinger of future battles, as Chi Chi was the only player in the field with a lower score than Bruce. It was his 4th victory of a season that wasn't at the halfway point yet.

The following week we were in Castle Rock, Colorado for the Denver Post Champions of Golf played at the TPC Plum Creek. Bruce played steady the entire event and won the first of many with me on the bag. As we walked up the 18th, with victory a certainty, he told me, "Larry, savor this. It's what we strive so hard for."

I truly appreciated the wisdom he bestowed on me and relished my first individual win as a pro jock. I was also surprised and pleased when he mentioned me in his victory speech at the awards ceremony. Incidentally, Bruce's share of the purse for his victory was $37,500, which is about a third of what a PGA Tour caddie makes for packing for a winner today.

The following week wasn't as exciting, and was actually a rerun of Oklahoma City, as Chi Chi carved his sixth notch in his gun belt and Bruce finished in second position. We were playing with Chi Chi in the final pairing Sunday in Dallas as they dueled it out. Bruce opened up a cozy four-shot lead over Chi Chi, his nearest pursuer, with nine holes left to play. He shot even par 36 on the back side and lost by one. Chi Chi scorched the same nine holes, making five birdies, and shot 31 coming in. Twice he was Adolf Hitler (dead in the bunker) with impossible lies. In each instance I said, "Let's see what the little son-of-a-bitch can do with this," and he nearly holed them both. He would amass seven victories on the Senior Tour that year.

The Senior Tournament Players Championship was even more of the same, except that Bruce's final score tied Chi Chi. This time Gary Player was the spoiler, taking home the trophy and the oversized check.

Billy Casper decided to jump on the bandwagon the next week in Grand Rapids, winning the event. I'll give you one guess who finished in the second slot.

The rivalry between Bruce and Chi Chi extended beyond the golf course; it evolved into a personal battle that bordered on the infantile and resembled what you might witness on an elementary school playground. For instance, Bruce was well aware of Chi Chi's superstitious nature and used it against him as often as possible. When he was in Australia, Bruce purchased a little black satchel that contained Aboriginal bones. They were your run-of-the-mill novelty item, but Bruce had an alternate and sinister plan for them. Every time we got paired with Chi Chi, he tied the satchel to a loop on the golf bag just above the front zipper pocket in plain view. I was instructed to always have the bag situated so Chi Chi would see the bones. It was a weak and infantile attempt to get under Chi Chi's skin and hit him right in his island mentality. But it didn't work, and after a couple of outings with him, Chi Chi approached me and said, "Hey Pards, you tell Bruce I don't care about no #$@&in' chicken bones! They don't bother me!"

Bruce also took the time to paint three golf balls black, and would putt around Chi Chi on the practice green. To this day, I'm not quite sure what this was supposed to accomplish, and the childish prank pretty much backfired. Chi Chi never really noticed, which just reinforced everyone's belief that Bruce's antenna wasn't picking up all the stations.

The battle continued when the Senior Tour came out with electronic scoreboards that couldn't accommodate Chi Chi's full last name, so they just used Chi Chi instead. Bruce found this unacceptable and let the tour officials know it. He said that it gave Chi Chi an unfair advantage and went so far as to point out that Chi Chi wasn't even his real name (how he figured this was advantageous to Chi Chi, I have no idea). In an effort to appease Bruce, they started using as much of Chi Chi's last name as would fit. When he saw RODRIGU displayed on the scoreboards he was red hot. I can still hear him, "What the #$@& do they think I am, spaghetti sauce?!"

Our travelling band of fun made our way to Sam Snead's backyard for the American Express Championship played at the famed Greenbrier Resort in the mountains of West Virginia. You won't believe this, but I once hit a golf ball *a mile.* You won't read about the feat in any record book because it happened at the Grand Canyon with only a couple of my distinguished colleagues present. Over the course of our travels, we got our kicks from launching drivers at strategic locales, teeing the balls up on anything we could stick a tee in, which was usually a beer can. Our favorite launch pad was a precipice we discovered on the south rim of the Canyon near the Bright Angel Lodge. From that spot, you could top it a half a mile and we weren't overly concerned that there were hikers below us. We smacked 'em into the ocean from the beach in Ponte Vedra, across the vast cornfields of

Nebraska, from our hotel room balcony on the 6th floor in Lahaina, Hawaii, and down a dormitory hallway on Long Island. Truth be told, we were jackasses. We could have killed someone. So en route to Greenbriar, while traversing the winding Route 60 just outside of White Sulphur Springs, we discovered Hawk's Nest, a tiny viewpoint towering almost 600 feet above the New River Gorge and a perfect spot to let it fly. We launched shot after shot and timed how long the ball would stay in the air until landing in the New River below, which from that height seemed like an eternity. It was great fun until a park ranger showed up and threatened to throw us in jail if we didn't stop.

Lettin' it fly!

The caddie master at the Greenbrier was an unsophisticated rural gentleman who reminded me of Otis Campbell, the town drunk from the *Andy Griffith Show*. A couple of his country-bumpkin caddies got into a bit of a tiff with a few of the African-American caddies from our itinerant clan, prompting him to announce in a voice akin to the warden's in the movie, *Cool Hand Luke*, "You tour caddies betta' watch ya'selves. My boys all carry knives." I was inclined to tell him to research the John Gerski shooting back in Oklahoma City, but judging by his appearance and apparent absence of grey matter, I was fairly certain reading anything was not in his immediate future.

During the first round of the tournament, Bruce was in the zone and had a 12-footer on the last green to shoot 63. Unfortunately, a weather system blanketed the area and play was halted. We spent the remainder of the day at the clubhouse waiting for the skies to clear, but they never did, and play was to resume the following morning. That meant Bruce was going to have to come out early just to hit one putt.

It was overcast and considerably cooler the next morning as we made our way to the last green. Regardless, Bruce proceeded to bury his putt, giving him the first round lead, which he never relinquished. To review, I had been packing for Bruce for five weeks and didn't finish out of the top two spots, which included two victories. I was riding high and felt like giving Orville a big kiss the next time I saw him.

The glorious mayhem continued when we picked off another one at the MONY Syracuse Senior Classic several weeks later. I left town with another big check and the flag from the 18th green, a practice that would become the norm anytime a victory was had. Syracuse now held a special place in my heart. Wiz had migrated over to the Senior Tour with me, but his impression of Syracuse was vastly different than mine. He thought *Sadexcuse* was a more appropriate name for the city.

As happy as I was with my newfound wealth and success, there was an aspect of caddying for Bruce that was not mentioned anywhere in the job description; I should have been given white gloves and a whistle, because I was required to be an on-course traffic cop. Bruce possessed the uncanny ability to hear birds walk, and he was distracted by the slightest movement of anything. A big part of my job was to make sure that everyone and everything was completely still when he played his shot. This became a sore spot between us because I'd catch flack if I neglected to stop someone or something for disturbing him. The conversation usually went something like this:

"Larry, you should have stopped that man from moving."

"When he moved I told him to stand still."

"You should have told him before he moved."

"I didn't know he was going to move."

"The next time, stop him before he moves."

I was the usual target of Bruce's ire but every so often, one of his competitors found himself in the crosshairs. We were paired with Miller Barber, a.k.a. Mister X or just X, who had the nervous habit of jiggling the change in his pocket. This is a strange little idiosyncrasy, and the perpetrator is usually oblivious that he is doing it. Bruce was on the tee, trudging through his meticulous and torturous pre-shot routine. He had the hearing capability of the six million dollar man, so when X began his annoying little habit from five feet away, Bruce looked up to see who was causing such a huge ruckus, and X stopped jiggling his change. Bruce restarted his pre-shot, X restarted jiggling his change, Bruce looked up to spot the culprit, and X stopped jiggling his change. For the 3rd time, Bruce readdressed the ball, and X started his annoying habit again. It was like watching an Abbott & Costello routine. Bruce finally pulled the trigger, snap-hooking his drive into a hazard on the left. Then he figured out that X was the guilty one, got in his face and said, "Goddmmit it, Miller! Keep your bloody hands still when I'm trying to play!" and stormed off the tee. Miller, oblivious to his infraction, approached me and said in his high, soft, Texas drawl, "Son, I'm gonna tell you something. All that money you're makin' is gonna go towards your rehabilitation. He's goin' over the edge and he's gonna take you with him!" As amusing as this observation was, I wondered if Miller might have a valid point.

The biggest culprits I had to deal with were the very people who were there to help. For whatever reason, the marshals got in the way more than the general public. I fully understood that they donated their time so generously, but I just wished they would be more considerate of golf etiquette. Their two main concerns should have been staying out of the way and staying still. A lot of the marshals were retired military and didn't want some snotty-nosed tour caddie telling them what to do, and some were just there because it was a front row seat to the golf.

Over the course of my tenure with Bruce I had to stop or move people, birds, squirrels, ducks, geese, cars, trucks and more. Once I had to call NASA to stop a satellite from orbiting above the golf course. Another time I had to move a hot air balloon that was tethered next to the driving range because the sound of the burner bothered the delicate genius while he practiced. When I informed the guys manning the balloon that they had to move it, they thought I was kidding. The expressionless look on my face told them otherwise. They began the monumental task of disassembling it, but not before I heard one suggest to the other that they tie the balloon to Bruce's leg and release it.

Some of his fellow competitors had a zero-tolerance policy when it came to Bruce's antics—most notably, former 49er quarterback, John Brodie. He was used to dealing with 300-pound linemen and surely wasn't going to put up with the crap of some powder-puff golfer. When he saw his unfortunate draw for the following day, he came to me and announced, "You tell Bruce not to #$@& with the gallery tomorrow because they may be *my* gallery, and if he #$@&s with them, I'm gonna #$@& with him!"

One of the perks of caddying for a top player came in the form of clothing deals. The Senior Tour was nationally televised and advertisers were looking for any exposure possible. I became friends with most of the t.v. cameramen, which assured me of getting in the shot when Bruce was on television, which was by design. At the time, there was a clothing company by the name of La Mode Du Golf, which was shortened to La Mode. I signed a deal with them that compensated me in clothing, and I ended up with the nickname Larry La Mode. We all have embarrassing eras of our lives, where we look back and say, "What the hell was I thinking?" with regard to clothing, hairstyles or a combination of the two. This is one of mine. Don't get me wrong, I looked professional and it wasn't bad clothing, but I made the mistake of telling them that I would wear any color. Hence, they sent me outfits in aquamarine, bright red, purple and salmon. I was adorned in the salmon one day and Wiz told me that I looked like I had been dipped in Thousand Island dressing. Couple that with the fact that the predominant fabric of their line was polyester and you have some pretty hideous attire. Maybe a better company moniker would have been Ca Mode.

Another difficult aspect of working for Bruce was the constant Jekyll & Hyde routine he put me through. I never knew who was going to show up at the course. One day he'd show up chatty and upbeat; the next he'd get out of the car looking like he just found out he had cancer. I'd ask him how his evening was and he'd tersely tell me to get the clubs out of the trunk and get to the range. I learned very rapidly not to speak until I assessed who I was dealing with.

He also made it abundantly clear that he did not want me talking with anyone other than him while on the golf course. And under no circumstances was I to whistle on the golf course. I committed this horrendous gaffe once and got bitched out because he said that my whistling told him that I didn't have a worry in the world, and that really bothered him. I wanted to tell him, *"Oh, I got a worry. I got a great big worry! I'm worried X knew what he was talking about!"*

An adrenaline junkie is one who performs death defying stunts, eventually becoming hooked on the thrill and danger, and I was becoming one from the pressure I was exposed to on a weekly basis, minus the threat of loss of life, of course. Although, hanging out with Bruce for a prolonged period *did* hold a psychiatric danger. At the Northville Long Island Golf Classic, an unofficial, fledgling event with a $100,000 first prize, and a $60,000 second prize. Bruce looked over at me as we walked off the 15th tee and said with a smirk, "Boy, you are some lucky s.o.b." inferring that I was privileged to be working for him.

"Oh yeah, I was just thinking the same thing about you," I replied.

Bruce finished tied for first with Gary Player for the title, leading to a sudden death playoff. They arranged a split of the prize money so instead of one leaving town with $100K and the other with $60K, they'd both take home $80,000. This is now illegal in official events, but was a normal occurrence back when players weren't making zillions of dollars playing the game and actually needed the money. I was honored that Bruce asked me if I was okay with this arrangement. I told him it was fine as long as I get my victory bonus.

After making more money than I ever believed possible in this racket, I went and did what any red blooded American caddie would do; I bought a Cadillac. I'm not talking about a brand new one.

I found a clean '73 Coupe De Ville owned by a little old lady in the Desert who drove it very little and garaged it a lot. It was mint, metallic green, with a white vinyl top and skirts over the back wheels, to boot. Man, was I styling! It was a nice machine that served me well the first part of my stint on the Senior Tour. As much as I loved that Caddy (incidentally, I didn't buy it because of the name), it wasn't the perfect vehicle for the task at hand. Sure, it was roomy and had a ton of space for hauling luggage, but sleeping in it wasn't much fun, and it was also a lead sled, with an engine that would power an M-1 Abrams tank. I was getting three gas-stations-to-the-mile in it, and that was on the open road, so I began a quest to find something more suitable for the life of a professional tour caddie.

I found the perfect solution at a used car lot in Lexington, Kentucky. She was a used Chevy van with a custom package that included four captain's chairs, a bench seat in the back that folded down into a bed, a television and VCR, and a hanging clothes rack across the back. She was dressed in gold, bronze and brown tones, and after I made her mine, I added chrome wheels, an upgraded stereo and a few other goodies. The *Caddie Wagon* was our home away from home on four wheels. We maintained her fastidiously, and she returned the favor by never breaking down once in all of our treks across the continent. The road trips could be brutal, but the knowledge that no matter where we were, a comfortable night's rest was ahead, made it a lot more bearable. Some of the best times of my life were spent with my cohorts, cruising across the breadbasket of the nation in that vehicle with Eric Clapton and Steely Dan oozing from the speakers.

The timing of my vehicular acquisition could not have been better, as the Crampton train rolled along and we picked off our 4th victory together that week in Lexington. Like always, Bruce thanked me in his victory speech, and a local newspaper wrote an article on yours truly (I was getting more press than most of the golfers). Couple that with the fact that I was caddying for Mr. Sunshine, and I was well aware that I was not the flavor of the month in the eyes of some players. Also, I heard one of them bitching that I dressed better than most players, but it wasn't my fault that I outshined them in polyester.

I adore the quaint borough of Newport, Rhode Island, from the opulent mansions on 17 Mile Drive to The Black Pearl, which serves the best bowl of clam chowder in the world. Newport Country Club is one of the oldest in the U.S., and was founded by the Astors and Vanderbilts, which made it the epicenter of serious wealth a century ago. The site of the inaugural U.S. Open, it wasn't the most modern course around, but it reminded me of many we played on the European Tour, which may explain why I was so fond of it.

The tournament was a Pro-Am format, so we were competing in official rounds with amateurs in the group with us. This was like having outsiders in the operating room while Dr. Crampton was performing elaborate brain surgery, and he wasn't too happy about it, which made my life hell.

Bruce hit his tee shot in the middle of the 18th fairway, and as we made our way to forward tees, one of the golfers in the group in front of us picked up Bruce's ball.

"Goddamit, Larry, go and get my ball from that guy and have him place it back where he got it. Take one of the amateur's carts. Go!"

I hopped in a cart and carefully navigated my way under the gallery ropes, mashing on the gas as soon as I was clear. What I didn't know was that the rope had caught onto one of the golf bags and was now being pulled taut, forming a huge bow and arrow. I hadn't gotten very far when a bystander yelled to alert me of the potential disaster. I turned just as the rebar gallery rope holder released from the ground, the projectile flying directly at me. Luckily for me, it struck me across my head instead of impaling me and turning me into a human shish-ka-bob. Instantly I had a gaping wound above my eye and was bleeding profusely. Someone wrapped a towel around my head and I was whisked away to a local hospital, where several stitches were needed to close the laceration. Bruce was so concerned about me that he went on to birdie the hole, which I jokingly gave him grief about later.

In October we found ourselves in the golf Mecca of Hilton Head for the Seniors International Golf Championship, played at the famed Harbor Town Golf Links. Bruce continued his torrid run, and on the final green was taking dead aim on a putt to tie for the lead. In an unbelievably bad case of perfect timing, a private jet cruising about 50 feet above the deck flew down the waterway adjacent to the 18th right as Bruce pulled the trigger. It startled him and he missed the putt. The tail number on the Citation was N1AP. It was Arnold Palmer.

"Goddammit! Who the hell was that?" Bruce bellowed.

"Take a wild guess," I told him.

Arnold was notorious for his golf course fly-bys, and I thought for sure I was going to have to carry signal flares to keep that from ever happening again.

The end of a very long but also very fruitful year finally arrived, but not before the final event played down in Jamaica at Tryall. The Mazda Champions was a mixed team format pairing the top 10 Senior Tour golfers with the top 10 from the LPGA. Bruce was coupled with lady tour stalwart Betsy King, who oddly enough, possessed the same no-nonsense, all businesslike approach to the game. The shenanigans between Bruce and Chi Chi had diminished for the most part, but were instantly rekindled when Chi Chi found a voodoo doll on his golf cart before play commenced in the first round. It was sporting a little hat like Chi Chi's, and was stuck full of pins. He was fighting mad, and was totally convinced that Bruce was the culprit. I'm fairly positive that he wasn't, but sure wished that he was. A devious third party was trying to fan the flames, and to this day, I would love to know who it was.

On Saturday we encountered another low-flying aircraft, but this time it was a scheduled event, and Arnie wasn't in the cockpit. The tour officials announced that their air horns would be blown at exactly 3:00, halting play as that legend of an aircraft known as the Concorde would make two low passes over the golf course. I will never forget the sight and deafening sound of the SST as she swooped directly over us, her nose down and delta wings outstretched, looking like a majestic bird of prey going in for the kill. She went out over the ocean and circled back, allowing us to take in her splendor once again. Maybe it's just a guy thing, but it was an incredible spectacle.

We closed out the year without a bang, Bruce and Betsy finishing in the top five, but Bruce laid an unexpected surprise on me before we parted. RJ Reynolds was one of the tour's title sponsors and held a yearlong points contest that paid handsomely. People still smoked back then, and tobacco dollars flooded professional sports. He cut me a hefty check from his Vantage Cup bonus money, which I was not expecting. It was such an awesome gesture that I decided on the flight home to splurge and buy him a gift to show my appreciation for the unbelievable year we had together. They say the road to hell is paved with good intentions and I learned how true that is.

The gift I decided to bestow on my generous boss was one that he had expressed interest in a while back. While in Dallas, Bruce worked with golf guru Hank Haney, who videotaped his swing. Bruce instantly fell in love with the technology and the ability to break his swing down to every movement of every muscle at every point, so I bought him a video camera. Nowadays, they give you one if you fill your tank at the local gas station, but this was back in the day when they were very pricey. He was extremely appreciative, and we began to analyze his swing from stem to stern. In retrospect, I must have had a lapse of rational thinking. This was a dangerous item to buy someone already obsessed with the technicalities of a golf swing, and I found myself taping and reviewing countless hours of his. While the rest of the lads were unwinding in the local boozer, I was the Oliver Stone of the driving range. Bruce was a range rat long before I bought him the camera, and I wanted to shoot myself for giving him a reason to extend his practice time. I could have saved myself a ton of money and frustration and just bought him a damn sweater.

I basked in the glorious sunshine of the California Desert during the short off-season in the knowledge that I had a top-notch bag. With Bruce finishing in the second slot on the money list, I knew the previous year was going to be a tough act to follow, as I made my way over the mountain to La Costa for the Tournament of Champions. I was a T of C virgin, having never caddied for an official tournament winner up to that point. This was the only event where we played with the flat-bellies but each in their own respective fields. We played our practice rounds with Payne Stewart, which I thought was a bit of a mismatch, but there was an indirect connection, as Payne's wife also hailed from Down Under, and he and Bruce got along famously.

Payne was an easy-going, fun-loving guy, and it was painful to witness his untimely public demise years later. I cannot even begin to imagine how excruciating it was for his loved ones to watch that pilotless plane soar across the sky inevitably crashing in that South Dakota field.

Besides my driving range woes and on-course crowd control, another duty was laid on me a couple weeks later in Naples, Florida. The 16th hole of The Club at Pelican Bay was a short par 4 with a water hazard fronting the green, forcing a lay-up off the tee. The landing area for the tee shot was divot central, and Bruce knocked his tee shot right into one. Even though it wasn't more than 120 yards to the green, he was basically playing from a bare lie. He chunked it right into the drink and ended up making double-bogey, which didn't do much for his radiant demeanor. Apparently, this little fiasco kept him up that night and he came to the conclusion that a divot was ground under repair in its purest sense, and that a free drop should be granted when a golfer finds himself in one. While he did have a point, there's also a term known as *rub of the green*, which means *tough shit... You hit it there, you play it from there.* He drew up a lengthy petition that he wanted every player to sign so this miscarriage of golf justice could be overturned. Initially, he was the one obtaining the signatures on the document. Some of his fellow competitors signed without a fuss, some signed to make him go away, and some just said no. After a while, the chore was dumped in my lap, and I guess they found it easier to say no to me. I could have been asking them to sign a petition that only large breasted women were allowed to caddie topless and they still would have told me to get lost simply because Bruce authored the legislation.

It was nice working the Florida swing every year. Everyone was fresh after the off season and there were four events clumped together in the sunshine state. The Chrysler Cup was a President's Cup for geezers, teaming the top eight U.S. Senior players against the top eight from the rest of the world. The event was held at The TPC Prestancia in Sarasota, and it was one you wanted to be part of due to the prize money of $50,000 for the winners and $25,000 to the losers.

In Sunday's singles matches Bruce lost, getting closed out on the 16th hole. Players and caddies shook hands and we made our way to the clubhouse to watch the events unfolding in the other pairings… or so I thought. I had just barely gotten comfortable and was ready to dig into some much needed lunch, when one of the event staff came into the cart barn and yelled, "Where's Crampton's caddie?"

"Right here. What's up?" I asked curiously.

"Bruce is on the 17th tee waiting for you and he's pissed!"

"What are you talking about?" I asked.

"He sent me to come and get you. C'mon, I'll give you a lift."

The ride out to the 17th was spent trying to reason why Bruce could possibly be waiting for me, but an answer eluded me. When we pulled up to the tee, Bruce was standing with his arms crossed and a perturbed scowl on his face. I had seen this expression before and it sent shivers down my spine.

"Larry, we haven't finished this round yet. We have two more holes to play!"

"Whaddya' talkin' about? We lost our match. You shake hands and call it a day," I retorted, which really fueled his fury.

"The round is over when we finish playing the 18th hole and not before then!" he yelled at me angrily.

We proceeded to play the final two holes in absolute silence and all the while, I mulled over X's comment after the change-jiggling incident.

It was really cool to rub elbows with the likes of Palmer, Nicklaus, Player and Trevino, especially for a former country club caddie from the suburbs of Chicago, but there was an upper echelon to the legends of the game. They were living, breathing antiques of the sport, and Sam Snead was the head of this rat pack. His competitive years had been used up, but he came out from time to time, usually to play in the Legends of Golf. Art Wall was a true gentleman and a genuinely nice man, but I just could not get myself to call him Art, always addressing him as Mr. Wall. It was just the opposite with British Open Champion Kel Nagle, whom I used to refer to as "dad." Roberto De Vicenzo was a good guy, but I had to bite my tongue to keep from asking him what the hell happened at The Masters in '68. JT, one of our crew, worked for Bob Toski, a.k.a. Mouse, and we spent considerable time shooting the bull with him. Mouse was a real kick in the ass.

We were loading up the Caddie Wagon getting ready to depart Sarasota when one of these relics of the game inquired about hitching a ride. Peter Thomson, that pioneer of Australian golf, wanted to catch a lift on the short hop to the next event. We had the extra space and figured what the hell. If Aileen "Monster" Wuornos was a five-time winner of The British Open and asked to hitch a ride, we would have told her to hop on in. As we were loading up his gear, Wiz whispered to me, "Five-time winner of my national championship."

Me and five-time Open Champion Peter Thompson.

"Pretty impressive, huh?" I said.

"Not bad for a #$@&ing convict," he replied sarcastically.

Peter was pleasant and chatty, and it was incredible to hear his stories from golf's yesteryear. I only wished that he were traveling with us on a longer journey.

Sixth Street in Austin, Texas, is no Champs-Elysees, but it is one of the better party spots we visited, and just one of the reasons why we liked playing The Legends of Golf there. Another was that Onion Creek had been very kind to the Moody/Crampton team, affording us a victory the previous year. The humungous difference of returning to the scene of my first taste of tournament victory was that this year I'd be packing for the other half of the team. My good friend and travelling partner Evan had been looping for Sarge since my exodus, and would be on the bag until Orville's daughter made her caddie debut later.

The sexagenarian team of Arnold Palmer and Miller Barber experienced a collective flashback, playing like the Arnie and X of old, instead of the old Arnie and X. They manhandled Onion Creek over the first three rounds and led going into Sunday's final round, but we were lurking not too far behind. Paired with the team of Masters champion, Tommy Aaron and U.S. Open victor, Lou Graham, the Moody/Crampton machine took command of the lead early on the back side. We were poised and in position to repeat as victors until Aaron threw a monkey wrench into our works, hitting a shot from under a tree limb on 16, right in the jar for an eagle 2 and sole possession of the lead with two to play. Standing on the 18th tee and trailing by a shot, we were in desperate need of a birdie or better to force a playoff. Orville obliged us, hitting driver-driver onto the front edge of the par 5, giving him an easy 2-putt birdie, which was uncontested by the other pair. We were heading for overtime.

There had been only one other playoff in the 11-year history of the event that was decided after six grueling holes. I sincerely hoped Tommy Aaron blew all the miraculous shots out of his system and we could claim the top spot on the leader board. The teams matched shot for shot, birdie for birdie, and the second playoff in Legends history ended the same as the first, when Orville sank a long birdie on the sixth playoff hole, giving our team consecutive victories.

Awesome is the only word to accurately describe winning an event with one of your brothers-in-arms. Evan and I each grabbed a flag from a couple of greens, which were proudly displayed on the Caddie Wagon as we made our way out of town to the next venue.

There was nothing like being in the circle of the Senior Tour during these Camelot years, especially on the driving range before the round. It was incredible to see Trevino cutting up with Palmer, Player jawing with Nicklaus, Chi Chi kibitzing with the crowd and amusing them with his antics, and Doug Sanders telling off-color jokes to his assemblage. I regret that I was too close to the action and didn't fully appreciate this epoch of professional golf, the likes of which will never be witnessed again.

Unfortunately, Bruce was all business when it came to the game, and practice time before the round was no exception. He stayed as far away from the revelry as possible, sometimes going to the opposite end of the range. If that wasn't an option, he'd choose a spot to at the very end of the range line. I pretended like I was paying full attention to what he was doing but truthfully, I was straining my ears to ingest just a fraction of the commotion. It was like being locked out of a party, watching through a window and wishing I was smack dab in the middle of it.

Playing at Inglewood Country Club on the northern shore of Lake Washington in mid-July was always a nice respite from some of the hotter and muggier venues we visited during the summer months. In an omen of good fortune on the horizon, Bruce knocked his 5 iron on the 185 6th hole right in the jar for an ace during the first round. Then, in an odd and rare display of golf prowess and uncanny luck, Bruce's playing partners, Bill Collins and Charlie Sifford, both holed their approaches from about 100 yards on the par 5, 7th. You spend enough time around professional golfers and you'll witness some supernatural happenings, but three lengthy, holed shots on consecutive holes was off-the-charts weird.

There must have been something in that unpolluted air, because I really had my hands full tending to crowd control duties that week. Needless to say, I was not the darling of the links in their eyes. Couple that with the fact that Bruce edged out the hometown favorite, Don

Bies, for the victory and I wasn't sure which one of us they wanted to lynch more. This triumph was his third of the year and our seventh as a team, as the Crampton Train kept chugging along.

There was an exception to Bruce's gracefulness under fire if the event he was vying to win was a Major championship. I'm not inferring that he choked in the big ones, but victory just didn't seem to be in the cards for him. He'd have a hiccup on the way to the clubhouse and someone would edge him out by a nose. On the regular tour he finished second in four Majors, every time to the same man...Jack Nicklaus. Unfortunately, history was repeating itself for him on the Senior Tour.

In early August we were in my hometown of Chicago for the U.S. Senior Open, held at the notorious Medinah No. 3. Packing for one of the top dogs on the "over 50" circuit, and with three victories under our belt for the year, I had lofty expectations for the week, especially since I'd have my own little gallery of family and friends present. I honestly figured this would be Bruce's best shot at a Major title.

The USGA had Medinah set up on the extreme edge of challenging, and a trip around the course was like holding your breath for four hours. There was no place where you could relax, even for a brief moment. The greens were so slick it was like putting on granite, and ball placement was of paramount importance. The rough was lush and thick, and hitting fairways was as important as ball placement on the greens. In the event of a miscue, you just took your medicine and played for par, but hopefully, no worse than bogey.

Bruce adhered to the rule of hitting fairways and greens, and stayed away from the big numbers. He was near the top of the leader board going into the weekend. When the final round commenced, he was in a position to finally smooch silver after a Major championship. He continued his solid ball striking and strategic maneuvering around a demanding track. After a perfect tee shot at the par 5, 10th hole, Bruce laid up to approximately 70 yards to a hole cut at the front of the green, just over a false front. He nipped his approach with the dexterity of a surgeon, the ball dead on line with the flag. It hit several feet short of the cup, took a healthy bounce forward, hit the flagstick and spun back off the front of the green. Looking back, I wish I had advised him to aim to the left or to the right of the pin (I'm being sarcastic; no caddie could make that call). It's really amazing that the intended target is less than an inch in diameter and yet, can act like a backboard and wreak such havoc. It's just the macabre humor of the Golfing Gods.

The timing of this bad luck was poor, but was right in line with the Crampton Major Curse. He failed to get it up and down, and we left the green dropping a shot instead of gaining one. The thought occurred to me that I was going to be soliciting signatures on a petition once again. This time to diminish the width of the flag sticks so they are as thin as possible and still able to support a flag.

The snafu rattled Bruce a bit, but he righted the ship and managed to gain possession of the lead as we stood on the 15th tee box. After weathering the setback at 10, I felt it was Bruce's time to shine; all we needed was get it in to the clubhouse and post a score. I fantasized about being magically teleported to the 18th green hundreds of times while watching a hack flail at it during a scorching summer loop at North Shore, but I never, ever wanted a round to be over more than I did standing on that tee.

Bruce hit another commercial drive, which he followed up with a Thurman Munson (a dead yank) mid-iron into a bunker left of the green. Then he blasted out well past the hole and proceeded to play green hockey, three-putting from 15 feet. The quick double bogey felt like the thrill ride at Disneyland where the bottom drops out of the elevator floor and you plummet to the ground. It's a daunting task to make birdies at a USGA event, especially on one set up so brutally. Bruce parred in to the clubhouse, and we missed the Gary Player/Bob Charles 18-hole playoff on Monday by one shot. It was absolutely amazing how quickly the situation went from me salivating just thinking about caddying for the winner of the U.S. Senior Open, in my home town, to me dumping the clubs into the trunk and Bruce slamming it shut and driving off in a huff.

Even though Bruce was already victorious three times and had numerous runner-up finishes for the year, the near-miss at Medinah stung like a swarm of jellyfish, and the best finish we had through the end of that season was another second place at the PaineWebber Invitational in Charlotte, North Carolina. That one had an interesting completion that didn't tickle our fancy. Bruce posted a score and was leader in the clubhouse with one group left on the course. Dave Hill was the only player who could bump us from the top spot, and he drove it into a fairway bunker off the 18th tee. I was feeling pretty chipper about winning our fourth event of the year as I watched Dave play from the trap. Bogey was a very real possibility from there. He hit a stellar shot up the hill that came to rest about 15 feet past the cup. The ball was now in Dave's court as we now just hoped for a playoff. I stood beside the 18th green and watched with bated breath as he stood over the winning putt and fiddled with a collection of different grips. He started with a conventional right hand low, switched to some kind of a claw grip, and eventually decided on left hand low. I figured there was no way he was going to bury this putt with the demons he was wrestling with, but I figured wrong. He stroked it with authority and drilled it dead center, the ball making that painful journey six inches straight down. Everyone in professional golf lives and dies by the adage that every shot makes *someone* happy.

In early December we visited Maui for the season-ending event at Kaanapali. Bruce may have been the Iron Man, but I was not the Iron Caddie. I was more worn out than Paris Hilton after film festival week at Cannes. Most of the players didn't grind too hard that week and just enjoyed the tropical surroundings, but not Bruce. We hit the range like it was U.S. Senior Open week and did our usual six-hour practice rounds preparing for the tournament. While all the other caddies were sunbathing, snorkeling and chasing grass skirts, I was watching Bruce hit so many balls on the range, he wore down the sweet spots of his irons.

I decided to go to Chicago and visit my family for the holidays, which did wonders for my soul, but I had to leave just before New Year's to be in San Diego for the Tournament of Champions. I drove solo across the country, as all the lads had scattered for the off-season. The vast majority of the year I was flying high, traveling to exotic locales and living large. I admit that I was a braggart, telling anyone who would listen about my glamorous life, but sometimes there was an expensive price to pay for the high-falutin' lifestyle of a professional tour caddie. The loneliness I felt driving across the Arizona Desert as the clock struck midnight ringing in 1989 was almost unbearable. I thought about all my family and friends kissing and hugging each other and singing Auld Lang Syne. And then I cried.

While the previous season was fruitful and lucrative, Bruce's antics were beginning to weigh heavily on me. He developed a nasty little habit after holing out when his score didn't meet his expectations. He would drop the putter on the green next to the hole and walk off, leaving me to pick it up. You had to witness this to fully grasp how rude it was, and it was difficult for me not to take it personally. A few times, when I saw the galleries' reaction to it, I fantasized about doing a flying drop-kick on his ass.

In Tampa, he was more dour than usual, and during one round, he rode me relentlessly. He chewed on me more than Bob Lorenz did during my inaugural loop at North Shore. I was so pissed off afterwards, I failed to notice a telephone pole behind the Caddie Wagon when I left the course, and backed right into it, caving in not one, but both rear doors in the process.

I was granted a psychiatric reprieve a few weeks later when we picked off our eighth victory together, winning the MONY Arizona Classic at The Pointe Resort in Phoenix. It lifted my spirits to hear him mention me during his victory specch, telling the crowd that I was an integral part of his team and that my assistance was invaluable to him. But the warm, fuzzy feeling vaporized when he was back to his old tricks at The Murata Seniors Reunion in Texas a couple weeks later. I guess it was no different than any other abusive relationship. He was loving me one minute and kicking me all over the place the next. At least I was getting paid for it, which basically made me a whore, and I'm not debating that label. Plenty of people asked me why I put up with his crap and my answer never varied. "For the #$@&in' money, why else?"

Bruce always cut me a check right after completion of the tournament, but writing this one, he informed me that he was not going to pay me a percentage of his winnings. His exact quote was, "You don't deserve it." He left the club and went to his home in north Dallas, just a stone's throw away, leaving me to stew over our altercation. Like a pot set atop too high a flame, my blood began to boil and I made a decision that I was well aware would have huge ramifications on my future employment with him, but not really giving a rat's ass. It was that low point in a relationship where you ask yourself, "*What am I really holding on to?*"

I was an emotional wreck by the time I pulled up in front of Bruce's house (proof of that was the rubber I laid when I locked up the brakes with both feet). I pounded on the front door, and when his son answered, he knew from the look on my face that I wasn't there for a social visit. I stormed past him and made my way to the kitchen, failing to even notice that Bruce had guests. It wouldn't have made an iota's difference if he had Byron Nelson visiting; he was getting a piece of my mind. He was standing at the kitchen island making a sandwich when I confronted him.

"I don't know who the hell you think you are, telling me I don't deserve my percentage! I deserve twice my percentage for having to put up with you!"

I was half yelling and half crying as I took my caddie card and frisbeed it at him and announced, "WE'RE THROUGH!"

I turned and started to leave when Bruce piped up and said, "Wait, Larry…"

I cut him off and said, "Stay away from me, Bruce. I can't guarantee what I'll do in this state!" as I stormed out the door.

We were finito as far as I was concerned, and I must confess that a large part of me was going to miss being in the hunt, not to mention how much I would miss the dough I was pulling in. My solace came in the knowledge that no amount of victories or money was going to do me any good in a rubber room. John Brodie always preached to me that I should never compromise my standards for money, and I took to heart the wisdom he was laying on me, but that's easy to say when you're a rich man.

I resigned myself to the fact that I needed to explore my options, but decided to take a couple weeks off to decompress. It was during my brief sabbatical that I came to the conclusion that I owed Bruce a final phone call to thank him for employing me and allowing me to partake in his success. Mentally and emotionally, I had moved on, and figured he had also. I called him, but the conversation took a detour and we ended up deciding to reconcile, (another characteristic of an abusive relationship).

They say insanity is doing the same thing and expecting a different result. In the world of professional caddying, insanity is expecting your man to change. Don't get me wrong; my brief period of baglessness gave me a newfound appreciation of packing for one of the premier players on the tour, but we stepped right back into our old routine. It was about this time that I coined a damn good caddie axiom: *Life is a shit sandwich, and if you want the bread, you're going to have to eat some shit.*

You may recall that when Orville Moody, out of the kindness of his big heart, gave me up to Bruce Crampton, he told me that his daughter was going to come out and caddie for him. There was no way for me, or anyone, to know that Orville would go from being one of, if not *the* worst putters on the tour, to one of the better ones. As awesome a ball striker as he was, this meant that he became a force to be reckoned with. He had won a handful of tournaments, including The Vintage Invitational, where he obliterated the field. I'm not a jealous man and was sincerely happy for his success. I firmly believed that Orville was being rewarded for his generosity. It also didn't hurt that I held on to Bruce's coattails as he stepped into the winner's circle as many times as he did.

Bruce had been signing my checks for two seasons, and the psychological toll of working for him was beginning to leave a bitter taste in my mouth. Basically, I was beginning to taste more shit than bread. Then, to compound the situation, Orv went out and seized the title at The Mazda Senior TPC *and* the U.S. Senior Open. His daughter Michelle had blossomed into the best caddie in the universe (according to the media) and was getting more than her fair share of press. I think I saw her on *Letterman,* and I pulled into the parking lot at one tournament where a vendor tried to sell me a tee shirt with "I Caddy for my Daddy!" emblazoned on it. Again, jealousy is not in my nature, but when things got rocky with Bruce and I saw all the green Michelle was rolling in, I almost felt like Orville threw me under the bus.

There was a thinning of the proverbial caca and another psychiatric reprieve in late July when Bruce notched his ninth victory with yours truly on the bag, winning The Ameritech Senior Open at Canterbury Country Club outside Cleveland. Unbelievably, the Iron Man actually took the following week off, so I went to nearby Chicago to visit family and friends, savor the win, and most importantly, recharge the caddie battery. Little did I know, it would be the last time Bruce Crampton would mention my name in a victory speech.

Up to this point in my illustrious career I had been to 15 countries. Australia was always a place I wanted to see but was not on the list. That was about to change as Bruce invited me to his motherland for an event held at the infamous Royal Melbourne Golf Club.

Don't ever let anyone tell you that you can go to Australia for two weeks; it takes half that time just to get there. You could probably board a spaceship and travel to another galaxy in less time. I wanted to get off that plane so badly, I considered doing a D.B. Cooper…and

I was in Qantas Business Class! I sincerely felt the pain of the poor schmucks stuck behind me in coach for a flight that long.

Jack Newton was an unbelievably talented golfer from Australia who won 13 times on the European Tour and finished runner-up at two Major Championships, the '75 Open and 1980 Masters. Unfortunately, his days as a professional golfer ended on July 24, 1983, when he accidently walked into the spinning propeller of an airplane. He lost his right arm, right eye, and sustained traumatic abdominal injuries. It's unbelievable the catastrophe didn't kill him. He swears that he wasn't drunk, but he had the reputation of being a loose cannon, and I heard from a knowledgeable source that he was pretty pissed when the tragedy occurred. I'm not a gambling man but I'd have to bet on the latter.

I mention Jack Newton, a.k.a. Newt the Beaut, because he was paired with Bruce in the Pro-Am at The Coca-Cola Classic. In typical Aussie fashion, Newt's verbiage was riddled with a four-letter word starting with f; thus, he referred to Bruce as "the old fockin' fart" all day long. He was funny as hell and it was another miracle that he didn't lose his sense of humor while lying on that airport tarmac some years ago. It was also utterly amazing to see him play a difficult golf course well with only one arm. He played with specially made clubs that were extremely light and easier for him to control.

The apex of his unilateral golf dexterity occurred when he hit his tee shot on the par 3, 5th hole, over the green. The ball came to rest in a hairy lie just off the back fringe, leaving him a downhill chip onto an Augusta–like green. It was a tough shot for a seasoned tour player with both hands. I seized the opportunity to inject my two cents before he played the shot. "Hey, Jack, that gonna be a little quick?" He answered without a hint of hesitation, "Larry, this is gonna be slicker than cum off a gold, fockin' tooth." He proceeded to take his putter and bump it through the heavy grass separating his ball from the putting surface. It just barely made it on and for a split second, looked like it was going to stop above the hole and leave him a putt that wasn't much easier than the chip, but it continued rolling slowly and steadily down to a resting place about two feet from the cup. He tapped in for his par from there, as the rest of the group watched in complete awe. It took Jack Newton 84 strokes to get around The Royal Melbourne Composite Course that day.

Hanging out with Newt the Beaut was the only pleasure I was going to derive on the golf course that week. Bruce's psychological shenanigans reached an excruciating zenith on that trip, and my tolerance meter was peaking. I was shouldering the burden for every negative occurrence on the course, and I thought I had witnessed just about every calamity that could befall a professional golfer, but I was wrong. Bruce actually hit himself with his own golf ball, which is a violation of 19-2b under the rules of golf and a cozy little one-shot penalty. This was all my fault of course, even though I wasn't the one who hooked the tee shot into a bush and then tried to play it from there.

It's pretty safe to say that when a caddie begins to fantasize about knocking his player into next week, he should consider a new employer or a new line of work. I knew I had to make a change, but decided I'd wait until we were stateside. We were slated to go to Sydney the following week for a vacation, and my informing Bruce we were history would definitely dampen the mood. Plus, there was another minor issue. Bruce had my return ticket to the U.S. and I didn't want to be left stranded in Australia.

What happened next, I should have seen coming. The following week spent running around Sydney reminded me of the old days in Europe with my pal Wiz, only we actually paid for all our meals, and my digs wasn't a polyester pup tent, but the ultra-tony Regent Sydney overlooking the iconic Opera House. Bruce was a completely different guy, and even shelled out the dough for my room. We hit all the tourist spots and took in some off-the-beaten-path sites, like a topless beach he knew about. He introduced me to what friends he still had there, and the highlight of the visit was a Saturday Night dinner cruise around Sydney Harbor.

I had such a blast in Sydney that I was overcome with a case of amnesia boarding the 747 back to the states, forgetting about what a complete ass-wipe Bruce was in Melbourne. My pact with myself to can him when we got back to the U.S. was a distant memory.

The jumbo-jet leveled off as I prepared myself mentally for the marathon flight, much the way a convict does at the commencement of a 20-year prison term. Just about the time I was getting comfortable, an official looking gentleman walked up to our seats and asked, "Excuse me. Would you happen to be Bruce Crampton?" He was a tall, distinguished-looking fellow wearing a powder blue blazer, the Qantas logo prominently displayed on the front pocket. His face was adorned with a snow white, handle-bar mustache that perfectly matched the comb-over that sparsely covered his head. His name was Reginald, and he was the steward in First Class. Apparently, the flight crew was crazy about golf and noticed Bruce's name on the passenger manifest.

"The pilots request your company up in First Class. Would you care to join us?"

I don't know a seasoned traveler who would pass up that offer, and Bruce was out of his seat and gathering his belongings before Reginald finished his invitation. Bruce hadn't begun his glorious trek up to first class when I grabbed hold of the back of his shirt. In the blink of an eye, business class wasn't making it any more.

"Hey, what about me?" I asked pathetically.

Bruce, standing in the aisle with his arms full, asked Reginald, "Can my caddie come, too?"

"Absolutely." he proclaimed.

Passing through the curtain that separated business from first class was like driving up the front drive of North Shore Country Club for the first time. There was a palpable feeling of wealth and decadence that I knew I could easily become accustomed to.

Reginald escorted us to unoccupied seats that were the size of queen beds folded to look like chairs. Once we were situated, he returned with supple leather pouches jam-packed with toiletries, cologne, one of those sleeping masks worn by Hollywood types, and some plush footies. Apparently, you want to air your dogs whilst travelling at the front of the bus. He also handed us each a parchment paper dinner menu that rivaled the wedding invitations Prince William and Kate sent out for their royal union. My eyes widened as I opened it, like a child's when dining in a restaurant for the first time. The fare included Russian caviar, broiled shrimp, and a choice of poached salmon in a white wine cream sauce, or authentic Australian lamb as the main course. The coup-de-grace was eating with sterling silver dinnerware instead of the plastic crap they give you in cattle class.

I could feel eyes on me as I stuffed a caviar-laden cracker in my mouth, a Russian vodka chaser not far behind. Bruce was watching me with the most amused look on his face. "Oh, sorry," I said as I kicked my pinky finger out, evoking a chuckle from him. I seized the opportunity to take it a step further. "Reginald, could you come here please?"

"Yes sir, may I help you?" he asked.

"Reginald, what kind of caviar is this?"

"It's Beluga Caviar from the Caspian Sea," he replied.

"Of course it is. Thank you, Reginald," I countered, my voice now assuming the accent of a Briton.

Bruce was in stitches by this time. "The one-and-only reason you like that caviar is because it's expensive," he observed.

"And your point would be?" I asked.

After gorging on one of the best meals I've ever had on land, and 50 times better than any while jetting across open skies, Bruce and I reclined in our massive seats and let the digestive juices do their thing.

A short while later, the airliner was fairly quiet as everyone was asleep or trying, when a gentleman approached our seats and said, "Excuse me, Mr. Crampton." He was wearing the standard issue clothing worn by a member of an airline crew. "The pilot would like to know if you would care to join us on the flight deck."

Bruce possessed a latent affinity for aviation and had expressed an urge to get a pilot's license on numerous occasions. Again, he was up out of his seat before the man could finish his invitation and before he took one step toward the cockpit, I reached out once again and grabbed the back of his shirt. I felt like the tag-along little brother.

"Bruce, I wanna come too," I whined. He asked our escort if I could join them and he replied, "Sure."

We entered the flight deck and were warmly greeted by the captain, co-pilot and navigator who offered us open seats toward the back. The coolest part of being in the cockpit of an airplane, especially a large one, is the ability to see looking forward. Normally, you're looking out the side of the craft and usually have your face uncomfortably pressed against the window in an effort to expand your field of view. It was night and there wasn't a lot to see, except for the heavy canopy of stars above, but it was gorgeous nonetheless.

My assessment that these guys were crazy about golf was an understatement; they were rabid about golf. They gave us a quick overview of the controls and the myriad of switches covering every square inch of the confined space, but they were considerably more interested in Bruce's profession and fired off question after question.

We had been in the cockpit for what seemed an eternity, and I really thought we were overstaying our welcome, but the flight crew continued to absorb any golf-related morsel we threw at them. I looked out the front right windshield of the aircraft and noticed a faint glow off in the distance. I continued to peer through the thick glass as the most magnificent full moon slowly climbed from beneath the horizon, illuminating the Fijian Archipelago floating serenely below in the South Pacific. It's a sight I will never forget.

I can't tell you how many times I was asked what it was like to caddie for Bruce Crampton. My standard tongue-in-cheek response was, "It's like being in the military." A lot of truth is said in jest, and this statement was no exception. Bruce could be a real hard-ass, but he instilled in me the importance of a good work ethic, a laser-like focus on the task at hand, and total professionalism. Packing for him was the equivalent of caddie boot camp, but I give him credit for transforming me into an efficient tour caddie and giving me the confidence to know I was capable of working for anyone. He won nine times while I was on board with him, and finished in the top five more times than I can remember. Bruce taught me the importance of striving for a goal and more importantly, he taught me to savor the thrill of victory. Unfortunately, the devolution of our working relationship was a certainty, and it was only a matter of time before we parted ways. A couple years ago my wife ran into Bruce's wife at the grocery store and one thing led to another, culminating in an impromptu dinner engagement for the four of us. I was happy to see that Bruce, 12 years removed from the game, looked as jovial and contented as I had ever seen him. Golf dominated every fiber of his being for more than 50 years, and he hadn't touched a club in over a decade, quitting the game absolutely cold turkey. It took me a couple of minutes to wrap my head around that concept.

It isn't too hard to understand the negative effect professional golf can have on certain individuals. Bruce was all business on the golf course, and that enabled him to achieve all that he had. Sure, he wasn't the crowd pleaser that Chi Chi or Trevino was, but it was his living, and he ran his ship the way he saw fit. Everyone handles pressure differently. Chi Chi smoked and Trevino yammered on about any subject under the sun. Bruce just had a caustic personality. I'm not going to make any excuses for him and why he conducted himself the way he did, but the fact of the matter is, once removed from the golf course and the game, he was and is a good man.

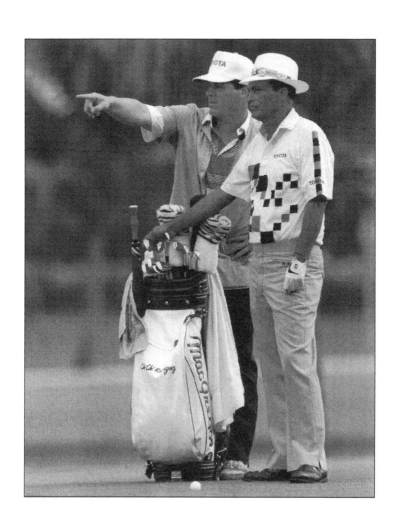

THE PUERTO RICAN
ROBIN HOOD

SOMETHING INTERESTING HAPPENS when one becomes a professional tour caddie that involves a partial forfeiture of one's personal identity. You cease to exist as your former self, and are now identified by the player whose name adorns your caddie bib. "He's Billy Casper's caddie." "Has anyone seen Don January's caddie?" "Did you hear what happened to Miller Barber's caddie?" Sometimes it goes beyond just adopting the player's name; you were an extension of your man. If he wasn't liked by his tour colleagues, you could very possibly bear the brunt of their loathing. Believe me, I learned this firsthand in Bruce Crampton's employ. There were guys who looked at me like they hated my guts, just because they hated his.

It was the late 1980s and Chi Chi Rodriguez knew me only as Crampton's caddie. I was pretty sure he didn't know my proper name, since he always called me Pards, but he used that name for everyone. It derived from the word partner and was used in the same way one might use "bro" or "dude" today.

With the history that Chi Chi and Bruce shared, it is absolutely amazing that he even considered hiring me, but unique circumstances led to our amalgamation.

It was December of 1989 and the tour made its way to Dorado Beach, Puerto Rico, for the Mazda Champions, where the top 10 players of the Senior Tour were paired with the top 10 of the LPGA Tour. Bruce was slated to play with then LPGA stalwart Colleen Walker, but had to withdraw at the last minute with a debilitating muscle pull in his back. The pain must have been really excruciating, because this was a big money event. Knowing how fond Bruce was of the almighty dollar, you could have hacked both his arms off and he still would have tried to tee it up. Chi Chi and I ended up thrown together, as he was sans caddie and I was now bagless.

It felt pretty weird to be working for Bruce's enemy, almost a bit kinky, but Chi Chi and I hit it off from the get-go, and there was good chemistry between us. Unfortunately, the first round didn't go as smoothly as either of us would have liked. Chi Chi knocked it stiff all day long, but his putter abandoned him, and he couldn't get anything to drop. He also missed a couple of short ones. Little did I know at the time that this was a harbinger of things to come in my professional future.

We hit the practice green for a marathon session of finding a panacea for an ailing blade. After several hours of tinkering, Chi Chi assured me that he had discovered the cure. He had his legs spread wide, toes pointing outward, hunched over completely, with the butt end of the putter stuck in his navel. He looked exactly like the Ping logo.

After knocking his approach to 12 feet on the first hole the following day, Chi Chi assumed this new putting stance. Colleen took one look, and not being one to mince words, asked, "What the

#$@& is that?" I responded, "I haven't got a clue, but whatever you do, make sure you tell him it looks good."

Colleen and Chi Chi gelled pretty well, and even though victory was never within their grasp, they finished respectably. Chi Chi cut me a check and said he was extremely pleased with my work. He caught me totally off guard when he inquired if I would be interested in caddying for him full time. I declined, telling him that I had been with Bruce for three successful years and wasn't interested in a change, but that was just my mouth talking. My gut was telling me otherwise.

Even though I felt slightly indebted to Bruce for molding me into an efficient tour caddie, after three years with him, I was tiring of his antics. The player/caddie union is similar to a marriage, and our relationship was well beyond repair. It was June of 1990 and we were destined for divorce court. About this time, Bruce was now on a lengthy sabbatical, and I was looking for a new horse. Fortunately for me, Chi Chi took a liking to me, and he was looking for a new jockey.

I had a little taste of what it was like to caddie for Chi Chi before, and I was particularly fond of the fun that was associated with being in his circle. Bruce was always so serious about every aspect of the game, as if we were on a bomb squad and any miscue could mean certain death. But Chi Chi was fun, and we meshed extremely well on the course. Proof of this was the 63 and 64 that he shot in the Pro-Ams of the first tournament we worked together. I felt like a surfer on the north shore of Hawaii who just caught a big one. Things were looking up, until Chi Chi took it upon himself to call Bruce and let him know that I was only caddying for him until Bruce decided to come back out. This was a kind gesture on Chi Chi's part, but I had absolutely no intention of going back to Bruce. I was exactly where I wanted to be.

I consulted with Chi Chi about working for him permanently. When he said the job was mine, I had a very difficult phone call to make. I called Bruce and told him of my decision, and it really caught him off guard. Pros are accustomed to doing the firing, and it must have been a blow to his ego. I explained to him that the situation was based purely on economics. Truth be told, it was based on a plethora of reasons, including the fact that The Rodriguez Show was a ton of fun (the vast majority of the time), and it paid better. Chi Chi covered my expenses, and he had his own jet. Hell, I would have caddied for Attila the Hun if he had his own jet. Bruce and I said our goodbyes, ending a very lucrative and educational period in my caddie career.

I was packing Chi Chi's bag down the fairway of Nashawtuc Country Club outside Boston when Mike Hill, walking alongside me, looked over at me and did a double-take. "What are you doing?" he asked.

"I'm caddying for Chi Chi," I answered.

"I thought you were Crampton's caddie," he followed.

"I was."

He stopped me in my tracks and squared off with me. "You mean to tell me that you left Crampton for Rodriguez?"

"Yeah, that's right."

"Boy, can you #$@&in' pick 'em," he shot back dryly.

One of my biggest beefs with Bruce was his absolute refusal to pay me 10% when he won a tournament. Any professional caddie will tell you that we're a tax write-off; your player's going to give the cash to you, or the government. The huge flaw in this thinking is that it's caddie logic, and unfortunately, not player logic. After a trial period of a couple of weeks with Chi Chi, I was making a decent wage but not a great one, and no 10% on victories. I felt I had more than proven myself as an asset on the course, and the time was right for a contract renegotiation. I asked Chi Chi for a raise on my base salary and my base salary on tournament weeks that he didn't play, as he made it quite clear that I would only work for him exclusively. Most of all, I asked for 10% on tournament victories, explaining that we were a team and when he won, I should win too. I pushed the envelope, stressing that we were going to win numerous events together, which was no guarantee. He mulled it over with his management team and they succumbed to my terms. I'm pretty sure the confidence I showed by dangling the victory carrot didn't hurt me at all.

We were at The Grand Traverse Resort in Traverse City, Michigan, for The Ameritech Senior Open the following week. It's a gorgeous area located in the upper section of the state, and the Nicklaus-designed golf course lived up to its name—The Bear. I was well aware that Chi Chi played difficult courses well, and he proved it by firing solid rounds leading into Sunday's finish.

The final day we were paired with Don January and playing the par 5, 3rd hole. Chi Chi drove it in the left center of the fairway; January, a.k.a. "Pops," who was also in the hunt, drove it in the thick rough, right of the fairway. We were teetering on the borderline of going for it in two, inhibited by a creek that dissected the fairway, just in front of the green.

One of the first weeks I worked for Chi Chi, he asked me for input on club selection. I went into a rambling dissertation on all of the elements involved, including yardage to the hole, wind velocity and direction, and how there were a number of different club options that could be implemented. I sounded just like a politician; I answered the question without really answering the question. Chi Chi jumped my shit and scolded me. "Don't you get vapor lock on me! When I ask for your opinion, give it to me. That's what I'm paying you for." The foundation was set and I made a mental note to have a club in mind, whatever the situation.

"Whaddya' think here, Pards? Think I should take a crack at this?" he asked.

This was a precarious and monumental juncture in my future caddying for him, as any input from me could affect the outcome of the tournament. I'm not inferring that I was calling the shot, but I knew that I could sway him either way. If I talked him into going for it and he knocked it in the hazard, my nuts would be on the chopping block and I'd look like an idiot. If he knocked it on the green, *he'd* look like the hero. From my perspective, the safe play was to lay it up. As good as he was with a sand wedge in his hands, it was only a matter of how close the birdie putt would be. I asked him how he felt.

"What do you think? You feeling pretty good about hitting your 3 wood in there?"

He looked over at Pops, who was forced to lay up because of his poor lie in the rough and said, "If that old man was in the fairway, he'd take a crack at it."

Without any hesitation, he yanked his 3 wood out of the bag and dead-nutted it at the green. The ball travelled through the air, bending just slightly to the left as it carried over the creek, landed just on the front of the green and ran past the hole to about 15 feet. He drained the slick putt for eagle 3 and set the tone for the rest of the day. That shot defined the event, and all the other players were playing for 2nd.

Standing on the 18th tee, Chi Chi held a 7-shot lead over the field. My first victory with him was sealed, barring a catastrophe, like a bolt of lightning striking him. Besides being our inaugural victory as a team, it was particularly sweet for several other reasons.

First, the tournament was televised by CBS, and Chi Chi dedicated the win to Kenny Davert, a very special young man with cerebral palsy who came to any event in the Michigan area. Chi Chi shared the limelight with Kenny, bringing him out on the 18th green during the awards ceremony. There wasn't a dry eye in the house. Second, I was on Crampton's bag the previous year when he won the same tournament at Canterbury Country Club outside of Cleveland, so that made me the defending caddie champion. Lastly and most importantly, the win solidified my position with Chi Chi. He now had concrete evidence that he could win with me on the bag. This was extremely important when going to work for a player who was accustomed to winning tournaments. And I was getting 10% for wins!

Bruce emerged from his time away and won the PaineWebber event in Charlotte, North Carolina, and I was honestly happy for him. But, I was looking ahead, not back, and I was positive of one thing; his caddie didn't receive 10% for the victory.

The Sunwest Bank Charley Pride Senior Golf Classic was held at Four Hills Country Club in Albuquerque. Charley was one nice man, and must have been one a caddie at some point in his past, because he treated us like human beings. There was a tent set up specifically for caddies, where they served barbeque and other fare. He spent a good bit of time eating, bullshitting, and cutting up with us, so much so, I got the impression he would rather spend time with us than with the players.

Four Hills was located on the side of a mountain and every putt broke toward The First National Bank located in the valley. It was imperative that you find that landmark before you even thought of reading your putt. On Saturday, Chi Chi was 10 feet from the hole with a putt that he figured was going right. Even though this seemed correct, the bank was to the left, which meant it had to go that way. I told him to start it right edge of the hole. He went with my read, starting it right edge, and it drifted slightly left, hitting the hole dead center. Walking off the green he said, "Pards, I'm glad I listened to you—it did go left. That putt was an optical 'disillusion.'"

Chi Chi hung on to win the tournament by two shots over Jim Dent and Jim Ferree. It had been three short weeks since our first victory together at the Ameritech, and we were proving to be more than a formidable team. My arm was getting sore from patting myself on the back for insisting on 10% on victories. My working relationship with Chi Chi was blossoming at a faster pace than I could have wished for, prompting him to tell David, the pilot of his private jet, "That Larry is one helluva' caddie!" David let me know what Chi Chi said, but I found it odd that Chi Chi didn't tell me himself.

The event in Park City, Utah was always one we looked forward to. I was reminded of the tournament at Crans-su-Sierre in the Swiss Alps, except that I wasn't lodging in a tent or bathing in a lake. It was off-season for the ski industry, so renting a fully furnished chalet with some of my caddie brethren was a nice change of pace from the usual hotel stay. We prepared our own meals and invited some of the other loopers over, which gave us a small taste of normal living and broke up the monotony of the usual grind.

On the course it was not nearly as stress free, as Chi Chi's play was less than stellar. He came to the conclusion that the air was too thin for him to play well, and even went to the extreme of sending David to a medical supply store to buy bottled oxygen. I figured that would go over well with his smoking. Of course it didn't help one iota, and he made the declaration that he wouldn't be returning to the event.

One of the first things I had to get accustomed to when I made the change from Bruce to Chi Chi was the difference in their speed of play. Bruce was deliberate and methodical, analyzing every aspect of the shot as if we were splitting the atom. He was not one of the faster players, and coupled with his sparkling personality, I guarantee there were plenty of his fellow competitors who blurted out, "Aw #$@&! We got Crampton!" on seeing the pairing sheet for the day.

Chi Chi, on the other hand, was one of the faster players. In fact, the first week on his bag, I was calculating the yardage to the hole when I heard the swoosh of the club and the strike of the ball. I looked up to see that he'd hit his shot without even waiting for me. I said to him, "Hey, Cheech, in case you were wondering, you had 157 yards to the hole and the breeze was helping from the left. I liked the 8 iron."

Once I asked him, "Why do you need to play so fast? It's not a track meet."

He replied, "Pards, I know I play fast, but old habits die hard. When I was a kid, we used to sneak onto the golf course. We'd hide in the trees, run out to the fairway, hit our shots and run back to the trees. If the greens keeper saw us, he'd take shots at us with a shotgun full of rock salt. You get hit in the ass with rock salt one time and believe me, you learn to play fast!"

Another facet of being employed by Chi Chi was dealing with the most superstitious person I had ever encountered. Proof of this was the numerous good luck charms and talismans he carried in his pockets. He would only pick up a coin from the ground if it was heads up and mark a birdie putt with a quarter (heads up, of course) and par putts with a nickel.

He once went through a prolonged period of extremely poor play on the course. He made adjustments in every aspect of his game but nothing seemed to help. While back at his home in Puerto Rico, he realized there was a palm tree planted directly in front of the entry doors of his house. This is apparently very bad luck, and needed to be remedied immediately. He had the tree transplanted to a new location, and upon returning to the tour, started playing considerably better. I don't think you'll ever hear golf instructor extraordinaire David Ledbetter proclaim, "If you're having trouble with your game, check your grip, your stance, and your alignment, and if that doesn't help, check your trees."

Another time he sent me to the locker room as we made the turn, to get a different pair of shoes. "What's the matter?" I asked. "Are those hurting your feet?" "No," he answered, "I'm just not playing worth a shit in them, and I might play better wearing a different color." There's something else I don't believe you'll hear the aforementioned Mr. Ledbetter say to pupils, "If you're not playing well in your brown shoes, try the white or the black ones."

It was also frowned upon for me to wear red on the golf course. He told me that it was too aggressive a color for him to look at while he was playing. He went so far as to tell me that he wanted me to wear green on Sunday, because that was payday and green is the color of money. I tempted fate once and didn't wear green on Sunday and quickly realized that he was not kidding. Incidentally, I find it very interesting that Tiger Woods wears red every Sunday.

I showed up at the range one morning with cart number 78. Chi Chi saw it and asked me if I was crazy, then ordered me to return it for cart number 64 or 65, but no higher number than 69. Some tournaments we played at clubs that had carts with triple digit numbers only. These were extremely tough weeks for me.

Chi Chi shot 65 in the opening round of the event in San Antonio one year. The following day, his pilot David was driving us to the course when Chi Chi adamantly ordered him to pull the vehicle over.

"Which way are you going?" he asked.

David replied, "Cheech, I've found a faster route to the course. It shaves 10 minutes off the trip."

Chi Chi quickly returned, "What did I shoot yesterday?"

"You shot 65," David replied.

"That's right! Now turn this car around and drive exactly the same way you did yesterday!" Chi Chi ordered.

Chi Chi believed that Arnold Palmer had serious spiritual connections. We were paired with The King one day when the weather became very bad, very quickly. There was no place to seek shelter from the lightning, forcing us to wait patiently until the transportation vehicles came to pull us off the course.

"C'mon, Pards, we're going to stand by Arnie," he announced.

"Why?" I asked naively.

He looked at me like I was a moron and said, "Pards, Arnie ain't gettin' hit by no lightning!" He took it a step further and swore that when it began raining, it was holy water.

The Good Lord has a purpose for each of us, and it is undeniable that Chi Chi's was to go from rags to riches through the avenue of golf, and also to entertain those who came to watch him in the process. He was part professional athlete and part comedian, and the golf course was his stage. He was the consummate showman, and gave those who were fortunate enough to be in the gallery their money's worth. It was this facet of his employ that I am eternally grateful for. There was nothing like watching him on the driving range warming up, throwing out quips and one-liners between shots. The money I was making was great, but it was a distant second to the pleasure I derived from watching the gallery smiling, laughing, and hanging on every word that emerged from his mouth. This relationship between athlete and fan was an anomaly, and I was blessed to have a front row seat to witness it. Here's just a sample of the world according to Chi Chi Rodriguez:

"My wife says I can do anything I want…as long as I don't enjoy it!"

"I was misbehaving in school once, and as a punishment, my teacher told me to go out and count all the holes in the chain-link fence around the playground. I came back 15 minutes later and she said, 'Juan, I told you to count all the holes in that fence.' I told her, 'I did!' and she said, Okay how many are there?' I told her, 'There's 3,333,333 holes,' and she said, 'Juan, there is no way you could have counted all those holes that fast.' And I told her, 'Oh yeah, well you can prove me wrong!'"

"I'm not a stupid man. I just don't understand numbers unless they got a bunch of zeros after them!"

"This guy wasn't feeling well so he went to the doctor. The doctor checked him out and said, 'You're fine. Go home.' The guy walked out of the doctor's office and keeled over. The doctor and his nurse rushed outside and the nurse said, 'Oh my God, Doctor, he's dead. What are we going to do?'

The doctor said, "Quick, turn him around. Make it look like he's coming in!'"

"That Arnie is something else. He's so dedicated to his sponsors, the other day I saw him drinking Pennzoil."

"I stayed in a hotel once that was so bad, I called the front desk and said, 'Hey, I gotta' leak in the sink!' and the guy at the front desk told me, 'Go ahead!'"

"What do you get when you cross a Jew with a Puerto Rican?" he asked. The answer: "A chain of empty stores."

"Most people don't know that Lee Trevino has written 2 books on golf. *How to Get Distance Out of Your Shanks* and *Taking the Proper Stance on Your 4th Putt.*"

Chi Chi is patriotic to the core, and once proclaimed, "I believe it's perfectly okay to burn the American flag…AS LONG AS YOU'RE WRAPPED IN IT!"

One of his Pro-Am participants was playing horribly, so Chi Chi went over to the guy, put his arm around him and said, "Can I give you a tip?" The guy answered, "Absolutely!" thinking Cheech was going to lay some golf wisdom on him and ease his pain. Chi Chi pointed down to the guy's ratty looking golf shoes and said, "You need to start tipping the locker room guy a little better."

Chi Chi's Seinfeld routine was usually geared to the time spent on the driving range before the round. He was still funny on the course, sometimes more than others, but when the gun went off, he'd bear down and get more serious. He would b.s. with the gallery if the opportunity arose, but every so often it came at the expense of his playing partners.

Such was the case years ago in San Antonio when Chi Chi was paired with Dave Hill. Dave was a bit of a loose cannon and apparently wasn't afraid to shoot off more than his mouth. He managed to piss off the whole state of Minnesota with his Hazeltine comments, which didn't earn him an honorary membership to the club. Anyway, leading the event, he was disturbed by a rambunctious gallery on more than one occasion while playing his shot. Dave asked Chi Chi to refrain from kibitzing with them until he played his shots. Chi Chi agreed but the crowd inevitably disturbed Dave anyway, causing him to lose the tournament. His already short fuse now gone, he sent his caddie out to the car to get his pistol. He told me this story over numerous cocktails in a hotel lobby. "Larry, I was a stone's throw away from shootin' that lil' son-of-a-bitch!" he declared, his eyes afire and nostrils flaring.

Make no mistake about it; he was as serious as a heart attack. Chi Chi needed the local law enforcement to escort him from the property after the tournament was over.

Besides the front row seat to The Chi Chi Rodriguez Comedy Hour, another extremely fulfilling facet of working for him was the post-round autograph sessions. He would sit on his cart amongst a sea of fans and sign everything from visors, to hot dog wrappers. As the fans lined up to get various items John Hancocked, they would watch Chi Chi curiously, while ingesting his witty banter. Observing the children was the best, as they stood patiently, wide-eyed, like they were in line to see Santa Claus. At the commencement, Cheech would announce, "The kids are first, women are second, Puerto Ricans are third and men are last…and I don't sign no autograph for any man wearing an earring. I'm old fashioned—a man's gotta' look like a man!"

At the Cadillac NFL Golf Classic, one of the pranksters on the tour coaxed Lawrence Taylor of the N.Y. Giants into asking Chi Chi for an autograph with his huge "LT" earring dangling from his ear. We watched from a distance as Chi Chi glared up at the earring, hesitated for a moment, and then half-heartedly signed the hat.

The Matador.

Once, Chi Chi refused to sign an autograph for an earring-clad man in Melbourne, Florida. He told the guy if he took out the earring, he'd sign for him, but the man wouldn't, and Chi Chi held firm on his end, refusing to sign. The guy was a local disc jockey who went on the air later that day and urged all the listeners to go to the tournament and root against Chi Chi. Gary Player, always one to take advantage of a great situation, showed up on the first tee the next day wearing one of his wife's earrings. It was a big Carmen Miranda-looking thing that looked ridiculous. Everyone was hysterical; everyone except Chi Chi, who wouldn't shake hands with Gary until he took it off.

The hat, the accent, the superstitions, the clever quips and the trick shots are all trademarks of Chi Chi Rodriguez, but the one thing people will always associate with him is his patented sword dance. From the time he was a participant on the Regular Tour, he has been thrilling galleries with this routine. In his early years at the professional level, he used to throw his hat over the hole to keep the ball from jumping out. He claimed he once lost a match as a kid in Puerto Rico because a frog popped out of the hole, along with his ball. Complaints from his professional cohorts halted the practice, so the matador was born.

Once the ball disappeared in the cup, he would begin waving his putter overhead, sometimes so vigorously I thought he was going to get airborne; then, back and forth in front of him, eventually pointing at the hole, in mock victory over the bull. Finally, giving the routine authenticity, he would wipe the "blade" (putter shaft) with his handkerchief and return it to an imaginary scabbard on his side. Every so often, he would add a special touch by propping the putter against his shoulder, like it was a rifle, and march off the green. The crowd devoured this performance, and I never tired of it myself.

Chi Chi's clinic was another spectacle of golf from a bygone era. These displays consisted of 45 minutes of imitations, instruction, lessons for the kids, trick shots and of course, plenty of comedy. The highlight was a trick shot where he announced, "What you're about to see is one of the greatest things in sports. I'm going to hit one ball with a slice and another one with a hook, and they're going to collide in midair." It was ludicrous to think he could do this every time, but he could usually come pretty close, and a few times, he pulled it off. When he did, there was quite a response from the crowd.

The pride I felt being associated with the entertaining aspect of Chi Chi Rodriguez couldn't come close to that pride I felt having an up close, personal view of one of the biggest humanitarians professional sports will ever see. Kids were always center stage with him, especially the sick, underprivileged and handicapped. If he spotted one in the gallery, he'd bring them out and make them feel like they were the center of the universe for a brief moment in their challenging lives.

Some pictures just say it all.

Chi Chi was warming up on the range at White Manor Country Club outside of Philadelphia when he noticed a boy in a wheelchair behind the gallery ropes and instructed me to bring him over. I noticed that the lad had severe cerebral palsy, as I approached him and asked if he would like to meet Chi Chi Rodriguez. To say that he was enthusiastic would be a huge understatement. After meeting the boy, Chi Chi proceeded to put on a clinic, catering solely to him. The guest of honor watched intently as Chi Chi described each trick shot to him before he executed it. I, like the hundreds of people lucky enough to witness this spectacle, was totally engulfed watching, when I realized we were next up on the first tee. I informed Chi Chi that we had to go. He pulled off his golf glove, signed it and shoved it in the boy's atrophied hand. Then, he placed his hand on the boy's head and told him that he was very special, and that God made him that way. He told him there was a special place for him in Heaven. As we departed, the boy looked up from his wheelchair and said in an angelic voice, "I love you, Chi Chi." There wasn't a soul in the gallery not tearing up. I caddied the first hole of that tournament with a humungous lump in my throat. It was truly an incredible moment.

Juan "Chi Chi" Rodriguez was born into a very large and very poor family in Rio Piedras, Puerto Rico, and was working in the cane fields by the age of six in an effort to contribute what he could to the family. In his early life, Chi Chi was plagued with rickets and tropical sprue, a vitamin deficiency that causes the softening and bending of the bones. He wholeheartedly believed that God purposely inflicted him with the disease, and that's why a golf club fit so perfectly in his smallish hands. To this day, I can vividly envision his brown, weathered hands on the grip of the club, while he declared, "Look at that, Pards. It was just meant to be."

Like Hogan, Sarazen, Nelson and a score of other golf greats, Chi Chi was introduced to the game through caddying. Spending his days at Berwind Country Club was considerably better than working the fields, and a heck of a lot more lucrative. He always said that when he first started in golf, he was so small they used him as a tee marker. He learned the game by watching, and taught himself by hitting a tin can fashioned into a ball with the limb of a guava tree as his club. He later acquired a sand wedge and practiced lob shots on a local baseball diamond. He told me he became so proficient with that wedge that he could stand directly behind the backstop and pop the ball over it, bouncing it on home plate. His skill for the game developed rapidly, and he claims that he shot 67 when he was just 13 years of age, holing out four times from off the green. He eventually became an assistant pro at the Dorado Beach Resort, where he now has a home.

Because Chi Chi came from very meager beginnings and made more money than he ever could have fathomed, he loved to share his wealth. Generosity is as big a part of him as humor; thus, the title of this chapter. One year, he won the tournament in Oklahoma City and donated the winner's check to a nearby town that was recently ravaged by a tornado. On more than one occasion, he sent me to the finance trailer to cash a check for him for operating capital, only to discreetly pass it all out to the Mexicans he saw maintaining the golf course. I stress the word 'discreetly' because he was not pretentious about his generosity in any way, and didn't want anyone to know that he was handing out hundred dollar bills. He taught me that the true beauty of giving, was never expecting anything in return.

Not many of the pros openly expressed their appreciation for the job we do for them, but Chi Chi was one of the exceptions. He did this by throwing a caddie party any time he won an event. He gave me a budget (which I always exceeded), and I would scout out an appropriate dining location. Usually we'd have a buffet dinner with an open beer and wine bar. At one of these soirees I made the faux pas of showing up a tad late, and some of the caddies took it upon themselves to order some very expensive bottles of wine from the wine list. A gang of hungry caddies can clear out a buffet faster than a bunch of piranhas can strip a steer down to the skeleton, and after completion of the meal, the real fun began. Rampant stories about caddies, and more specifically, their blunders, stories about pros, swing impersonations (I was always called upon to grace them with my Chi Chi, Miller Barber, Arnold Palmer and Don January routines) and other mayhem was always on the menu.

It was no secret that Chi Chi was generous to the bone and was, therefore, the man to see when a caddie was down on his luck. They'd always promise to pay him back and he'd always cave. One time, a caddie approached him on the range and asked if he could borrow $100. Chi Chi took $50 out of his wallet, handed it to the caddie and told him he didn't have to pay it back.

"Cheech, you're *giving* me this $50? What's the catch?" he asked curiously.

"The way I look at it, it'll be the quickest fifty we both ever made," Cheech answered.

We were paired with Jim Dent, who had his nephew PeeWee caddying for him. Jim had the reputation of being one of the tougher guys to work for, and on this particular day, he was in extremely rare form. He was all over PeeWee like a bad smell, abusing him for everything, including the clouds in the sky. Watching a caddie get treated so poorly didn't sit well with Chi Chi, especially since they were related. The abuse escalated, and Chi Chi, having witnessed enough, told PeeWee right in front of Jim, a man who towered over him, "Pards, you don't have to take that shit from any player—even if he is your uncle. Drop that bag right now and don't worry about money. I'll give you $2,000 when I get to the clubhouse!"

PeeWee glared up at Jim and gave the proposition some strong consideration but declined the offer. It was one of the most impressive and upstanding things I ever saw a player do.

One of the best perks of working for Chi Chi Rodriguez was the fact that he had his own jet, and I was lucky enough to fly with him, schedule permitting. I always said that I didn't have to be a millionaire; I just wanted to live like one. There is absolutely nothing like flying privately and after having done so, even flying first class commercially sucks.

Not bad for a poor kid from Puerto Rico.

Every Sunday was a mad dash to get out of town, like we just robbed a bank. I could never understand it. If we were stopped at a red light on the way to the airport and it was taking longer to turn green than he would like, he'd tell me to run it. I'd ask him, "Cheech, what's the rush? It's not like you're going to miss a flight or something. It's your plane—it doesn't leave until you say so!"

The jet would be sitting on the tarmac, awaiting our arrival, engines whistling, and ready to take to the skies. One thing was certain; he was going to tell me not to hit the wing of the airplane as I pulled up. I always came back with, "I managed to get us here without hitting anything. I promise I won't crash into your jet."

He had an older plane that was equipped with turbo-jets instead of the newer and quieter fan-jet engines. I adored the sound of the engines roaring as we thundered down the runway. Once the wheel was in the air and we were climbing, he'd instruct me to get him a glass of Johnny Walker Blue Label. He'd laugh, sing and eventually doze off to sleep. It was really good to see him relax and not have to worry about autographs, interviews, or people wanting something from him.

Besides being very generous with his money and his time, he was very hospitable to his tour brethren with his plane. Rarely were we flying without at least one hitchhiker, and many times the jet was completely full. The daughter of one of the players was in a freak accident that left her a quadriplegic, and she was in a facility on the west coast. Chi Chi offered the golfer a lift any time he was heading in that direction.

Another beauty of working for a marquis player was the invitations he received to special tournaments. One of these events was The Shark Shoot-Out, hosted by Greg Norman and played at Sherwood Country Club in Westlake Village, California. It was a team format, and Chi Chi was invited to pair up with John Mahaffey, who does a pretty comical impersonation of Chi Chi, but that was the height of the fun between them. On the golf course, they mixed like oil and water. John's pretty uptight, and Chi Chi sounded like a broken record saying constantly, "Don't worry about it, Pards. It's only money!"

The last sojourn of the season was to Dorado Beach, Puerto Rico for The New York Life Champions. This was the first tournament I ever worked for Chi Chi when they used to pair up with the LPGA players, but was now just the old guys.

I flew down a week early, per instructions from Chi Chi. He was all fired up and said he wanted to practice and prepare for the tournament, but he lives there, and I hardly saw him that week. I did my course preparation, walking the yardages and diagramming the greens, which took a couple of days.

During the tournament week I spent some my free time visiting nearby towns, some of which were smaller than the Buick station wagon Chi Chi let me use. It amazed me that there was such poverty just outside the gates of the luxurious compound. It was in one of these towns that I noticed a dirty, disheveled woman standing in the doorway of a dilapidated shanty, two semi-clad children clutching her thighs. As I sped past, I was thinking about how cruel and difficult life was for some and how I had just experienced my most prosperous season as a professional tour caddie. The farther I drove, the more compelled I felt to turn the car around. An idea sprang into my head and I dared myself to do it. Pulling the car in front of the shack, I approached the woman and couldn't help but notice a look of suspicion written all over her face. There was an uncomfortable silence created by her intrigue, and the communication barrier. I handed her a couple of $100 bills, rolled up and cupped in my hand and seeing as it was a couple of weeks before Christmas, said, "Feliz Navidad." She grasped the bills in her filthy hand and replied in a soft voice, "Muchas Gracias."

I made my way to the car, but took one final look their way. The three of them were standing in the doorway, all waving to me in unison. As I began my short trek back to Dorado Beach, I was enveloped in a warm and very satisfying feeling, thinking about what kind of Christmas they were going to have. I don't want to sound like I'm tooting my own horn, and I didn't do this to be the big shot. I'd like to think that I was following Chi Chi's example and that he would have been proud of me for giving to someone less fortunate. Keeping in line with his credo that you give without expecting anything in return, including accolades, I never told anyone about it until now.

On Wednesday of the tournament week, Inside the Senior PGA Tour approached Chi Chi about doing a segment on him, and the town he was raised in for the show. He agreed, and asked me if I wanted to go with them. After hearing all the stories about his childhood, I jumped at the chance. I figured it would give me some vital insight into the man I was dedicating a large portion of my life to. And so Chi Chi and I, along with a film crew, hopped into a van and left the elegant realm of Dorado Beach for a place called Rio Piedras. Years ago, I was a land surveyor in Chicago and had been in some of the nastiest and scariest neighborhoods you wouldn't want to see. They were Beverly Hills compared to this place.

It was like a war zone, battle weary people and all, and the fact that we had thousands of dollars worth of audio/video equipment in our possession didn't help the situation. Chi Chi was asked to bring a sand wedge with him for a still photograph. I held it the majority of the time, ready to swing at anyone who came within three feet of me. Fortunately, no one messed with us. As a matter of fact, they recognized Chi Chi, being the national hero that he is, and honked as they drove by yelling, "Hola, Chi Chi!" out of open windows. He reminded me of the Pope in Rome, as he waved to them in a dignified manner.

First on the agenda was a visit to the infamous baseball diamond I had heard so much about. Incidentally, this was the same field where a young Roberto Clemente honed his baseball skills. Chi Chi looked like he was seeing an old friend. He took us to various locations around the diamond, a yarn for each spot, then became extremely unnerved when he discovered some used hypodermic needles on the ground.

Next we went to the location that was once his childhood refuge—The Berwind Country Club, and once again Chi Chi took us on a trip down his memory lane, reminiscing about his early days as a caddie. Showing no signs of once being a lush, green country club, the property was now dotted with shabby tenement buildings.

What I remember most about that expedition was Chi Chi's reaction when we finally arrived at his childhood home. A myriad of discarded auto parts and trash was strewn about the grimy surroundings, and it was evident that the place hadn't been occupied for some time. Chi Chi strolled slowly around the house, not saying a word. He peered through the barred front windows and then stood back, his arms crossed in front of him and a very disturbed grimace on his face. I wondered what horrible memory he was replaying in his mind. At that point, he became overwhelmed with emotion, causing us all to back off and give him some space.

From a distance, I could see that he was extremely upset, and it was hurtful to witness his pain, but as I watched him, I couldn't help but notice his Rolex, alligator loafers and custom-tailored clothing. I thought about his palatial estate at Dorado Beach and his private jet. In that moment of clarity, I had a full and vivid picture of the seemingly insurmountable odds that he overcame. In that moment, I realized that he really is the epitome of the American Dream.

Chi Chi possessed a ton of willpower. Proof of this was the fact that he could stop smoking on command, anytime he liked, even though had been plagued with the habit most of his adult life. The nicotine not only helped his nerves, the physical act of smoking was a part of his pre-shot routine. He'd stand behind the ball, ala' Nicklaus, stare it down, take one last drag off the cigarette, throw it off to the side and begin his rhythmic approach. I always thought that if the smokes didn't kill him, the pesticides from the golf course would.

He had decided to quit smoking at the end of the previous year and was now a couple of months sans cigarettes. His putting stroke was fundamentally unsound to begin with, and the lack of nicotine wasn't helping his nerves any. That being said, Chi Chi went out the first round of the tournament in Naples, Florida, and shot 78 (that's cart top, snowman in caddie lingo), missing six putts from inside six feet. When he arrived at the course the following day, he got out of his Lexus and handed me three packs of smokes. I took them and gave him a quizzical look without saying a word. His rebuttal, "Pards, I know what you're thinking but I'm gonna tell you something. Those cigarettes are going to kill me slowly. Shootin' 78 is gonna kill me quick!"

He quit smoking another time, and then, out of the blue, had a cigarette in his hand. I inquired about the resurgence of the vice and he said, "Ya' know, Pards, I was thinkin' about it and I came to the conclusion that I'm gonna smoke, I'm gonna drink, I'm gonna eat red meat and I'm gonna die just like everyone else. And when I die, I wanna look bad. There's nuthin' worse than going to a funeral and everybody says, 'He looks good.' I want 'em to look in my casket and say, 'Oh, Chi Chi looks really bad. He really did a lot of livin'.'"

Chi Chi was a fantastic driver of the golf ball and could shape it any way to ride the wind and achieve maximum distance. I always liked when the wind blew because he was extremely proficient at keeping it under the wind, and held an edge over his competitors. For a man of his stature, he could be especially long when the pressure was on, and the adrenaline was pumping. During the Pro-Am, he just bunted it around the course, but when the gun went off and the gallery was behind him, he could turn it up a notch or two. He may have had the quickest hands of anyone ever to play the game, and he got all of his 130 pounds moving in perfect sequence. His swing was far from Hoganesque, but it was efficient, and pound for pound, you couldn't find anyone who hit it further.

Chi Chi was an excellent long iron player, which came in handy on the longer par 3s and par 5s. Again, he could shape it any way to produce a desired result. I saw him lay up on a long par 5 with a waist-high 3 iron, because the fairways were saturated and he wanted to keep the ball from picking up any mud.

When it came to mid and short irons, he was an artist and the golf course was his canvas. He could slice it, cut it, draw it, rope hook it, saw the legs off it (punch it), hold it, or just hit it straight. I get a kick out of hearing the golf announcers of today say, "This shot's a tough one for Steve, because he likes to play the ball left-to-right." Chi Chi had no shape preference, and played whatever the shot called for. Oddly enough, he didn't play easy golf courses well, because he didn't feel challenged. If you gave him a 10,000 square foot green with the flag cut in the middle of it, he'd have a hard time getting it close. But, test him with a flag cut back right on a small tier close to a bunker, with water to the right and thick rough behind, and he'd stiff it.

His wedge play from 100 yards in was impeccable. From this distance, he expected to be no farther than 10 feet from the hole and was totally pissed off if he wasn't. The great Japanese player, Isao Aoki, would be what I consider a comparable wedge player and incidentally, played with a similar 'handsy' style.

Around the green was Chi Chi's forte. Some of the incredible shots I witnessed remind me of some of the magic I see Mickelson performing today. I saw Chi Chi hit a pitch shot with a full swing, off a bare lie, carry the ball 40 feet over a bunker, and land like a butterfly with sore feet. When he got into what I figured was an unplayable position around the green, he'd survey the shot, his left arm across his chest and his right hand caressing his face. I could almost hear the wheels turning and knew I was going to witness a masterpiece.

One of these stands out in my mind. We were playing the Legends of Golf in La Quinta, California. Chi Chi was paired with Jim Dent and had knocked his second shot over the 16th green of the Stadium Course at PGA West. The 16th is a par 5 with a deep, treacherous bunker guarding the left side of the elevated green. There's some Bob Hope Chrysler Classic footage of Speaker of the House Tip O'Neill trying unsuccessfully to extricate his ball from the chasm, flailing wildly at it and eventually throwing it out. Chi Chi wasn't in the bunker, but was some 35 feet below the level of the green, with a tight lie, that was sitting down and away from him. The hole was cut back, and from where he was, he could barely see just the top of the flag. The shot was nearly impossible, but would have been a fraction easier if he were in the bunker. He assumed his pose behind the ball, looking down at the lie and then up toward the flag, down at the lie and then up toward the flag. After this thorough examination of the predicament, he snatched his lob wedge from the bag and exclaimed, "Pards, there's only two people in the world that can handle this shot—me and Hogan."

He set up to the ball, took one waggle and said, "Scratch that, Pards, I don't think Hogan could handle this."

He laid the face of the wedge wide open, picked it up abruptly as he took it away, came into it hot with a ton of club-head speed and made contact about an inch behind the ball, like a bunker shot. It sounded like he hit a dog in the ass with a wet newspaper. The ball popped up, travelling parallel to the steep hill right in front of him, dropped on the green like it fell out of someone's pocket and rattled in and out of the hole, finishing a tap-in away. Jim Dent was in awe.

Chi Chi was more comfortable in the sand than Frankie Avalon. He was such an awesome bunker player that if a flag was cut just over one, he'd aim for it, knowing that an up and down was almost certain. Every so often he'd be in a trap and tell me to pull the pin. He didn't always hole it, but most of the time he'd scare the hell out of it. It was a given that if he did can it, I'd be walking to the next tee and some rocket scientist would ask, "Hey, Caddie, was he trying to hole that?"

What amazed me about his kitty litter expertise was that he relied solely on his instincts. Today, you watch a player faced with a tough trap shot and he spends 12 minutes taking 50 practice swings of different lengths, only to hit a mediocre shot. Chi Chi would grab the wedge, climb into the bunker, take a peek at the flag, and the shot was on its way.

Like Lefty, Chi Chi had an incredible imagination around the green. Once, he buried a tee shot under the lip of a bunker and it was so plugged you almost couldn't see it. Chi Chi climbed the steep face of the trap, pointed the toe of the club straight down, and played the shot with the top edge of the wedge. With the club in that position, it cut through the sand like a knife and drastically eliminated resistance. He caught the exact center of the ball, which he'll be the first to admit is extremely difficult and lucky, and popped it onto the green. His philosophy was, even if he caught the ball off-center, he would free it from the buried lie and leave it in the bottom of the bunker.

I used to believe that every professional golfer has an Achilles heel, even Tiger Woods (though his is not related to golf). Jack Nicklaus' chipping and bunker play were the only weaknesses in an otherwise flawless game. Unfortunately, Chi Chi's one-and-only nemesis in the bag was the one club you want to be best buddies with—the flat stick. I wish that I had a dollar for every time I heard him say, "If I could have putted, you would have *never* heard of Nicklaus or Palmer." As great a ball striker as this man was, if he had been just an average putter, he would have won at least one Major on the PGA Tour and a score of other events. I got so sick and tired of leaving an event, griping to my travelling partners about how we should have won the tournament, and I knew they were tired of hearing it.

We were paired with Bob Charles at the Doug Sanders Celebrity Golf Classic in Houston, and Charlie Bob was in his usual zone, making everything within 25 feet of the hole. He was the trailblazer for left-handed players, being the only one at the time to ever win a Major championship, the 1967 British Open. I loved getting paired with him because I loved to watch him roll his rock, even though I did get a little jealous, wishing Chi Chi could make just ¼ of the putts he did. He putted with an old Acushnet Bullseye putter, and his stroke was as pure as the driven snow. Chi Chi was in his usual mode and couldn't get anything to drop. By the end of the round he was fed up and said, "Can you believe I'm gettin' beat by a #$@&in' lefty?!"

At the root of Chi Chi's putting dilemma were poor fundamentals, plain and simple. He played a handsy game from tee to green, then tried to employ the same technique on the moss. Isao Aoki was about the only player to successfully pull that one off. He didn't really take the putter back as much as he picked it up with a wrist cock and then dropped it on the ball. This is a technique that you'll never hear the great putting guru Dave Pelz recommend. Aoki was a great putter using this unique and extraordinary putting style, but Chi Chi was not as fortunate. He set up to it with an open stance, a really weak grip, and his hands almost resting on his front left pocket...thus, the origination of the dreaded Tomahawk Chop, as I called it. From this position, it was a guarantee that he was going to take it away outside and then cut across it on the way through. I had to manipulate my read to accommodate his stroke. If the putt was a right-to-left breaker, I needed to read less break into it, as he was cutting it up the line, making it break less. The less popular alternative was a putt breaking from left-to-right. I had to read more break into it, because he was basically slicing it, which made it go considerably more right. I guarantee that he missed 90% of the left-to-right breakers low or right of the hole.

You might be asking, why not just advise him to play considerably more break on those putts? And that would be a correct assumption. But (there's always a but), it was a little hard to tell him to play it a ball outside left on a 3½ footer that didn't have any slope to speak of. Every so often he'd hood it coming through, negating the hideous chop. Plus, he tended to move his head and come out of it on the short ones. I can't tell you how many times he missed a short putt and then blamed it on me because he chopped it more or less than I anticipated. Needless to say, when he had a short one, the pucker factor was in full force, especially if it was early in the final round and he was in a position to win. If he had a 4 footer on the first green and he made it, it was a building block of confidence. If he missed it, I just said a prayer that he didn't see that range for a while, which was usually the next hole. Once again, the Golfing Gods at work.

He tried everything to remedy the problem, God bless him. He tried long putters, short putters, heavy putters and very light putters. My mentor, Scotty Gilmour, caddied for Chi Chi in the 60s and said that he used a putter that was one foot long. Scotty said it was so small he had to keep it in a satchel in the zipper pocket of the bag. Chi Chi attempted to use a long putter a few times when I worked for him, but saw a picture of himself using it and said that it made him look like he was drilling for oil. He trash-canned it, saying that if he was going to be a bad putter, he was going to look good doing it.

At the risk of sounding wishy-washy, Chi Chi was not a horrible putter all the time. He was a streak putter, and when he got in a zone, he could make some putts. You don't win as much as he did on ball striking alone.

I was walking the golf course in San Antonio while on Crampton's bag, and witnessed a putting lesson that was going to cost me dearly. Bob Toski was working with Chi Chi, and was brilliant enough to know that he would never be able to teach him how to stroke it like the putting masters, i.e. Bob Charles, George Archer, etc. So he worked with what he had. I watched from a distance as Bob instructed Chi Chi to put the ball way back in his putting stance. When I say way back, I mean off of his right toe. He placed balls with the Titleist logo as far to the right as possible, but still visible at address. Then he told him that he wanted him to strike the ball at the logo. I remember hearing him say, "Cheech, I want you to 'pop' it."

Basically this transformed a swiping, slicing stroke, into a trapping, driving one. The trick here is that the putter has to have some loft on it; otherwise you'll drive it into the ground and it'll squirt on you. Bob was ahead of the game, and had Chi Chi's putter set at about 6-7 degrees of loft. The ball was coming off the putter head with a good departure and a super roll to it. The instruction was worth its weight in gold, or actually winner's checks, as Chi Chi won seven events that year. Unfortunately, Crampton was in his rear view mirror on several of them…with me on board.

One of the luxuries of working for a superstar was that his corporate outings scheduled early in the week afforded me a couple of free days. Don't get me wrong, these were big money days for Chi Chi, and I would have given my left nut to have been involved in them. Such was the case after the Chrysler Cup. Chi Chi had a gig to do somewhere, so I flew to the Desert and after a couple of days rest, made my way to the Ojai Valley north of Los Angeles for the next tourney.

From the time I arrived at The Ojai Valley Inn and Country Club, it rained so heavily that both Pro-Ams and the first official round of the event were cancelled, shortening it to just 36 holes. This didn't happen very often but when it did, there had to be a change in strategy. Playing conservatively was out of the question, and your man really had to play with a balls-to-the-walls mentality. There was also less margin for error due to the lack of time to catch up. Chi Chi followed these guidelines, playing solidly and vaulting himself into contention for the second and final round.

Standing on the 15th tee at Ojai, Chi Chi was leading, but drove his ball into the right rough, under a small tree. From this lie, most players wouldn't have thought twice about chipping out to the fairway and trying to save par from there. Chi Chi had other plans. He crouched under the limbs of the tree and contemplated the shot, which required hitting the ball 130 yards uphill out of a heavy lie and taking a waist-high backswing. It was extremely possible that he could hang the club up on the tree limbs and whiff it, and the outcome of the tournament hinged on this one shot. He took his 7 iron and assumed his stance under the tree, completely bent over at the waist. After a series of practice backswings, he drew the club back slowly and took an abbreviated swipe at the ball. He made solid contact, and the ball traveled in a low trajectory, covering the distance easily and running 20 feet past the pin, narrowly missing it. He went on to hole the putt, transforming a possible bogey into a birdie. That was one of the top five most miraculous shots that I ever saw him play.

Playing the par 5, 18th, Chi Chi was still leading, but was faced with one last hurdle. He was short right of the green in two, with his ball nestled down in the rough. Gary Player was also in striking distance of victory, but had a much easier shot in the greenside bunker. As phenomenal as he was out of the sand, I knew Chi Chi needed to knock it close to avoid a playoff. He had to carry it over the bunker and run it up to a flag located on the back tier of the green. It was one of those moments when I was ecstatic that my name wasn't on the bag.

Chi Chi took a really deep breath, addressed the ball, and took a lazy, full, half-speed swing at it. The ball came out high and soft, landed on the green just over the trap, and ran up to the hole, finishing two feet away. It was another superbly executed shot when he really needed one. After the tournament, he confessed to me that he prayed he didn't chili-dip it. It was his first official win of the season and it earned me $7,400 for two day's work. Now, if I could only find a job that paid as well on a consistent basis!

A couple of weeks later, I was working in my own backyard. The Vintage Invitational was played at The Vintage Club in Indian Wells and located within walking distance of my condo. One of the most elite clubs in the world, I was very familiar with it because I caddied there with Scotty and the boys when we weren't chasing the European Tour. We had the best of both worlds—summers in Europe, winters in the Desert. In fact, I was getting ready to go back to Europe for my third season abroad, caddying for a Vintage member during the tournament, when I was enticed by our pro in the group, Orville Moody, to pack for him on the fledgling Senior PGA Tour. It would prove to be a very lucrative fork in my road.

Chi Chi continued his stellar play from tee to green, and more importantly, his putter was behaving. He positioned himself for glory and was tied for the lead standing on the 17th tee of the final round. A downhill par 3 of about 150 yards, the flag was cut front right just over a lake. There's a lot of luck involved in professional golf, and I'm not just talking about a fortuitous bounce here or there. The luck I'm referring to is being dealt yardages that take the guesswork out of club selection. When your man's vying to win, you want to stay away from the in-betweeners. Such was not the case on that tee; we were dead between 7 and 8 iron. There was a slight breeze into us, and the hole always seemed to play to the yardage, even though it was downhill. The hole was located precariously close to the hazard, and there was a slope behind it that would serve as a backstop. Accordingly, I talked Chi Chi into going with the 7 iron. I figured the worst place he could hit it would be short.

Man, was I wrong. He caught it dead flush, which can happen when a player has plenty of weapon in his hands, and flew it over the flag into the back sand trap. He wasn't Adolf Hitler, but he *was* Eva Braun; he wasn't dead in the bunker, but death was on the horizon. It wasn't the best call in my annals of club pulling, and had I known he was going to hit it that solid, I would have had him go with the 8.

Chi Chi later quipped that the bunker shot he was left with, was faster than Billy Graham running through Harlem. He had a downhill lie with a little clump of sand behind the ball, which made it even harder to stop. The green was sloping drastically down to the hole, it was straight down grain, and the water past the pin was waiting patiently to gobble up a bunker shot. Chi Chi didn't say anything about the club selection on the tee shot, but I knew if he didn't get it up-and-down, he was going to. I needed him to pull off one of his patented bunker masterpieces, and then I needed him to make the putt. In other words, I needed him to bail my ass out. He obliged me by blasting out of the trap, landing it just on the green with a bit of stuff on it, and trickling it down the hill to a cozy little resting place about a foot from the hole. My wish was granted.

The 18th was a reachable par 5, but Chi Chi drove it into a fairway bunker, forcing him to lay up. I actually didn't mind and thought it might be a blessing. The right side of the green dropped off severely and included a deep, hellish, grass bunker that we dubbed "The Devil's Asshole." Getting it up and down from there would be next to impossible, even for Chi Chi. I'd rather he took his chances with a wedge from 100 yards than go for it and have to dabble in some agronomy proctology.

Chi Chi, still tied for the lead, flew his wedge right over the flagstick, which was five paces from the back right edge of the green.

The 18-footer he was left with was identical to a putt we had earlier in the week to the same pin location, so the read was pretty clean cut. The ball had to be started about 3 feet right of the hole and he needed to get it there. This was no time to leave one in the jaws. A dead silence blanketed the gallery around the green as Chi Chi addressed his putt. I was tending the flag and could see that he was right where he needed to start it. In classic Rodriguez fashion, he jabbed the ball toward the hole. It had covered half the distance when he threw his arms in the air and looked to the heavens. Chi Chi buried that putt without ever seeing gravity work its magic as the ball dropped six inches down to the bottom of the cup. The crowd erupted into a thunderous roar and I let out a pretty good one myself, as Chi Chi capped off the performance with an extended version of his sword dance.

My old friend and mentor Scotty was caddying for Mike Hill, who finished tied for second in the tournament. He was so pissed at me for the miscue on 17 that the only thing he said to me was, "Nice #$@&in' club on 17, wanker! I can't believe he got that #$@&in' thing up-and-down!"

I stood my ground and told him, "Hey, we set up our par with that club." It took him a while to cool off before he would speak to me.

I celebrated Chi Chi's third victory of the season at my condo that night with some friends. Things were going so well it was almost scary. My father used to tell me that I'd never make any money caddying for a living. I called him to see if he had changed his mind.

It is an unwritten rule in professional golf that the Pro-Am participants are supposed to tip the pro's caddie, but unfortunately, very few of them do. I always felt that maybe it should become a written rule, printed in large red letters on the entry form. I never bent over backwards for the guys in our group, knowing that I'd probably get stiffed, but I still tried to help, time permitting. I'd fix a pitch mark here or there, give them a read on a putt, or tell them an off-color joke or two. One time I had one ask me how far he was to the hole. After a quick calculation, I informed him of his distance and he questioned my expertise. "Are you sure?" he asked. With a hint of irritation in my voice, I said, "Sir, Chi Chi Rodriguez pays me well over a hundred grand to know exactly how far it is to that hole. If he can trust me, you can too."

The Monday after Chi Chi's thrilling finish at The Vintage, he was playing in a charity Pro-Am at Big Horn Country Club and was paired with some very heavy hitters. The group consisted of Alan Paulsen, founder and CEO of Gulfstream Aerospace; Michael Smurfit, owner of Jefferson-Smurfit, one of the largest packaging manufacturers in the world; Robert Wagner, the actor; and a little guy named Sam Smith. I'm not quite sure what he did for a living but judging by his clothing and equipment, I think I made more money than he did.

I put in a little more effort than usual with gentlemen from such a high socioeconomic level in our midst. I went out of my way to do everything possible to enhance their golfing experience. I could almost hear Wizzie's voice telling me to stop sticking my tongue down the back of their trousers. The round complete, they disappeared like a hit of Ecstasy at a rave. All of them except for Mr. Smith, who laid a $50 slide on me. Every so often, Chi Chi would inquire about the tipping situation.

"Did you get any tips from those guys, Pards?"

"Yeah, I got 50 bucks from one of them," I answered.

"Who'd you get it from—Paulsen?"

"No, not Paulsen," I answered.

"Oh, Smurfit gave it to you?"

"Nope, not Smurfit."

"Wagner then, huh?"

"Nope."

"Pards, you're not tellin' me that little guy gave you a tip?"

"That's what I'm telling you," I said.

He shook his head and said, "Pards, you gotta' be kidding me. You make more money than that guy."

When we were in Houston for The Doug Sanders Kingwood Celebrity Classic, everyone from athletes to movie stars was in attendance, and Chi Chi was paired with Vice President George H. Bush in the Pro-Am. Accordingly, a chain link fence was installed around the perimeter of the course (your tax dollars at work), and the Secret Service conducted background checks on everyone, including yours truly. My mind was racing, wondering how deep they were going to delve into my past. What could I possibly say if they asked me about getting kicked out of the U.K. and then sneaking back in, or the little filly in Florida who swore she was 18?

With all due respect, George Bush looked more like he was swinging an axe than a golf club. Talk about the lack of executive power. It's a used and abused cliché, but I've seen a better swing on an outhouse door. And he was dangerous, to boot. He dead topped it off the 2nd tee and almost killed a woman. It hit her just above the breast, leaving a perfect imprint of the Titleist logo. I'm totally amazed more spectators aren't seriously injured at golf tournaments.

What our soon-to-be president lacked in golf ability he more than made up for in personality. He and Chi Chi got along famously, and I exchanged a few niceties with him myself. I had the inclination to inform him that my grandmother always thought he was a pantywaist, but decided against it when I caught a glimpse of the Uzi one of the Secret Service agents was packing.

At the tournament in Las Vegas a couple of weeks later Chi Chi returned to the scorching form that had helped him win twice already that season. He was tied for the lead and paired with Gary Player on Sunday. Standing on the putting green that morning, Gary asked Chi Chi if he could catch a lift on his plane to L.A. in the event of a playoff. "It is imperative that I make my connection to the far east," he said emphatically. Chi Chi gave it a few seconds of thought and then replied, "I tell you what. I'll just win the dang thing and you won't have to worry about it!"

Chi Chi had it on cruise control most of the day and maintained a two shot lead over the field. Then he drove it left toward a fairway bunker off the 17th tee. I took it as a given that he was in the trap and just prayed for a clean lie. When we arrived there, we were mortified to find the ball in heavy rough just outside the bunker with a side hill lie. He was going to have to execute this shot standing in the trap. He only had 155 yards, which normally would be a good 7 iron, but with the lie he had, it would take two of those. He examined the situation thoroughly and then grabbed his 5 wood out of the bag, pulling the head cover off in the process. At first, I thought he was going to take an unplayable and needed the club to measure out his drop area. I quickly realized he was using it to extricate the ball from the horrid lie when he entered the bunker and set up to it. Before I could tell him that was way too much club, he took a 60% swing at the ball and knocked it right on the putting surface. The club looked like it weighed 20 pounds during the execution of that shot, and one word came to mind: control.

Chi Chi birdied the last to finish in style by three over his nearest pursuer. For the awards ceremony, it was tradition at The Desert Inn to bring a wheelbarrow full of the winner's share of the purse, all in silver dollars, onto the 18th green. With armed guards flanking him, Chi Chi ran his fingers through the shimmering coins as television cameras soaked it all up and beamed it to golf fans around the globe. He reminded me of a pirate who had dug up buried treasure; all he needed was an eye patch and a parrot on his shoulder.

Clan Rodriguez adjourned to Chi Chi's suite to celebrate the victory. His wife's family lived in the area, so there were more participants for the bash than usual. The only thing standing between us and a great time were the corks in the bottles of Johnny Walker Blue Label. We were just approaching warp speed when Chi Chi took a phone call in the other room. He came back a few minutes later with a look on his face like he just received word someone shot his favorite dog.

"What's the matter, Juan?" his wife Iwalani asked.

He had a faraway gaze in his eyes as he answered, "That was my sister."

"Is everything all right?"

"Yeah, but she told me something that I totally forgot about." he answered.

He went on to tell us all about a recurring dream he had when he was a boy in Puerto Rico. He would dream that he had a wheelbarrow full of money, the shiniest coins he could ever imagine. He had this dream on a regular basis and would tell his sister about it every time it happened. She told him that it was a crazy dream and that he was poor and would always be poor. She told him to stop torturing himself. Forty years later, she flipped on her television set and realized that some dreams really do come true.

Our next destination on the traveling circus known as the Senior PGA Tour was Stonebriar Country Club just outside Dallas, for the Murata Reunion Pro-Am. Chi Chi edged out tour newcomer Jim Colbert and won his second tournament in a row, fourth of the year, and it was only mid-May. Things were going so well, I was bummed there was any time between tournaments.

Sleepy Hollow Country Club is named after the book written by Washington Irving, and is located in Scarborough-on-Hudson, just north of New York City. The famed setting for the tale, the grounds possess a real cool and creepy aura.

Chi Chi was paired with his old adversary and my former boss, Bruce Crampton in the second round of the tournament. Ill feelings between the two had diminished greatly, but that was about to change.

Chi Chi was first up and struck his tee ball before the name "Rodriguez" passed from the 1st tee announcer's lips. Bruce was next up and began his painfully lengthy regimen, which included a couple of minutes of tee manicure (at one point I thought he was going to break out a leaf blower), followed by club maintenance (a thorough cleaning of his driver grip with a towel, and then the cleaning out of the scoring lines of the clubface with a tee), and then his pre-shot routine. It was taking so long for him to play, I could feel my beard coming in. He was finally ready to pull the trigger when a fly landed on his ball. He waved off the fly and began the whole routine anew.

After completing his tedious regimen for the second time, he was once again ready to play, when church bells began to ring in the distance. Bruce stopped and assumed a stance behind the ball, arms crossed, resting on the butt end of his driver. At first I didn't think there was any way he was going to wait for those bells to stop ringing, but having seen worse from him, I knew that was exactly what he was going to do. As we waited, tension blanketed the tee like a thick fog. I could hear Chi Chi behind me muttering in Spanish. After an extended version of Ave Maria, the bells finally ceased and Bruce hit his damn tee shot.

Chi Chi missed a couple of short putts on the first few holes and was hotter than a lava flow. It's hard to hit greens when you're seeing red. He played lousy all day long and after the round was so angry, I'm convinced he would have fought Apollo Creed. David whisked him from the course to avoid the inevitable altercation.

Two winless months had passed and Chi Chi was on a quest to find out why. He forgot that he had won four events and the season was barely at the halfway point. The fact was that he played in eight and hadn't picked off one of them, and that bothered him. He tinkered incessantly with his game, trying desperately to regain his winning form. I tried to be the voice of reason, telling him that he needed to be patient and we'd be in victory lane again. I told him he couldn't make it happen—he had to let it happen, but it was a waste of breath, going in one ear and out the other. He turned into Vince Lombardi on me. Winning wasn't everything. It was the only thing.

The reason for his slump, if you can call it that, was the ineffectiveness of his putting. He and his putter were getting along like The Crips and The Bloods. He was having a difficult time converting the 10 to 15 footers for birdie, and he was really starting to get shaky on the short ones. When he putted well it was fairly pretty, and when he putted poorly, it was pretty ugly. He attempted to remedy the problem with unorthodox stances and grips, assuring me that each was the panacea for his putting woes, but if one short putt missed, he was on to the next possible corrective.

By that point I was battle-hardened enough to know that it was only a matter of time before a big ole finger would be pointing in my direction. I'd get a call every Monday from his manager, Eddie Elias saying, "What's goin' on out there?"

The answer was always the same.

"You know what, Eddie? I didn't make one bogey last week!"

Sure enough, I was informed that the basis for all of Chi Chi's putting woes was my lack of expertise in the green-reading department. It pissed me off something fierce. I never tried to take credit when he was getting it in the hole, and I sure as hell wasn't bearing the load when he wasn't.

Chi Chi came to the outrageous conclusion that if I charted every slope of every green like a topography map, that I'd give him the perfect read and he'd make everything. He even went so far as to say that my green diagrams should be so detailed that I should be able to look at them and tell him where to play the putt! This was a load of absolute rubbish and there was no telling me otherwise. The only way to read a green is to look at it from as many angles as possible, determining the slope and grain. Your eye will tell you these things—not a pad and pencil. I was a team player, and would have walked through fire if there was a sliver of a chance that it would help.

Regardless, I still had to start charting the greens of every golf course we played to appease Chi Chi. My diagrams were so detailed, Leonardo Da Vinci would have raised an eyebrow. This practice was extremely time consuming. I'm not sure what was more irritating, the added length of time needed to prep for the tournament or the fact that I knew I was beating a dead horse. Creating schematics for every green of every golf course wasn't going to rectify the horrible fundamentals of Chi Chi's putting technique. I wisely reverted to the adage I adopted while on Crampton's bag. As long as I made my living as a professional tour caddie, caca was going to be a staple of my diet.

You know a golf course is a brutal one when the great Ben Hogan dubs it 'The Monster.' The U.S.G.A held the 1991 U.S. Senior Open Championship at Oakland Hills Country Club outside of Detroit. The good news was that Chi Chi tended to play extremely difficult courses well. The bad news was that he hadn't performed worth a poop in the past two months.

Chi Chi played solidly from tee to green the first two rounds, even though birdies were scarce, and made the par putts when needed. He was in favorable shape for the weekend, and anyone in professional golf will tell you that you can't win an Open on Thursday or Friday, but you can sure lose one.

The morning of the final round it dawned on me that this was probably going to be my best and possibly last shot at packing for a U.S. Senior Open champion.

Standing on the 18th and final hole, Chi Chi was tied for the lead. A par 4 dogleg right, this hole had gotten the better of us previously. His adrenaline level was at full throttle as he blistered his drive over the right bunker, cutting the corner. We were left with 167 yards to the hole, uphill, to a flag cut front left over a bunker, with a healthy breeze hurting from the right. Chi Chi asked me what I liked. I must admit, I was feeling the gravity of the situation, but knew this was no time for even a hint of vapor lock. I took a deep breath and just threw it out there, "I like 5 iron, and hold it." This was a lot of club, but we had been short twice on this hole. Carving it up into the wind was going to take a lot off the shot and would enable him to bring it in high and soft, which the shot called for.

Chi Chi rebutted, "No, Pards—I'm bringing a 6 in the other way."

He answered without a whisper of hesitation, and I knew the worst thing I could do was doubt the call. This was no time to be a hero. I just let him go and gave him one last word of positive reinforcement, "You got this shot, Cheech," as I pulled the bag away. He stood behind the ball and contemplated proper execution, then started his rhythmic approach. His address completed, he drew the club back and took a wild slash at it. I was under the impression that he was going to draw it in there, but I was wrong. The ball left the clubface about 80 yards right of the hole. It's an exciting moment when the ball first separates from the club and you learn in an instant if the shot is going to make you happy, sad, or somewhere in between. At that initial moment, I wasn't too enthused.

In classic Chi Chi Rodriguez style, he contorted his body to left and ran a few steps in that direction as if to impart English on the shot. Approaching the green, it was still miles right, but almost as if the ball was pre-programmed, it made a hard left turn, landed in front of the green and spun sharply to the left. Chi Chi would later dub this shot his 'masse' shot.

The crowd sprang to their feet with an explosion of applause. The green was elevated, making it impossible to see how close it finished, but when you've been around professional golf long enough, you learn to read the crowd and they were telling us it was close. I didn't know it at the time, but I had just witnessed the greatest golf shot of my caddie career, and I was having a tough time controlling my emotions.

When we arrived at the green, we were pleased to learn the ball had come to rest three feet from the hole. That was about two feet farther than I would have liked. The exuberant crowd cheered wildly as Chi Chi marked his ball. He still had to sink a tester from above the hole, and with the combination of his stroke and the pressure, this was no gimme. He tended to miss short ones when he got tentative on them, so before he putted, I gave him one last ditty of input, "Left of center here, Cheech. Nice and solid. The hole will stop it."

I would have rather watched an open-heart surgery as he set up to the putt and coaxed it in the jar. The response from the gallery was deafening as Chi Chi rewarded them with his sword dance. He was 2 over par and leader in the clubhouse.

We were in the scoring trailer and feeling pretty comfortable with our position, when a huge ovation emanated from the distance. The Golden Bear, Jack Nicklaus, was Chi Chi's nearest pursuer at 3 over par, and almost holed his tee shot at the par 3, 17th. Chi Chi's reign at the top was short lived as Jack tapped in for birdie and a share of the lead with one to play.

Jack was only human, and a bogey on the last wasn't out of the question. But in retrospect, that was wishful thinking. He drilled his drive on the same line as Chi Chi, and his approach was pure Nicklaus as it came in high and soft, settling about 13 feet from the pin. As Jack surveyed his putt, I felt nauseated. He carved out his historic career making these putts to win major championships. The crowd quieted as he prepared to strike what could be the winning putt. He rolled his ball toward the hole, and it appeared to be in all the way, but at the last split-second it decided to dive right and miss the hole by a micro-fraction. The crowd emitted a collective groan as Jack stared disgustedly at the ball hanging precariously on the lip, a *don't you understand who I am?* look on his face. Chi Chi was now in a Monday playoff with Jack for the U.S. Senior Open.

That night I experienced what can only be described as anxious exhaustion. I was physically spent from the day's events, but my mind was in overdrive pondering tomorrow's.

The following morning, *USA Today's* sports section was inundated with stories surrounding the tournament. One segment described Chi Chi's heroic shot to the 18th green by stating, "Against the advice of his caddie…" but it really didn't bother me. No caddie in the history of the profession could have called that shot. Under those circumstances, suggesting an 80-yard rope hook into that green could get you hauled off in a straightjacket.

The playoff commenced and Chi Chi was in control of his game and his emotions, parring the first 5 holes. But there was a proverbial fly in the ointment. The Bear had it on cruise control, making birdies at 2, 4 and 5, and was ahead by 3 strokes. It was painfully apparent that he was going to blitz us. We needed to break his momentum, and we accomplished that with an assist from Mother Nature. The sky darkened and unleashed a vicious thunderstorm as we approached the 6th green. There may be only two ways to beat Jack when he's on his game…get him off the course or shoot him.

The skies cleared and we journeyed back out to the 6th green. Before play was interrupted, Chi Chi was putting for birdie from 30 feet and Jack had a 4-footer left for par. Chi Chi miraculously holed his long putt and The Golden One was unsuccessful in his par attempt. A two-shot swing endowed us with a renewed sense of vigor and hope, and we took the delay as a gift from above.

Now facing only a one shot deficit, Chi Chi put his ball in a bunker left of the green on the par 4, 7th. Jack missed his approach short and to the right of the green on a tight, wet lie. This was definitely not the same opponent we faced the first five holes. At that point, I felt that momentum swung in our favor and Chi Chi was destined to win the tournament. But that feeling evaporated when Jack holed his pitch shot.

On the next tee Nicklaus drove into a sand trap and Chi Chi was safely in the fairway. I figured we had the advantage again, but Jack made bird from the bunker and Chi Chi 3-putted for bogey. Two holes earlier, Chi Chi walked off the green trailing by only one shot and full of optimism. Now the deficit was four, and I felt like someone kicked me in the balls. The skies were clear, so another helping hand from old Mother Nature wasn't likely to happen. I wondered how hard it would be to get a gun.

On the tee of the 9th, a par 3 of 215 yards, Chi Chi showed his resolve by sailing a 5 wood over the flag. There was a very steep slope to a back tier directly behind the hole, and his ball hit into it, ran to the top and then slowly began creeping backward toward the cup. As we walked off the tee, the ball was still inching closer, the crowd's applause increasing with every rotation. It wasn't as frenetic as the scene at the 18th the day before, but it was gaining on it by the moment. As they walked, Jack shot Chi Chi a smile and extended his hand for a low five. Chi Chi reciprocated with a grin back at him as he slapped his hand. Witnessing that small gesture was a poignant moment for me. It was awesome to see two superstars dueling valiantly, but still rooting for each other. Chi Chi sank his putt for birdie and we made our way to the 10th trailing by 3 shots.

Sadly, consecutive bogies on 11 and 12 took the wind out of our sails. Chi Chi never got any closer than 4 shots; the last couple of holes were a mere formality. We might as well have been spectators in the crowd. Chi Chi fired a very respectable 69, but Jack sealed his first U.S. Senior Open with a solid 65.

To this day I believe that Chi Chi Rodriguez would have his name on that trophy if he had climbed into the ring with any other senior golfer except Jack William Nicklaus.

It was my second near-miss caddying for the winner of this event. The first was in '88 when Crampton missed the Gary Player/ Bob Charles playoff by one shot at Medinah. My gut was right; I never again came close to grabbing the brass ring of caddying for a U.S. Senior Open champion.

Just a short month later, Chi Chi had consecutive 2nd place finishes at the GTE Northwest in Seattle and The Charley Pride Senior Classic he'd won previously. He played well enough to win either or both events, but the putts weren't dropping like they did earlier in the season. It was as if the Golfing Gods decided that he had won enough tournaments that year. I was having my best financial year as a professional tour caddie, leaving no room for whining.

The end of the season arrived and we found ourselves at Rancho Park in Los Angeles for the Security Pacific Senior Classic. By this time I wasn't just burned out, I was charred. It had been a long year, and one tires of seeing the same old faces. Some used to say that we were one big happy family on the road. By that point in the year, I didn't give a damn if I ever saw some of those people again in my life. I did find solace knowing that I only had a couple more tournaments to work before I had some time off.

At the end of the 2nd round, Chi Chi was once again within striking distance of victory. After a solid round on Sunday, he was tied for the lead with Masters Champion George Archer and former San Francisco 49er quarterback, John Brodie. On the first playoff hole, Brodie put his drive in the left-center of the fairway; Chi Chi's was on the same line but a bit farther. Archer's drive was on the right edge of the fairway, bringing some trees into play. Brodie was first to play, giving me the opportunity to do some club selection recon. He had an 8 iron in his hand, which was a bit strange because Chi Chi was 10 yards ahead of him and we were liking 7. I didn't believe there was any way he could get that club all the way there but he thinned it, striking it right in the forehead and it covered the distance, finishing 4 feet from the hole. I guarantee it was pure luck. I've heard just about everything, but I have never heard a professional golfer say, "Give me that 8 iron. I'm gonna thin it in there."

Chi Chi played his 7 iron to 20 feet right of the hole. George missed the green short and right, which he then chipped up close for a tap-in par. As close as Brodie was, it was imperative that Chi Chi hole his lengthy birdie attempt. I was immersed in reading the line on the putt, while Chi Chi clowned around with John. He had his handkerchief covering Brodie's eyes, feigning execution. They're good friends, but John wasn't all that amused. It took all my effort to get Chi Chi to concentrate on the task at hand, but he stood up and missed it like he was just going through the motions and was resigned to finishing second.

I knew he wanted to see John win his first Senior PGA. Tour event, but I sure as hell didn't want it to be at our expense. It was Chi Chi's fifth 2nd place finish, including two playoff losses since his last win in early May.

After the annual romp to Dorado Beach for the season ending event, I took a detour to Chicago to see my family for the holidays. Having just completed my finest and most lucrative year as a tour caddie, I was riding high and felt like things were only going to get better. This was a tall order after four victories and five 2nd place finishes, including two playoff losses, one for the U.S. Senior Open. I couldn't wait for the next season to start.

1993 commenced with another bridesmaid finish to Al 'Mr. 59' Geiberger at the Tournament of Champions. Finishing events with just one player ahead of him was really beginning to wear on Chi Chi's nerves. I couldn't help but think that if he would have tried a bit harder and won at Rancho Park, he'd have a recent victory under his belt and I'd have a little breathing room.

I worked my second consecutive Senior Skins game in Hawaii at the end of January. Palmer, Nicklaus, Trevino and Chi Chi were the contestants that year, which turned out to be a lucrative trip for me. Once again, Palmer played like the Arnie of old, and won the majority of the skins. He was cork-screwing himself into the ground on every tee shot, holing chips and coercing the ball into the jar.

All the way to the 17th hole it appeared to be a rerun for Team Rodriguez. He hadn't won any skins, but rolled in a long birdie from off the green for a four-skin carryover worth $125,000. I was beyond relief, leaving the Big Island knowing that my man won some skins and I made a healthy check.

One month later in Ojai, unbelievably, Chi Chi finished in second position again, and a debate was brewing in the Rodriguez camp about why he wasn't sealing the deal. It didn't help that he was a bridesmaid in events that he'd previously won, and fingers were pointing at me. I stuck to my guns and told myself that I never took credit for the wins and I sure as hell wouldn't take the fall for the near-misses.

Regardless, Chi Chi's office informed me that I was burned out and should take a week off. The funny thing was, they were right on the money, but Chi Chi needed a respite as much, or more than I did.

Instead, he played in San Antonio the following week and finished 2nd using a different caddie. Had he won that tournament, there is absolutely no doubt in my mind that I would have gotten the axe immediately. *Whatever happened to "Larry is one helluva caddie?"*

His putter was still misbehaving, and that was the root of all the evil. I tried to show him the elaborate charts I was required to compose to help him visualize the intended line, but he wouldn't even look at them. He said they confused him and made his vision blurry. One thing was a certainty; if Chi Chi wasn't making a victory speech in the near future, I was going to be down the road.

It was obvious the pressure was getting to him. One symptom was a conviction he talked himself into that he was receiving inferior equipment from the manufacturers, specifically the ball he was playing. I had a conversation with the Spalding rep on the issue, and he assured me that professionals got the cream-of-the-crop. Their balls were "tour select" and were put through a barrage of testing, including x-raying to make absolutely sure there were no defects.

But Chi Chi insisted they had tumors on them that prevented them from flying properly. On one occasion he teed off into a left-to-right breeze and came out of it a hair, putting a little cut on it. It was clearly a poor swing, and the wind accentuated the error, pushing it way right. He said there was no way he could hit a drive that badly and that it must be one of those "sabotaged" balls. I found it interesting that the story evolved from him just receiving sketchy equipment to a blatant conspiracy. He ordered me to take the ball out of play after the hole was completed, and I did, but I stashed it in my back pocket. We played a few more holes and now stood on the tee of a long par 5 with the wind blowing in our face. I handed him the ball

I had saved in my pocket, which he proceeded to smoke right down the pipe and long.

"That's a hot one!" he declared. "We'll use that ball on all the par 5's."

I was dying to tell him about my escapade, but figured it wouldn't be conducive to maintaining the small shred of job security I had left.

I was working on my third year with Chi Chi, and like a marriage headed for Splitsville, so were we. Our relationship was beyond thin; it was anorexic, and it was our big pink elephant in the room. I received a pretty clear omen that someone else would soon be endorsing my checks in the very near future, and had a hint about who it would be.

Returning to the scene of a previous victory, we were once again in Las Vegas for the tournament at the Desert Inn and Country Club. Even though my relationship with Chi Chi was as about smooth as a gravel road, I was totally immersed in my on-course duties of pulling clubs, reading greens and keeping him focused. I knew that loyalty was an important trait as far as Chi Chi was concerned, and I wasn't bailing out on him. I was committed to doing my absolute best, and if he decided to can my ass, it was his call.

We were paired with Gary Player, and as I packed the bag down the 14th fairway, he sidled up to me and said, "Laddie, you're one of the best caddies out here, and when Chi Chi fires you, give me a call."

Two things hit me right upside the head. First, one of only four men in golf history to win all four majors just paid me a huge compliment (of course that was before Tiger Woods joined that elite club). Second, he said "when" and not "if" Chi Chi fires me. The writing was on the wall, and it provided concrete evidence that Chi Chi had been airing his dirty laundry to other players in the locker room. Initially, I was really perturbed about it. I felt like the proverbial unappreciated

wife, because I was the only one putting all the effort into this relationship, and we didn't talk anymore and…*See? I told you it was just
like a marriage.* I stewed as I packed the bag up the fairway. It really
rubbed me raw that golf professionals think they have a monopoly
on frustration. I have emotions too, and my patience with Chi Chi
was wearing thin.

I cooled off by the time I reached the green, aided by the fact
that I would probably have the name PLAYER pasted across my back
at some point in the future. The more I thought about it, the more I
was in tune with the idea. Someone once said that a change is better
than a rest, and I really needed one.

Chi Chi loaded yet another club on the caddie's back when he
informed me that he wanted me to make an advance trip to the U.S.
Senior Open venue in Bethlehem, Pennsylvania, to do my prep work.
I had plenty of time early in the week to prepare for the tournament,
and taking a trip by myself to walk yardage and chart greens wasn't
going to guarantee a win or even a good finish. If Chi Chi said he
wanted to go there *together* to practice and get familiar with the track,
I would have crawled there, but sending me alone was basically an
attempt to project his non-victorious play onto me. I wasn't buying
it and he shouldn't have been selling it.

I begrudgingly agreed to go. Instead of having a full week off in
Chicago with my family, which I sorely needed, I had to travel to the
depressed steel town and find the Saucon Valley Country Club, which
was no easy task. By the time I finally found the club, I was so livid
I couldn't see straight. I made my way around that course faster than
Dale Earnhardt at Daytona, and acquired just enough information
to cover my ass in case Chi Chi grilled me.

The following week at the Kroger Senior Classic, I was expecting a deluge of questions from Chi Chi about the Senior Open site. As it turned out, he never asked me one. In fact, I tried to tell him about the course and he didn't even want to hear it. I could have skipped that freaking trip and he would have been none-the-wiser, but I've been around long enough to know that if I hadn't gone, he would have interrogated me about the course and I would have been looking for another bag, or applying for a job at Taco Bell.

When the Senior Open finally rolled around, I knew exactly how to get there (more sarcasm). My relationship with Chi Chi was still painfully skinny, but an incident occurred that made me realize, once again, why I loved packing for him.

Wednesday, we were playing a practice round with the Golden Bear, when Chi Chi spotted a deformed boy outside the gallery ropes. I was already making a move toward the lad before Chi Chi told me to bring him over. As I approached him, it was obvious that the boy had a severe cranial disorder that left his head considerably smaller than normal. "Hi!" I said. "What's your name?"

"Jimmy," he replied shyly.

"Jimmy, would you like to meet Chi Chi Rodriguez?"

He enthusiastically responded, "I sure would!"

I took his small hand in mine and we walked to the fairway, where I introduced him to Chi Chi and Jack. He was really jazzed. Chi Chi put his hand on Jimmy's head and said, "Jimmy, you may think you're different, but you're not; you're special. God made you that way. If anyone ever makes fun of you, I want you to give me a call and I'll come take care of them."

Jimmy shook his head as if to say okay.

"Now c'mon, Jimmy, you're gonna caddie for me this hole!"

I pulled my caddie bib over my head and put it on my temporary replacement. He was too small to carry the bag, so I packed it up the fairway while Jimmy walked and talked with Jack and Chi Chi. I had him pace to the nearest sprinkler head when we arrived at Chi Chi's ball.

"What do I got, Jimmy?" Chi Chi inquired.

After some quick calculating, I whispered in his ear, "148 yards to the hole, into a slight breeze from the left."

Jimmy relayed the information to his new boss.

"Do you like 7 iron here, Jimmy?" Chi Chi asked.

Jimmy nodded his head energetically. Chi Chi pulled his 7 iron and hit his ball on the green, then told him it was a good call. The boy smiled proudly.

When we reached the green, Chi Chi instructed his fragile protégé, "Okay, Jimmy, now I want you to read this putt for me."

Without hesitation, Jimmy squatted behind the ball, staring intently down the line, then took a stroll to the other side, to get a look from there. Chi Chi grinned, his eyebrows raised. I was thinking, *If this kid reads this right and Chi Chi makes it, I might be out of a job!*

Jimmy made his way back to the ball and told his new employer, "I think it's going to break a little to the left."

"Okay, Pards, I'll play it two inches outside right."

Chi set up to the putt and popped the ball toward the hole. It missed on the left, but he told Jimmy that it was a good read.

Jack had been relatively quiet during this whole scene. As a matter of fact, it may have been the first time in golf history that Jack Nicklaus was on a golf course and wasn't center stage, but he jumped on the bandwagon by telling Jimmy he wanted some help with his putt. Once again, Jimmy stalked the line and returned to

Jack, informing him that his putt was going to break to the right. In his classic fashion, Jack hunched over his 12-footer and prepared to stroke it. Everyone held their breath in anticipation, when he stopped and called to Jimmy.

"Yes, Mr. Nicklaus?" the boy replied.

Jack held out his putter and said, "Here, Jimmy. You hit it."

Jimmy looked totally astonished that the greatest player in the history of golf was making such a request. Nonetheless, he grabbed Jack's putter and made a couple of practice strokes. He was a frail boy and looked like he was swinging a sledgehammer, but his stroke was fairly sound. I almost wished Chi Chi's looked as solid. By this time, the multitude of people watching were totally engrossed watching these two golf heroes cater to this handicapped child. In fact, a nuclear device could have been detonated three holes away and I don't believe anyone around that green would have noticed. Jimmy stroked the putt and watched as the ball missed the hole wide to the right. The crowd emitted a collective groan. You would have thought, judging by their reaction, that Jack just missed a two-footer to win his 7th green jacket.

The ball hadn't stopped rolling when Chi Chi retrieved it and placed it in front of Jimmy. He told the boy that the secret to life is giving it your best shot and if it doesn't work out, then you try again. For a second time, Jimmy drew the putter back and struck the ball, sending it on a journey toward the hole. With positive vibes from everyone in the gallery and some divine intervention, the ball approached the front edge and fell gently to the bottom of the cup.

All in attendance broke into an exuberant cheer and lengthy applause, but Jimmy's reaction is what I will remember forever. He let Jack's putter fall to the ground, threw his arms in the air, and then made his way to the perimeter of the green, where he proceeded to high-five every person he could. He tore a page right out of Hale Irwin's book. The chaos eventually simmered, but not before Jack autographed his ball and gave it to his victorious fill-in. Chi Chi gave him his ball and his glove and would have probably given him his golf bag if he had a back up. We said our goodbyes and Jimmy returned to the gallery, where they surrounded the new superstar.

A reporter caught wind of the story and after interviewing Jimmy, wrote an article for the local newspaper the next day. It profiled a challenged boy and some extraordinary moments he shared with two of the greatest names in the game. I'd like to think that those are moments Jimmy still thinks about. I know *I* do.

The course at Saucon Valley was a challenging test, and Chi Chi played respectably, hovering around even par through the first two rounds. You will not be surprised when I inform you that he was underwhelmed with the performance of the ball he was playing and decided to play a different brand for the third round.

Chi Chi had been playing MacGregor CG1800 irons as long as I had been with him, and successfully I might add. The ball stayed on the clubface longer than most other irons, enabling him to really shape the shots, i.e. the rope hook he hit into the 18th on the final hole of the previous U.S. Senior Open. Plus, we knew very accurately, the distances he could hit each one. It takes some time for a player to "learn" a new set of clubs and their limitations. The same goes for the caddie.

When Chi Chi arrived at the course Saturday morning, he had an old set of Spalding irons in his bag. They looked like a set of clubs you'd see in a member's bag at North Shore, and I don't mean one who could play a lick. I inquired about the new and unfamiliar weapons and he told me he won the '64 Tallahassee Open with them.

He started out by saying, "Ya' know, Pards, I was sitting in my hotel room thinking…"

Those words are just like the words "we need to talk" in a marriage. Nothing good ever comes after them. He'd concluded that it was his iron play that was the chink in the armor, so he called his manager, who dredged up these relics and chartered a private jet to get them to Chi Chi in time for the round. When I thought about how much that probably cost, I was sick to my stomach. I wished they would've just given that money to me. Making that kind of extreme a change in the midst of a major championship was ludicrous, and definitely was not going to be conducive to my happiness or job security.

I ran them over to the club repairman and had him check all the lofts and lies. They were all over the board. Some were a degree or two weak of standard and a few were set strong. A couple were too flat, and one was upright. Our relationship was a house of cards, and with the combination of the new irons *and* the new ball, forget about being between a rock and a hard spot. I was screwed. But unbelievably, Chi Chi had an adequate showing at the Open, even with all the extraneous variables. I was granted a reprieve and would live to caddie another week for him.

The following week I was close to my roots as we played the Ameritech Senior Open outside Chicago. Family and friends were in abundance, and even though Chi Chi and I were on the rocks, I was proud to be his caddie. He returned to the form that earned him four victories the previous year when he birdied the final six holes of Saturday's round. I left a pass for a friend at Will Call, and he happened to show up just as we got to the 13th tee. He was fortunate to witness this rarity in golf, and asked, "Does he do that all the time?" "No," I responded, "And as superstitious as he is, if he finds out you arrived just as the deluge of birdies started, I'm gonna have to fly you to every tournament he plays."

It turned out to be a flash in the pan, as another weak and fruitless Sunday left us in the middle of the pack. My relationship with Chi Chi was a volatile one, and I knew that after changing clubs, balls and even shoes with no positive results, I would most probably be the next alteration.

Chi Chi took his sabotaged ball theory one step further by coming to the conclusion that not only was he receiving bad balls, but that Lee Trevino was getting the absolute best of the best. Lee had won five events thus far that year and had numerous 2nd place finishes. I made the asinine mistake of asking Chi Chi why the ball manufacturer would give Lee balls superior to his. He looked at me like I was a dithering idiot and explained his hypothesis that because Lee was under contract to play their equipment, the manufacturer would prefer to see him win. This was complete rubbish. They'd be just as happy if Chi Chi won playing their ball. But he didn't see it that way, and instructed me to ask Lee for a dozen of his golf balls. Even though I never swallowed the ball conspiracy, a caddie's got to do, what a caddie's got to do, and as I made my way to the locker room, it dawned on me that this was no easy task. What could possibly be my reason for asking Lee Trevino for some of his golf balls? The answer eluded me and I decided to wing it.

I found Lee's locker with him in front of it, preparing for the day's round. It was open and I saw the objects of my mission on the top shelf. I still didn't have the faintest idea how to pose the question. He was loading up his golf bag when he noticed me. "Hey, Lar."

"Hey, Lee, how's it goin'?"

I stood there nervously and couldn't for the life of me figure out how to ask him. Lee's no dummy and knew I needed something.

"What can I do for you?" he asked.

I decided to hit it head-on. "Lee, can Chi Chi have a dozen of your golf balls?"

"The ball rep is around here somewhere," he said. "Can't you find him?"

Why the hell couldn't he just give me the damn balls without asking a zillion questions?

"Well, uh…" I was beginning to stammer. "I, uh, need a dozen of your balls."

"Why's that?" he asked, a hint of irritation in his voice.

I decided that honesty would be the best policy, and blurted out, "Chi Chi thinks they're giving you better balls than they're giving him." I had a silly grin on my face, hoping that he would find the charade funny, but it was obvious that he was not amused.

"Why the #$@& would they do that?"

"Because they don't want him to beat you," I answered.

"And why the #$@& is that?" he asked, now really cheesed off.

"Because you have a contract with them and he doesn't," I finished, my back against the ropes.

With that, Lee grabbed a dozen balls from his locker and slammed them in my gut, and then he picked up his golf bag and slammed it down in front of me, nearly clipping my toes. He leaned forward, and with his finger in my face said, "There's some balls, and there's my clubs. Tell that lil' son-of-a-bitch that I'll caddie for him. HE STILL CAN'T BEAT ME!"

I scurried out of that locker room like a whipped puppy, relieved to have successfully completed my mission. When I got to the range, curiosity got the better of Chi Chi and he asked, "What did Lee say when you asked him for the balls?"

"Nothin,'" I replied, "He just gave 'em to me." I didn't feel it necessary to stoke the fire.

He played that day with balls that had the initials L.T. printed on them and it didn't make a damn bit of difference. He played a mediocre round and it didn't bother me one bit. Had he played well, I would have had to endure the Trevino gauntlet regularly, and that was something I did not want to do ever again.

I had charted the greens with the detail of a draftsman ever since it became an issue with Chi Chi. I did so not because I felt it would help me in any way, but simply to appease him. The fact that he would never even look at my creations gave the whole scenario a humorous, but kind of pathetic tone. With all this in mind, I made a corporate decision that would jump up and bite me in the ass.

I was doing my golf course preparation for the Northville Long Island Classic when I concluded that there was no reason to continue charting the greens to the extent that I had been doing. It was extremely time-consuming, but more importantly, the fact that Chi Chi thought I could read a green from a drawing went against all my caddie principles. Now there's an oxymoron for you.

As bad luck would have it, we were in the middle of our final round and it was status quo in the scoring department. Chi Chi hit every fairway and green, but was one over par for the round. Take a wild guess which club in the bag was not cooperating. He could not get anything to drop, and frustration was the emotion du jour.

Walking to the 12th green, he was deliberating possible putting correctives, which led him to ask, "Pards, can I see your chart of this green? Maybe that'll help."

I couldn't believe what I was hearing, and gave him a look like he just asked me to speak Swahili. It was too weird to be true. I'd charted every green, every week for months, because I was required to do so and I couldn't get him to even peek at the drawings. The very first week I abolish the practice, he asks to see them.

He knew from the look on my face that I didn't have them, but still asked, "You don't have any charts, do ya', Pards?"

In an effort to pull myself back from the brink of baglessness, I said defensively, "Cheech, I don't need a diagram of a green to help me read it. That is not the way I operate."

"Okay, Pards," was his response, and I knew from the brevity of it, that we were history. He pretty much ignored me the rest of the round, and afterwards, I was informed by his pilot that my services were no longer needed, which was not a huge revelation. Without seeing Chi Chi, I got in my van with a couple of my esteemed colleagues and drove to Newport, Rhode Island, where we got more twisted than usual.

I was whistling in the shower the following morning when I realized it had been a long while since I had done that. I was a bit remorseful that Chi Chi and I split, but I felt a massive weight had been lifted from my shoulders, and it wasn't his golf bag. The idea of being unemployed was intimidating, but remembering my conversation with Gary Player in Las Vegas soothed all my fears.

Boston was the next tournament location, and I made my way there not knowing what to expect. Word of my professional demise spread like wildfire, and I was peppered with questions from everyone. Even a hot dog vendor asked me, "So what happened with you and Chi Chi?" Twenty caddies notified me that he was out on the course with another caddie. Maybe C-A-T-T-Y would be a more appropriate spelling for the position at this point.

I was sitting on a golf cart by the pro shop when Chi Chi pulled up. Playing it cool, I turned the other way, purposely avoiding him. I didn't have anything to say to the man...or so I thought. He approached me and said, "Pards, the chemistry's not there anymore." That was all I needed to hear. I stood up from the cart with my hand extended and told him that we had a great run together and that I experienced times I will never forget.

As we shook hands, he thanked me and told me to give him a call if I needed anything. Then, before we parted, he said, "Pards, I think Gary Player's looking for a caddie." I replied, "Thanks, Cheech, that's what I heard."

THE BLACK KNIGHT

I LOVE THAT scene in the movie Brian's Song where Gale Sayers gives the locker room speech to the team about Brian Piccolo, the football player who died of cancer at a young age. I cry like a little girl every time I watch it, which is probably more information than you need. In that speech he says, "I love Brian Piccolo, and today, I want you to love him too." There is no more appropriate way to begin the chapter on my time with Gary Player; he is the epitome of class, and I cherish my time as his caddie. He taught me things about life, not just about golf, that I will take to my grave.

The way I looked at it, Gary owed me the opportunity to work for him, because he took a lot of money out of my pocket before I went to pack for him. I caddied for many of his bridesmaids, including in several Majors. I was working the Senior Open at Medinah for Bruce Crampton, who was leading with four holes to play in the tournament, when a quick double-bogey knocked the wind out of us and we missed the Player/Bob Charles playoff by one shot. Gary hoisted the trophy after that one. We also finished second to him at the Senior TPC and countless others. He reminded me of the spoiled kid in the neighborhood who always got everything he wanted, and it really bugged me. But therein lies one of his purest qualities; the man is a fierce competitor and absolutely loathes second place. I heard him once say, "The only ones who remember you finished second are your wife and your dog, and that's if you have a good wife and a good dog!"

Gary and I had a pleasant rapport prior to my employment with him. I had learned tons of sayings in Afrikaans, the native tongue of South Africa, from some of the South African caddies on the European Tour. When I saw Gary, I'd belt out, "Howzit, you hairy back rock spider?" which is the equivalent of calling a South African a redneck, followed by other crude rantings. Honestly, sometimes I wasn't really sure exactly what I was saying to him, but I was definitely thankful that bystanders couldn't understand it. Gary would laugh, always followed by the question, "Laddie, where did you hear that?"

Once I committed a major faux pas. Gary was walking around a corner and I blurted out something really lewd in Afrikaans. He had the strangest look on his face and I realized why when his wife Vivienne came trailing behind him. She is also South African and speaks the language.

"Vivienne, Oh, I'm so sorry! I didn't see you."

She was pretty smooth about it and didn't make a big fuss, but I must have been 13 shades of red. I made a mental note to be much more careful when throwing profanities his way. Looking back, it's really amazing that he ever hired me. That was the kind of thing that could land you on a wife's blacklist.

Beyond our casual friendship, Gary knew me to be a very capable tour caddie. Hell, I worked for Crampton for three years, and that spoke volumes in the eyes of the other golfers. Just imagine, a golfer pondering over whom to hire. *Hmmm, how about Larry? He put up with Crampton for all those years. He must be on the ball!* Trevino told me as much when I worked for him. He said, "Larry, I knew if you could handle him for as long as you did, you could easily handle me for a week."

Inevitably, after Chi Chi and I split up, I gave Gary a call. We consummated our business relationship (consummated may not be the best choice of words after the marriage analogy), and decided to start the following week in Birmingham, Alabama. I was full of renewed vim and vigor, and ecstatic about working for this icon of the game.

When you work for a guy for any period of time and then show up at a tournament with a different bag, you get pummeled with a barrage of the same questions from both caddies and players. "You and Chi Chi split up?" "How long has this been going on?" "Did you guys go for counseling?" (Just kidding. No one asked that). For the most part, the feedback from both players and caddies was very positive. Everyone thought Gary and I would make a formidable team. You could tell from the players' reactions that Gary was well liked among his peers.

There's some discomfort associated with a bag change. It takes a little bit of time to become accustomed to the way a player operates, getting to know his preferences and idiosyncrasies. One of the first things I learned about Gary's m.o. was that he never, ever practiced with a new golf glove on. Forget the fact that Titleist gave him as many as he wanted, and the inside of his bag looked like a mini Nevada Bob's Golf Shop. He was adamant about this personal law. Being the curious one, I had to know why, so he told me about growing up poor in South Africa and how his father slaved in the gold mines for a meager wage. They couldn't afford the luxury of a new glove, so when he got one he'd wear it until it fell to pieces, literally. Now, even though he was privy to all the perks bestowed upon pro golfers (free clubs, shafts, balls, clothing and other goodies), it didn't seem right to practice with a new glove on; he just didn't feel comfortable. I came to the conclusion that old habits really do die hard. The irony of it was, that the stack of new gloves in the bag would eventually be given away to friends and fans. The great Gary Player was wearing a used glove, while some chop was shooting 115 wearing a new one.

Another of Gary's idiosyncrasies was that he didn't want his ball marked with the sharp point of a lead pencil. For some reason he thought that it could affect the ball's performance in an adverse way. My theory was that it was being struck by a piece of metal traveling at somewhere around 100 m.p.h., so I didn't see how sticking it with a small pencil point was going to do any damage. But it wasn't my show, so I marked them with a Sharpie to appease him.

Gary is a rancher at heart, and had a strange habit before throwing the divot back to me for replacement. He would hold it under his nose and take a huge whiff of the soil and then proclaim, "Oh man, smell that earth. That's good stuff." Then he'd throw it my way and I'd take a little sniff and say to myself, "*Where you just hit it, smells like a bogey to me!*"

I also discovered very quickly that my on-course interaction with Gary would be different than it was with Chi Chi. This was evident the first time he asked me what club I thought he should hit. My reply was direct and uninhibited, "I think you should hit a hard 6 iron and turn it…"

Gary stopped me mid-sentence before I could finish my dissertation. "Don't tell me how to hit the shot," he snapped abruptly, his South African accent peppering me like verbal mace. "I'm the one hitting the shot!"

"Well, okay…6 iron," I replied. *So it's going to be like that.*

With Chi Chi I had carte blanche when it came to club selection and shot shape, which was immensely important. With Gary, I needed to be a minimalist; keep it short and sweet. This was going to thicken the plot. I felt like I was going to be pulling clubs with handcuffs on. Selecting the right weapon is really an art form; you have to know what your man's going to do with the shot. It is the essence of the trade. But I eventually stopped worrying about it when it dawned on me that Gary had won a few tournaments before I ever toted his satchel. He had a pretty good handle on what he was doing.

I really miss those days.

As I was looking through the photographs I had accumulated over the years, it dawned on me that in 80% of those featuring Gary and me, we are either smiling or laughing. I quickly discovered that humor would be the glue of our relationship, our special bond. I found Gary to be a very happy-go-lucky man who truly enjoyed a good laugh, and from the get-go I could really tickle his funny bone. During one of the Pro-Ams in the first month of my employ, I started hammering him with fat girl jokes, one after another. He doubled over; he was laughing so hard, and finally went down. It was a comedic TKO. There he was, one of golf's Big Three, lying in the middle of the fairway, belly laughing. The amateurs approached me after the round (I was hoping they were coming to tip me but that wasn't the case), and told me that when they drew Gary at the Pro-Am party, they were shitting in their britches. Someone told them he was a tight-ass on the golf course and they wouldn't have any fun. They were pleasantly surprised to see him so loose and more than enjoyed the round. "*That's really great,*" I thought to myself. "*Now how about a tip?*"

Once he came out of the locker room with the old-man-pants-syndrome going on. You know, where they pull them up real high. I had a shit-eating grin on my face, prompting him to ask, "What's up?" I gave him a sideways look and said, "You pull those pants up any higher and you're gonna have to unzip 'em to blow your nose!" He really liked that one.

I'm proud to say that I know Gary found me very entertaining, and especially loved my stories about, and imitations of, some of the caddies. None more so than Trevino's caddie, Herman Mitchell, a.k.a. Big Mitch. God rest his soul, Mitch was a real beauty. He and Lee had a love-hate thing going on, and it was fodder for my comedy routine. Gary loved hearing me tell these stories, and I knew this because he would prod me to tell them to our Pro-Am groups and then stand back and listen while I spun my yarns, looking proud and amused.

One of my favorite Mitch stories came from the time we were paired with Trevino and Nicklaus at the tournament in Cincinnati.

We were standing on the tee of a par 3, and it was Lee's turn to hit. He and Mitch were discussing club selection, and Lee wanted to hit 6 iron, but Mitch liked 5. They went back and forth, each sticking to his guns. Mitch was persistent and finally won out with one final, "You gotta' hit the 5 to get it there!"

Lee pulled his 5 iron out of the bag, went through his routine of tugs and gyrations and proceeded to hit his shot, doing his patented club twirl as it dropped to his side. The ball looked good in the air and Herman let out a "Be as good as you look!" The ball should have had 'par avion' stamped on it, because it absolutely air-mailed the green.

Uh oh. Can you say caddie #$@& up? To say that Lee was not happy would be the biggest understatement in this book. He threw the club at Mitch, who barely managed to catch it before it clunked him in the head, and then he got right in his face.

"You dumb son-of-a-bitch! Lemme tell you something! Did you see what those cops did to Rodney King in L.A.?" (this was right after that incident).

"Yeah. What about it?" Herman came back.

"That ain't nuthin' compared to what I'm gonna do to your fat ass if you don't get the right club in my #$@&in' hands!"

And then he stormed off the tee, leaving Mitch standing there with a whipped puppy look on his face. After witnessing this, being the good comrade, I went over to console him.

"Forget about it. You know what these guys are like. They never remember the good calls you make, but the minute you make a bad one, they're all over you like a bad smell."

Herman responded with a classic line.

"That Lee Trevino is a bad mother#$@&a' and someday I'm gonna throw these #$@&in' clubs in a lake!"

Then with a devilish grin creeping onto his round face, he finished, "But I'm gonna stuff my pockets first.

Gary especially loved one of the stories from my wild caddie past. It happened while I was caddying on the European tour. It was 1985 and The Open (the British are so snobby, they call the British Open just THE Open) was being held at Royal St. Georges in Sandwich, England. In those days there was no money in European golf, even for the players. Big sponsors like Epson and Volvo would eventually get on board and pump millions into that tour, but I was long gone by then. So in 1985, we were sleeping in tents to make ends meet and showering in the clubhouse locker rooms. I need to preface this story with a little info on the Royal and Ancient Golf Club of St. Andrews, or the R&A as it is called. They are the biggest bunch of stuffed shirts on earth. They are pompous asses who think they have some divine ownership of the game (there goes any chance of a special invite to THE Open for me). The thing that amused me most about them was their habit of starting every sentence with, "Oh, good god, man!" with an upward inflection of the voice when saying "man." I always wondered if they did this just at the golf tournaments or if it was normal in their every-day life. "Oh, good god, man! I need petrol for the motor." "Oh, good god, man! I've got to take a dump."

Anyway, Wizzie and I were smelling a bit gamey, so we gathered our toiletries and made our way to the clubhouse where an R&A member was manning the front door. He was a bald, chubby bloke, wearing the standard issue R&A blazer, a handlebar moustache and a monocle. I had never seen anyone wearing a monocle. If they gave him a top hat and a cane, he could've doubled for Mr. Peanut. We started to walk past him, straight into the clubhouse (we learned from experience that you had to act like you own the joint, in order to get in.) But he placed himself in front of us, blocking the door. "May I help you?" his voice dripping with condescension.

"We're just going to take a quick shower," I replied, still trying to maintain the "we're supposed to be here" attitude.

"But who on earth are you?" he asked.

"We're caddies," I replied confidently.

That was all he needed to hear. We had violated a basic rule of clubhouse penetration by using the "C" word.

"Oh, good god man! This is no *oooordinary* golf tournament. This is the British Open—THE most prestigious golf tournament in the whole of the world. Now, be off with you, you bloody urchins!"

I shit you not; he called us urchins. We ended up sneaking in the back, showered, and as we passed by him, made it a point to make sure he saw us leaving. Once he recognized us, he yelled out, you guessed it, "Oh, good god, man! Stop! Stop, you bloody urchins!"

Wizzie and I bolted, laughing our asses off as we fled. I had lived 23 years of my life without being called an urchin, and I got called it twice in an hour.

I realize that story is a bit of a digression, but it illustrates the kind of humor I shared with Gary. In 1993 I was flying on his jet to The Open, once again played at Sandwich. "I hope that pompous S.O.B. is there at that door again. If he says one thing to me, I'm gonna tell him that I'm with Gary Player and I don't sleep in a tent anymore. I flew on a private jet to get here. How do you like me now? "

What I didn't realize was that Gary could really identify with my view of the R&A. He experienced first-hand how stuffy they could be the first time he won The Open. Apparently he showed up at the trophy presentation wearing a flashy sport coat that they deemed inappropriate. I could just imagine them collectively gasping, "Oh, good god, man! What is that bloody rag our Open Champion is wearing? Doesn't he realize this is no ooooordinary golf tournament? It is the most prestigious tournament in the whole of the world?"

Happy Days with The Black Knight.

When we arrived at the course, Gary was like a kid hyped up on an overdose of Skittles. "Larry, do you see the pompous ass anywhere? Is he here? Do you see him? Is that him over there?" Unfortunately, he was nowhere to be seen. Sweet revenge had eluded me once again in my life.

A recurring comedic theme in our relationship was Gary's Last will and Testament, and more specifically, me getting into it. Chi Chi once said to me, "Pards, I got good news and bad news."

"What's the good news?" I returned.

"You're in my will," he said.

"Cheech, that's not good news—that's GREAT news!

"Yeah," he said, "But the bad news is, I'm gonna outlive your ass," followed by his infectious laugh. Then he would go on a tangent about how he really was going to live to be over 100 because his great, great grandfather lived to be 106, and his great grandfather lived to be 108, and his grandfather was 102 when he was shot by a jealous husband and his uncle Rico lived to be…

I constantly teased Gary about cutting me in on the Player pie. I told him "Larry Player" had a pleasant sound to it, and I did a fairly convincing South African accent. Some people even said I looked like him. Once, an old lady walked up to me and asked me if I was Gary Player. I told her, "No, lady, he looks better than me."

But I'm no dummy. If I were seriously trying to weasel in on some old golfer's turf, it wouldn't be: A) One who had enough children to make a Mormon green with envy. B) One who owned thoroughbred horses. Nothing will drain a trust fund like kids, vet bills and stud fees.

I told Gary's son Wayne that his dad was actually considering adopting me. He put his arm around me and said, "No, No, my boy; you must be a member of the lucky sperm club!" We all howled. After that, every time a grandchild was born, I'd mutter, just loud enough for Gary to hear, "Super, another member of the lucky sperm club."

One of my most poignant moments with him happened at the tournament in Tampa years later. I was blathering on about something, cutting up with Gary, my audience of one. He was laughing, and then he paid me a compliment I'll never forget. He told me his father, Harry, loved to laugh, and he went into great detail about what a great laugh he had. Gary even named one of his racehorses 'Laughing

Harry' in his honor. And then, at the end of his story, he gently pinched my cheek and said, "Son, you really make me laugh."

Gary and I were settling into our routine, getting to know each other personally and professionally. It was evident from the start that I was in the company of someone very special. Of all the big names in the game, he wasn't just down-to-earth, he was subterranean. He possessed an uncanny knack for making people feel like they mattered. When he spoke with people, you could tell that he was really listening and that he really cared. I was filled with a deep sense of pride just being associated with him, and felt lucky to call him my boss.

Packing for a legend of golf at The Masters.

One of the largest perks of working for Gary came the first week of April. I had been a professional tour caddie for more than 10 years, but was still a Masters virgin. I had never worked the event or even stepped foot on those hallowed grounds, and Gary was really excited for me. I am embarrassed to admit that by that time in my career I was looking forward to it, but caddie burn-out was on the periphery. I wasn't as jacked as I should have been. The novelty of working any tournament had worn off by then.

Aboard Gary's jet (affectionately dubbed "Air Player") after Sunday's final round at The Tradition in Scottsdale, Gary, Vivienne and I talked about the upcoming week, but more specifically, Gary's past wins at Augusta. He told me about the 1978 Masters in which he came from seven shots back to capture his 3rd and final green jacket. He had breakfast that morning with IMG founder Mark McCormick (Gary was represented by IMG, as are the majority of top ranked golfers), who was leaving afterwards.

"Why are you leaving before the final round, Mark?" he asked.

Mark's reply was, "Because none of my guys have a chance of winning. I've got things to do."

"What about me?" Gary shot back.

"C'mon, Gary, be serious, you're seven back."

"Larry, please believe me (his catch phrase when he was adamant about something), "that was all the motivation I needed. Nothing was going to keep me from victory."

After a brief trip down memory lane, he started to talk about winning the tournament again. He still believed that at the age of 57 it was possible for him to be cloaked in a green jacket. You might read this and question his mental health. I know I did initially, but then I thought about it further. If a 57-year-old man had any chance whatsoever of winning The Masters, he had to first believe that he could. The belief had to come before the reality. I'm sure there were a lot of people prior to 1986 who thought a guy winning the tournament at 46 was a ludicrous notion. Keep in mind, these old guys had experience on their side.

So there I was, flying privately to one of the biggest, if not *the* biggest event in professional golf. I would be working for a three-time champion, three-time runner-up, who would have incredible stories for every square inch of famed turf. The juices were starting to flow and I came to the conclusion that I would have worked the week for nothing. I conveniently refrained from sharing that with Gary.

We finally arrived at the small airport in Augusta. The place was packed with private aircraft. I saw several of the PGA Tour players in the terminal and I thought to myself, wow, times have really changed. Years ago there would have been two jets here, Arnold's and Jack's. Now everyone has their own plane, or is a fractional owner. I think I even saw Bones, Mickelson's caddie, getting off his.

Gary had transportation set up to take us to the house that they rented every year. Viv graciously asked me to stay the night, and I would check into my hotel the following day.

I awoke the next morning to the sound of rain pounding on the roof. It was raining hard and Gary received word that the golf course was closed for the time being. After breakfast and a shower, the driver picked us up to take us to Augusta National Golf Club. It was show time.

The hamlet of Augusta, Georgia, is small and unassuming. Were it not for the famed golf course that bears its name, you wouldn't have many reasons to go there. The course would be hard to find if it wasn't for the throngs of people heading in its direction. There's no grand entrance, just a simple wooden sign hanging from a post.

Magnolia Lane is to golf, what Penny Lane is to music, and the Yellow Brick Road is to cinema. I had heard so much about this historic stretch of asphalt, and now found myself traveling it with one of golf's legends. We sat quietly, enjoying the beauty and forgetting the inclement weather. As we neared the clubhouse, the driver made the right hand turn into the parking lot. Out the window I saw a large planter filled with yellow petunias in the shape of the U.S. with a red flag marking the location of Augusta. Call it an epiphany, or a moment of realization, it really dawned on me. I was at the Masters.

The car came to a stop and I happened to look over at Gary. He was smiling, and he asked me, "Well, what did you think?"

"Of what?" I replied sarcastically.

"The drive up Magnolia Lane."

"It was awesome! What I can remember of it," I returned.

"What do you mean, what you can remember of it?" he asked curiously.

I answered, "All the blood rushed to my erection halfway and I passed out."

I grabbed the clubs from the trunk of the car and Gary told me he'd meet me at the range shortly. At almost every event the routine is the same for caddie check-in, but this was no ordinary tournament. I was trying to look like I knew what I was doing, but it must have been evident that I didn't have a clue. It was a flashback to my first day at North Shore. I had to ask someone for directions to the caddie shack, where an African-American gentleman barked at me to go to the security trailer.

Let me fill you in on a little bit of pro caddie history. Years ago, when the tour made its way to Augusta, the pros used local caddies for the week, even though they had regular caddies who worked for them the rest of the year. These guys were great caddies and knew every nuance of that golf course. Whether they were worth a darn away from there, I couldn't tell you, but that week, a good local was worth his weight in gold, and the pros had their favorites.

As I alluded to before, at most tournaments we went to a tent and signed a standard form stating who we were and who we worked for. Then we'd be given a list of rules (which got tossed three milliseconds after we left the tent), and a caddie badge. The security trailer at The Masters reminded me of the border checkpoint between Holland and Germany. I really thought I was going to get strip-searched. They interrogated me, and then gave me a list of rules that was the size of an encyclopedia. Finally, they gave me the coveted caddie badge, adding that if I were to lose it, I might as well commit hari-kari, because there was no chance of getting another one. After all, a Masters badge is the hardest ticket to get in sports and could fetch one helluva' price on the open market, as I would later learn.

I was handed the white coverall worn by all caddies at the tournament and instructed to wear it whenever on the grounds. Penalty for failure to do so was death by firing squad. I took it and then stupidly asked, "Do you want me to put it on now?" The gentleman answered the question with the question, "Are you on the grounds?"

I slipped it on over my clothes, and I have to tell you, I was quite impressed with how clean it was. I think it was even starched. At other events that tried to mimic The Masters by requiring us to wear these, you felt like you'd been subjected to wearing a homeless person's clothes. You really didn't want to think about whose boys had been in that neighborhood. The final touch was the PLAYER name velcroed onto the back. It was official; I was an Augusta looper Incidentally, I heard that Masters' caddies are now required to submit DNA samples.

I was packing Gary's bag toward the driving range when I passed a man holding the hand of a small boy who had to be seven or eight years old. As I swept by, I heard the boy say with excitement in his voice, "Look Dad! There's Gary Player's caddie!" The hair on the back of my neck stood up. That moment signified the whole Masters experience for me, and like a gift, I appreciated receiving it.

Gary was already at the range as I walked up. The crowd parted like the Red Sea to let us through, and he picked a spot to set up. Even though it was a cold, rainy Augusta morning, there were thousands of people milling about, taking in all that is The Masters. I was a dual agent myself, part professional caddie, part spectator.

Gary proceeded with his warm-up, hitting some sand wedges off the tightly mown grass. I've putted on greens that weren't as nice as that practice tee. I perused the range line, taking in the swings of Els, Olazabal and the like, then looked out towards the far end of the driving range. They obviously didn't take into account the future technological advancement in the game when they built that range. The fence at the end was not that far. Still, I had heard that Jack was the only one to fly it, and that was in his younger days. They did take into account the fact that an ungodly long hitter named John Daly had won the PGA Championship the year prior and would be playing their tournament, so they perched another 20 feet or so on top of the existing fence. I guess they figured, "That'll show him."

Just about that time, we heard a commotion from behind the gallery. They parted once again to let Larry, the Cable Guy of golf through, the incomparable John Daly himself. This was during his meteoric rise to stardom days. He was thin and wearing a blonde mullet that just screamed redneck, and the people were hooting and hollering more than you'll ever see out of an Augusta gallery. His caddie set up camp right next to us. *Cool*, I thought, *I got a front row seat to the Daly Express.*

Before he could even take his waterproof jacket off, some wise-ass yelled out, "Hey, Daly! Let's see whatcha' got," which at The Masters is akin to yelling, "You da'man!" We all turned into spectators as Long John unzipped his jacket and very deliberately hung it on his umbrella, grabbed his driver and pulled the head cover off, reached into his bag and pulled out one of his own golf balls and teed it up. The crowd was really lathered by now. A hush worked its way across the gallery as he milked it and prepared to launch. And then, on a cold, damp morning, without any kind of warm-up at all, probably with a massive hangover, John Daly pulled the trigger on a backswing that ended in the Tropic of Capricorn and absolutely jackhammered that golf ball over the fence. What he did next was the icing on the cake. He put his driver back in the bag, placed the head cover back on it, took his waterproof jacket off the umbrella and draped it across his shoulders, and then casually made his way through the gallery, back to the clubhouse. It was really something to behold. Gary and I stood there dumbstruck until he piped up and said, "Larry, did you see that?" his voice filled with awe. "Did I see that? Gary, I'll be telling my grandkids about that shot."

After the Daly show ended and Gary's 57-year-old bones were loose, we made our way to the first tee to play a practice round. We were a onesome, and a nagging question burned inside me. *Why hadn't anyone asked to join him?* This man possessed so much local knowledge, a practice round with him would be a crash course in the do's and dont's at The Masters. I know that if I were a young player privileged enough to play in the tournament, I'd be asking to go around the course with a man filled with that kind of info, but I guess that's just me.

Gary hit his tee ball off the 1st and we made our way down the fairway. It was still very overcast and damp and the golf course was extremely saturated, but as long as Mother Nature obliged, Augusta National would show its teeth come tournament time. Jack Nicklaus wasn't the wittiest guy to ever play the game, but I did hear that years ago, when asked how he prepared for the greens at The Masters, he said, "That's easy. I just putt on the hood of my car." I was looking forward to finding out just how slick putting surfaces could get.

We made our way around the front nine, and Gary was my tour guide. He had incredible stories about shots that he had hit in the tournament years ago. I've always found it unbelievable that a professional golfer can tell you, down to the most specific detail, about a shot he pulled off 35 years ago, but he couldn't remember what he ate for dinner last night or where he was two weeks ago. He was also rattling off important information about the perils of the course. For instance, on the 3rd, a short par 4, it was imperative that you keep your approach shot below the hole. If your shot hangs up past the green and the course is rearing its ugly head, you'll be putting for par from 15 feet. That's if you can keep the chip shot on the green. The approach shot is a short iron which will have a lot of spin and could very possibly juice back off the front and could even go all the way down to the bottom of the slope, but you still have an easier chip going back uphill. Basically, if you knock it over the 4th, you're staring bogey in the face, or even worse.

The 4th is a par 3, and on the green he showed me a putt from the front left portion going towards the back. In '78, he had that putt, and was conferring with his local caddie about the break. Gary thought it was going one way, the caddie thought the other. They went back and forth, each sticking to his guns. Finally the caddie told him, "Please

Mr. Player, play it my way. If it doesn't break the way I say, I'll work the week for nothing."

That's what I call putting your ass on the line. Gary followed the caddie's read, the putt broke the way he said, he drained it and went on to win the tournament. Gary told me it was one of the greatest calls he had ever seen. I told you those locals knew their stuff out there. I wondered why he let me work that week. If he had any chance at all of winning, he was going to need all the help he could get. What good was a white kid from the suburbs of Chicago going to be?

On the 9th he showed me where the usual Sunday pin placement was on the front tier of the green and how it was absolutely mandatory to take more club coming in, especially if you hit a big tee ball. If your second shot in was a lofted club that imparted a lot of spin, it was really easy to spin it back off the green and all the way down to the bottom of the slope fronting the green. Greg Norman learned this painful lesson in his 1996 final round implosion.

After finishing the front side, we made our way over to the 10th tee, only to find Mr. Grip-It-And-Rip-It Daly and his sidekick Fuzzy Zoeller there. They were running mates back then, which was like Bill Clinton hanging out with Carmen Elektra; you just knew it was going to end in trouble. What John Daly needed was a guy like Jack, a mentor who could keep him on the straight and narrow and teach him the pitfalls of golf superstardom. More importantly, he needed a man who might be able to exorcise his demons. There's a great movie idea…The Golfcorcist. Couldn't you see Daly in a bed, his head spinning around, with Jack dressed up like a priest, chanting bible verses at him? Then Daly yells at him in a deep, diabolical voice that Jack's going to Hell, where he'll 3-putt every green…and then vomits slime in his face.

The dog-and-pony show asked Gary if he wanted to join them, and he agreed. We had just boarded the proverbial train wreck waiting to happen.

After all tee shots were struck without anyone getting maimed, we started our walk down the fairway. I stress the word down. Television does Augusta National no justice with regard to elevation. The golf course is way hillier than it appears. That being said, yours truly made his way down the slope of the 10th fairway. I was robed in my bleached white jumpsuit, and am embarrassed to admit that I had the collar up. I was paying minimal attention to the terrain, hit a slick patch of grass, and my feet were immediately where my head was supposed to be. I was instantly flat on my back, which was now atop Gary Player's golf equipment. My wipeout was witnessed by the three participants in the group, along with 6,000 spectators, give or take a few.

Never one to miss a great chance to mock someone, Daly ran up over me and did an umpire "safe!" call, his arms outstretched. Everyone was laughing at me, including the man whose clubs were underneath me. I seriously considered trying to climb inside the zipper pocket of the bag. What the hell though; I've always believed that you should get your daily dose of public humiliation out of the way as soon as possible. What really bugged me was that the side of my nice clean overall now looked like the starting grid at Daytona.

Our arrival at Amen Corner brought back the burning sensation in my loins that I felt driving up Magnolia Lane. It is, without a doubt, the most unbelievable stretch of holes in the game, and it inspires the same feeling you get at St. Andrews. Augusta National is similar to the Grand Canyon; it is an enormous outdoor cathedral and these holes are the sanctuary.

There's not an abundance of port-o-lets on the golf course at The Masters. I guess it's the ultimate in control; you'll go when they want you to go, or maybe they don't even want urination at their tournament at all. Since the 13th tee is set way back in a stand of Georgia pines and bushes, away from the prying eyes of the gallery, it's the perfect place to take a leak (or as Chi Chi put it, shake hands with the unemployed). There is history there. Everyone has peed in those woods, which explains why it stinks worse than any truck stop john you'll ever have the horror of using. Keeping with tradition, I went to take a leak, even though I really didn't need to. I imagined what it was like to be there with the legends of the game. I even held a pretend conversation with them as I tapped the lizard. "Hey, Ben. How's it hanging? Nice birdie, you made back there at 12. Byron! Holy shit! Now I know why they call you Lord!" Back to reality, I zipped up and joined the group on the tee.

The next few holes were rife with disrespect toward the tournament and the golf course, but mostly toward Gary. They were talking while he was hitting, messing around, and on one green, Fuzzy was tapping the pin with an iron while Gary was putting from long distance, saying, "It's over here, old man."

I love to cut up and have fun more than the next guy, but there's a time and place for it. The coup de grace occurred on the infamous 18th tee. Gary and Fuzzy had hit their tee balls, and Long John was up. He teed it up and was milking it like a dairy farmer. A half second before he pulled the trigger, some guy in the gallery yelled out, "Hey, Daly! Let's see whatcha' got!"

Oh, not this freakin' moron again!

Daly was still set up to it, but you could hear the wheels turning. He pulled out of his stance, flipped the driver over, held it by the head, with the grip end extended in the direction of the culprit, and exclaimed, "No, asshole, let's see what you got."

The crowd emitted a collective, "Whoa!"

We all thought this was a joke until the perpetrator emerged from the gallery and took off his jacket. The whole escapade started to feel surreal. I've seen grocery store aisles wider than that tee, and this had ugly written all over it.

Gary was in panic mode by now, and went to the front of the tee box, saying, "Move back! Move back! Folks, please believe me! This man is not a professional golfer! He could kill one of you!" His voice was full of angst. The crowd fanned out away from the tee, but as soon as Gary turned his back, they went right back to their original position.

By this time, Fuzzy had put his glove on this schmuck and a ball had been teed up for him. I was pretty good at looking at a guy and knowing in 3.4 milliseconds if he could play at all, and this man didn't look like he could play dead. He took a couple of practice swings, doing his best to emulate Ernie El's action. With the moment of truth having finally arrived, he set up to it.

To say he was nervous wouldn't suffice. I've seen drunks with the DTs who shook less. He was about to hit a shot that could change his life or end somebody else's. He was about to begin his swing when Fuzzy blurted out, "Hold on a minute there, son." The guy backed off and asked, "What?" in a bewildered voice.

Fuzzy took a leisurely stroll over to him, put his arm around the man's shoulder and asked, "When's the last time you cold-topped it in front of 10,000 strangers?"

The gallery erupted in laughter. It was golf's equivalent of the last-second timeout before the opposing kicker tries to kick the winning field goal. I have to admit, the timing was impeccable. The laughter finally died down, and once again, this clown set up to hit a drive off the 18th tee at Augusta National. Gary whispered to me, "Bobby Jones is rolling in his grave."

Mankind does not possess the technology to film this guy's backswing; it was that quick. He made poor contact and barely got it up over the gallery on the right when he finally hit it. Chi Chi would have called it a wounded duck, but luckily no one got hurt. The charade over, we made our way up the 18th fairway. As we walked, Gary said to me, "Larry, please believe me. Thirty years ago these men would have been escorted to the front gate, never to return." I didn't doubt it. Gary McCord was banned from all Master's telecasts just for saying "They don't cut the greens at the Masters, they bikini-wax 'em."

Word of the shenanigans back on the tee reached the clubhouse before we did. As we left the green, several tournament officials in green jackets and white hats were waiting.

"Mr. Daly, Mr. Zoeller, come with us, please," one of them said sternly. I was once again knee deep in schadenfreude. These guys were in a heap of trouble.

Gary waited by the clubhouse like a kid waiting for his friends to be released from the principal's office, wondering what sentence had been handed down. After a while, the pair came out and Gary peppered them with questions. "Well, what happened? Are you banned?"

Daly answered sullenly, "They said their insurance policy doesn't cover that and if we ever pull a stunt like that again we'll be escorted to the front gate, never to return." Gary shot me an, 'I told you so' look, and so ended my first full day at Augusta National.

The following day when I was making my way to the course, I found out just how valuable a ticket to The Masters is, when a guy on the street offered me $3,000 for my caddie badge. It was an intriguing proposition, but one that wouldn't be good for my job security. I didn't think Gary would appreciate me pawning my ticket on the black market. I told the man, "Sorry, but Gary Player is expecting me to show up and caddie for him. Frankly, you don't look like you could hack it." His buddies accompanying him got a kick out of that line.

This day was a little more normal than the previous. The sun was beaming down, Augusta National was in full glory, and we had a couple of the younger players ask to join us for a practice round. This time the round would be more productive than the carnival the day before.

Your's truly at Amen Corner. Photography by Gary Player.

I had the foresight to put a disposable camera in the golf bag and was snapping pictures as we went around. When we got to the par 5, 13th, I took it out and told Gary to pose with the gorgeous flowering landscape behind him. After getting the shot, he said, "Okay, now you." I went over and assumed a position where he stood, the golf bag sitting beside me. We could hear the gallery laughing behind the ropes. Gary acknowledged them with a stately wave and then spontaneously yelled across the fairway, "Folks, watch this!" Then he commanded me, "Larry, do your Arnold Palmer imitation."

"Are you serious? Here? Now?" I asked.

"Yeah, c'mon. They'll love it," he returned.

Then, like a first tee announcer, he bellowed out to them, "Folks, may I present to you, Arnold Palmer!"

I proceeded to pull one of his irons out of the bag and got into character by pretending to pull my chest hair and throwing it up to check the wind (I picked that up from Chi Chi's clinic.) Then I hitched up my britches and glared down the fairway. Next came the two-waggle pre-shot routine, followed by the quick, abbreviated swing, ending with the patented helicopter finish and head twitching from side to side.

Gary was right. They loved it and gave me a warm round of applause. He stood there like a proud father, wearing an ear-to-ear grin. For the second time in as many days, Bobby Jones was rolling in his grave.

One of the week's events that I looked forward to most, besides the drive up Magnolia Lane and just stepping foot on the pristine fairways, was the par 3 tournament. It's a shame that some players don't even participate, either because they'd played in it enough or because they're afraid of the alleged curse (no one has won the par 3 tournament and gone on to do the same in the big tournament). It really is a miniature version of the tournament course. It is as picturesque, immaculate and fast. The fact that nobody really tries to win it leads to a whole lot of tomfoolery.

Gary paired up with a couple of other old codgers, Billy Casper and Arnold Palmer. I was afraid he was going to have me impersonate The King right in front of him and the 5,000 spectators following us, but fortunately he didn't. Remembering the events of the Senior Skins Game, I made a mental note NOT to step in his line, even though Trevino wasn't there to broadcast it to the universe.

Frankly, I was surprised to see Arnie and Billy in the same group. There was never any visible animosity displayed between them, but let's just say that these two didn't pal around together or chit-chat on the telephone frequently. They had a history, and while many believe it started at the '66 U.S. Open when Casper came from seven behind in the final nine holes of the tournament to beat Palmer, I believe it was rooted in the fact that Casper played his entire career in Arnold's shadow. It is fairly safe to say that Billy Casper was the most underrated player to play the game in that era.

The 2nd is a hole of only 75 yards, and Gary put a flip sand wedge right in the jar. I have never seen that many people get airborne at the same time. I guarantee, it registered on all Richter scales around the country.

I had always gotten along with, and had a huge amount of respect for Billy Casper, a.k.a. Buffalo Bill, Mr. C., and my favorite, Captain Hook, which got shortened to just Cap'n. This last one he inherited because in his later years he resorted to playing a huge hook. Not a draw, but a rope hook. He played with the original Callaway S2H2 irons, which were hot enough to begin with, then added a 50-yard dive hook. He'd be hitting 8 iron from 190 yards. Normally, you want to know what club a competitor is hitting, as it is valuable information. Whenever Chi Chi got paired with Billy, he'd tell me on the 1st tee, "Pards, don't tell me what he's hitting today! I don't wanna know!"

Me & Billy Casper a.k.a. Mr. C.

Billy was always very friendly and personable, and he had a big heart (anyone who adopts six children would have to). I did see him really cheesed off once though. I was working for Crampton and we were paired with Cap'n and Gary Player at Senior T.P.C. in Ponta Vedra. Billy was looking feverishly for his ball mark on the green, and finally realized why he couldn't locate it. Black Rabbit, Gary's caddie, was standing on it. Stepping in a player's line is taboo, standing on his mark is in a totally different stratosphere of caddie blunders.

Thursday morning was the first official round of the tournament, and I was experiencing a range of emotions, from pure excitement to excessive fatigue. Walking Augusta National was physically tolling, not to mention the fact that I had gotten soft working on the Senior Tour with only three-round tournaments and the use of golf carts. I sucked it up as Gary prepared to tee off the first.

Gary hit a decent drive off the first tee and a commercial 3 iron onto the front of the green. The flag was cut on the top left tier, and as Chi Chi would say, the green was faster than Billy Graham running through Harlem. Gary was lining up his putt from 40 feet away, and I assumed the typical caddie position behind him.

"Larry, what do you see here?" he asked.

Crap, I thought. I was hoping this would be one of those moments where nothing is said between player and caddie. The pro has the line and no discussion is needed. Besides, the man in front of me had been around this golf course 50 times more than I had. What the hell was I going to be able to tell him? I was inclined to tell him to keep it low, but wasn't sure if he would see the humor in it.

"It looks like it's going a little left at the hole," was all I could contribute. And then I threw in, "C'mon, Gary, cozy it up there close," before my departure to tend the flag. This line is the equivalent of telling a player, "You're on your own."

He had a look on his face like he was being escorted to the gas chamber, and returned, "Larry, I'm just trying to keep the bloody ball on the green!"

He was successful in his attempt, running it up the slope and eventually stopping a few feet away, which he knocked in for an opening par (incidentally, four players putted the ball off that green and onto the 9th tee that day). The round progressed and Gary valiantly tried to hold par like a muscleman trying to hold a 500-pound barbell in a *World's Strongest Man* competition, but he eventually lost his grip and sputtered to an opening round of 75. I was physically and mentally spent, and staggered my way back to my hotel to watch the tournament on television.

The following day Gary's idea of winning the tournament had evaporated and transformed into the realistic notion that if he could post a good score, he could make the cut. Unfortunately, it was more of the same, and even though he bettered his 1st round score by two shots, he missed the cut by three. He was going off to do a corporate gig somewhere, and was extremely dejected as we parted ways, telling me he would see me Tuesday in West Palm Beach for the next event.

And so, I was no longer a Master's virgin. Even though we missed the cut, it was a magical week, at least from my perspective. I had the weekend free and had, in my possession, one of the toughest tickets to get in all of sports. As exhausted as I was, I wondered if I could find the guy who offered to purchase my caddie badge.

Over the course of the weekend I hung out at the tournament, but being outside the gallery ropes just wasn't the same. I was a spectator just like everyone else, and it wasn't working at all for me. I met a couple of guys who were heading down to Florida and caught a lift with them in an old VW microbus. Thus, the life of a professional tour caddie...from the penthouse to the shithouse in a matter of days.

When I met Gary at West Palm the following Tuesday, the bitter taste of missing the cut had finally worn off, but we had an interesting conversation.

"Larry, do you know what I did after missing the cut at the Masters last week? Something I haven't done in 40 years," he added.

"No, whadja' do? Did you get rip-roarin' drunk?"

"No," he replied.

"Did you go home and kick your dog?"

"No," he answered.

"You went home and broke something? Smash a television set?"

"Uh uh."

"I give. What did you do?" I surrendered.

"I cried," he said.

This was a monumental event in our relationship, putting into perspective just how important the game was to this man. I also came to the realization that I didn't love the game as much as he did. One of my caddie buddies was near death at the time, and the fact that Gary was shedding tears over a tournament, much less one he'd won three times, just didn't make any sense to me.

After working for the Black Knight for a period of time, a few stark realities became very apparent to me. First, his game, while still impressive for a man of his age, had deteriorated over time. His mind knew what to do and how to execute, but the message took a detour on its journey to his hands. It is ironic that the man who patented the walk-through golf swing (it is often referred to as the Player walk-through), battled the terrible habit of hanging back on his right side later in life. Commit this awful golf crime and it's either the open club face, shove to the right, or its dreaded counterpart, a quick rollover of the hands, which results in the insidious dive hook. Part of my job description was to keep my eye on every swing and report to him whether he transferred his weight to his left side or was guilty of this golf atrocity. I am a team player and didn't mind becoming a swing analyzer, but Gary was almost obsessive about this problem, and would grind me on the issue. After hitting a shot, he'd ask me, "Larry, did I hang back on that shot?" If he did, a simple, "Yeah, you sure did," would suffice. Well, almost suffice, as he would fire off a series of practice swings, executing the proper weight transfer. The rest of our group would be halfway up the fairway and he'd still be back on the tee trying to change the past.

If the answer was no, he'd follow up with, "Are you sure?"

"Yes Gary, I am sure, you got your weight over to your left side. You didn't hang back."

"You're absolutely positive?" he'd ask.

"I'm sure, Gary."

"You were watching?"

"Yes, Gary, I was watching, and you did not hang back."

"Okay, because I need you to watch me and make sure that I don't hang back."

"I know, Gary. I watch every swing you make. I'm a human freakin' video recorder" (the last line mumbled sarcastically and below audible level).

This redundant ritual became the Chinese water torture of our relationship, but I will say that it prepared me for married life. It was almost as if he wouldn't accept the truth, as if in some weird way, he wanted to hear that he hung back, even if he didn't. Heaven forbid if he committed this gaffe on a Sunday late in the round. Then he would want to hit balls, even though the range closed. He'd say to me, "Larry, there is no way I can leave this tournament after hitting it like that." I'd have to go find the guys who worked the range and ask them for some balls. They'd tell me the range was closed and I'd reiterate that Gary Player wanted to hit some balls. They'd give them to me, but were not pleased that they'd have to stay late and go out and pick them up after he was done. It could have been worse, though. I could have had to shag 'em.

One time down in Naples, Florida, Gary hit a crap shot coming down the stretch on Sunday. I was frosted, knowing that I was going to have to reopen another driving range. It was a long, tiring week for the range boys, and they refused my request for balls. They didn't care if the incomparable Walter Hagen rose from the dead and wanted to whack a few, they weren't opening the range. I thought Gary would accept it and just move on to the next event, but I couldn't have been more wrong. We went out to a large grass parking lot where he hit every ball he had in his golf bag amongst the vehicles parked there. I stood there and watched him hit driver after driver over a sea of Buicks and Cadillacs, just waiting for him to take out a windshield. As irritating as this whole scenario was to me, it gave me a deep insight into how this man honed his skill and strived for perfection. He squeezed every drop from the talent he was born with, and he achieved a level of greatness through drive, determination and perspiration. There were many endowed with greater physiques and more natural abilities who never came close to attaining what he did. It was a bit sad seeing an athlete so used to performing at such a high level for so long battle Father Time. We all know who's going to win that one.

Gary is renowned as one of the premier bunker players to ever grip a sand wedge. Watching him practice trap shots was really a treat, and I never tired of it. Bear in mind that I previously worked for another guy who was no slouch in the kitty litter. Chi Chi is also considered to be in the game's elite of trap shot artists. The amazing thing to me was the disparity in their techniques. Cheech weakened his grip and opened himself way up to the line, a textbook way to play a bunker shot. He picked the club up abruptly and swung with an outside/in swing path. Gary on the other hand, stayed very square to the line and kept his weight on his left side by digging the left edges of his feet into the sand. I can still vividly picture his feet dug into the sand at a 45-degree angle. He set the club extremely quickly on take away and retained the angle as long as anyone. The sound created by the club impacting the sand was, in a word, sweet. If Gary hit a poor bunker shot during a tournament round, you'd find him in the practice bunker for a good long while, but at least this didn't entail asking someone to reopen a closed driving range. Once there, he'd announce that he wasn't leaving that bunker until he holed three shots, which could take five minutes or a couple of hours.

One year, Gary was hitting some bunker shots prior to his round at the tournament in Park City, Utah. This event was situated between some of the Majors on the schedule, and was a good week to let our hair down and take a breather. Park City is a fun little town, teeming with some caddie faves in the saloon department. That said, I was standing there, hung over, watching him practice, when he pulled a ball over with his wedge, addressed it and executed perfectly. The ball landed with a controlled 'plop' on the green and ran into the hole. No big deal. I had seen this numerous times. He pulled another over, and proceeded to knock that one in the jar. I had seen this occur several times. After he canned the third in a row, he stopped and said to me, "Larry, I've holed three in a row several times, but never four."

By now I had totally forgotten about my hangover and was rooting for him to hole it again, even though he was in a practice bunker and it didn't mean anything. He took his address position, eyed the hole one last time, and popped the ball onto the green. It covered the distance, was heading right at it and just barely missed, catching the left edge of the hole.

"Ohhh, shit!" I blurted out. "So close!"

He pulled another ball into position and holed that one after the lip-out, but the streak ended there. To review, he holed four-out-of-five bunker shots from about 20 feet away and lipped out the fifth. Even after being a professional tour caddie for as long as I had been and witnessing some of the unbelievable shots I was fortunate enough to see, I was absolutely blown away by this. I've told that story to some who find it hard to believe, which is understandable, but it happened, and to quote one of my old caddie buddies, if I'm lying, then I'm dying.

Another facet of my job description was to make sure he didn't move his head or look up when putting, particularly on the short ones. Gary was one of the few players who developed the habit of striking a putt and not looking to see where it went, continuing to keep his eyes on the spot once occupied by the ball. He always said that this drill involved a good bit of self-control and discipline to master; it's human nature to want to look up and admire one's work. His philosophy was that you must keep your head down, after all, you're not going to lose it. Nick Faldo, in his prime, was another player who utilized this drill and it served him well. Remembering the 1970 British Open & 1989 Masters, I can't say the same for Doug Sanders or Scott Hoch.

It didn't take me very long to figure out that caddying for Gary was completely different from working for Chi Chi. Our interaction in regard to club selection was incomparable, as was the reading of greens. I simmered it down to the simple fact that Chi Chi needed a lot of help, and Gary didn't. That's nothing against either of them; it's just the way it was. Gary may be the best reader of greens on any tour, which put me in a tough spot when asked for my opinion. He was looking more for confirmation than anything else, and if I didn't concur with his initial read, the process would be rife with doubt and indecision. Any successful player will tell you these two elements have no place in the game and have been the root of countless tournament tragedies.

Chi Chi and Gary even differed in the way they expressed their displeasure at poor advice they received (or thought they received). Chi Chi would just come right out and rip me a new one, and it didn't matter who was around. Gary was more stealth-like in his griping. He'd come in the back door and say, "Damn it, man, I KNEW that was the wrong club, or I KNEW that putt was going the other way. I shouldn't have asked you." Then he'd follow it up with, "But it's my fault. I make the final decision. I take full responsibility." He sounded like a politician, and that really bugged me. I would have rather had him come right out and tear me a new one.

What dawned on me was that I had gone from one extreme to the other with regard to my man's game. Chi Chi was killer from tee to green, knocking it close all day long, but unable to get a putt to drop. Nothing will erode a player's confidence more than this. Gary on the other hand, wasn't as sharp until he was on the green, where he shined. The guy could really putt. It made me wish I could combine their games.

It's no secret that Gary Player is renowned as the Jack LaLanne of the links. He is as well known for that as he is for his success in the game. He worked out like a madman in the early years when naysayers preached that golf and weightlifting were not bedfellows, causing muscle-boundness, which was detrimental to the golf swing. We all know this is a bunch of hooey, as Tiger Woods dispelled this notion with a physique that rivals that of a defensive back in the NFL. I believe the players who held this belief were the out-of-shape ones searching for a reason not to work out. I heard the crusty Dave Hill once state, "I'm tired of hearing about how Gary has muscles in his shit."

Heaven forbid if the kid just blurted out, "Can I have your autograph?" followed by my mumbling, "Oh shit, here we go." Gary would commence a polite rant about how the words 'please' and 'thank you' are absolutely mandatory and that you must look a man in the eye when shaking his hand. When Mr. Charm School was done with his lecture, the kid would run off and surely remember all he was just taught.

I don't recall reading this in the job description!

One time a young man approached him and asked, "Mr. Player, may I please have your autograph?" *Good job, kid, you just saved yourself a lecture.* Gary took the lad's program and began to sign it, but as he did, I noticed him eyeballing the kid. I failed to mention that this young man was a bit on the chubby side, and I was well aware of what was coming next as I mumbled to myself, "Oh shit, here we go." Gary finished the request and handed the program back to him, which he kindly countered with, "Thank you, Mr. Player. This is awesome." Before he took one step in his departure, Gary said to him, "Son, hold on a minute, please." The boy looked befuddled and responded, "Yes, Mr. Player?"

"Son, you look like you're a champion with a knife and fork, and I am going to tell you something that your parents will not tell you. Why? Because they love you. I am going to tell you because I do not love you. Son, you're fat and you're going to die young. You must eliminate all animal fats from your diet—ham, bacon, sausage, butter and sweets."

Gary went on a tangent for about five minutes, preaching to this poor kid about diabetes, arteriosclerosis and a host of other insipid diseases that were surely going to befall the young man if he didn't change his ways. After Dr. Heart Attack was done, the kid ran off as fast as he could, terrified that he wasn't going to live to see next week.

I stood there with a grin on my face, prompting Gary to ask, "What? Was I too rough on him?"

"Nah, the kid's gonna run home and tell his folks that some old golfer told him that he didn't love him and that he better not buy any green bananas 'cuz he wasn't going to live much longer."

Gary laughed and said, "I see your point, but someone's got to tell the young people of today about diet and exercise."

When he was finished, I ran to a nearby concession tent and wolfed down a hot dog without him seeing me.

He used to read me the riot act about the same thing, telling me that I was a bit plump and needed to watch what I ate. He gave me hell for eating a donut once, and I told him, "Sorry, Gary, they ran out of garden salads at the caddie tent."

The only known picture of "Jack LaLanne of the links" consuming a hot dog.

He once visited a hospital that specialized in the treatment of cancer and asked the doctors if there was any organic substance known to be a cancer preventative. They told him that some of their studies showed that raw garlic had some effect in keeping the disease at bay. That's all he needed to hear. A couple of nights later, we went out for dinner and he asked the waiter for a saucer of raw garlic, which he proceeded to shovel into his mouth, a loaded tablespoon at a time. He ate enough garlic that night to keep Count Dracula away for the rest of his life. The following day, I couldn't get within three feet of him; garlic was oozing out of his pores.

After caddying for Gary for a while, I developed a huge sense of pride being associated with him. What his game lacked on the course, he made up for off of it, tenfold. I loved the fact that he was so cordial with everyone, and very rarely saw him get irritated with someone, even when they deserved it. Then an event occurred that ratcheted my pride up to another level.

Gary was on the driving range, warming up for the first round at the Country Club of the South, near Atlanta. It was about 20 minutes to tee time and as he hit balls, I tended to the myriad of pre-round tasks expected of me. As I was marking the day's allotted supply of balls (with a Sharpie), I noticed a man behind the gallery ropes with a cell phone to his ear, beckoning to me. I ignored him and went about my duties, but every time I glanced in that direction, he attempted to get my attention. After a few minutes of this, he started to look like someone stranded on an island waving to a rescue plane. It was evident that he wasn't giving up in his quest to talk to me. I hoped it wasn't someone I owed money to. Realizing that there was only one thing to do, I made my way over to him and asked, "Sir, what can I do for you?"

He said, "Thanks for coming over. I'm sorry to bother you, but I have my elderly father on the phone. He's dying of cancer and they've only given him a couple of months to live," the phone still stuck to his ear.

"I'm sorry to hear that," I replied, wondering where he was going with this.

"My dad was an avid golfer and Gary Player was his absolute favorite. He even used to wear black on the course, to emulate him. Do you think you can get Gary to say hi to him, just for a second? It would really make his day," he pleaded.

By that point in my caddie career, I was experienced enough to know that you don't make any promises, especially since it was very close to our tee time.

"I'll see what I can do," I told him as I made my way back to the range line. Gary was putting the finishing touches on his warm-up when I arrived back at the bag. I picked up one of the dirtied irons leaning against the bag and started cleaning it without saying a word. He had seen me walk over there and while standing at address, ready to fire off another practice shot, asked, "What's up? What did that man want?"

The door was opened and I started my pitch, "I know we don't have much time, but the guy's father is dying and he thinks the sun shines out your ass. Could you just say hello to him?"

I should have known, as he replied, "Sure, sure, bring the phone," motioning for the man to come under the ropes.

When he approached us, the man said to Gary, "Thanks, Mr. Player. I sure appreciate this," as he handed the phone to him. Gary held the phone against his shoulder and whispered, "What's your father's name?"

"Jim," he replied.

With that, Gary put the phone to his ear and started talking, "Hello Jim. This is Gary Player. How are you feeling today?"

I could hear the man's muffled response over the phone.

"Well Jim, just keep a positive attitude. Attitude is everything. And watch your diet…it's very important that you watch what you eat, especially now."

Gary proceeded to hold a conversation with this man for the next 10 minutes. You would have thought they were old Army buddies and hadn't seen each other since the war. It was now so close to our tee time that I was in a panic mode, and told Gary, like a mother scolding her tardy child, "Okay, Gary, that's great. Now we gotta' go and get to the tee. We're going to whiff our time."

"All right, Jim, you take care and stay strong. Good bye."

He handed the phone back to the man, who said, "Thank you so much, Mr. Player. I know you've really made his day. I just can't thank you enough."

"Don't mention it," Gary responded.

"C'mon, Gary, we gotta' get over there," I told him as we bolted to the first tee, just barely arriving before the first tee announcer started his presentation of the day's pairing. I must admit that I got so caught up in getting to the tee and playing that first round that I didn't have the time to fully recognize and appreciate what Gary had just done for a dying man…but I would.

One year later, we were once again at the Country Club of the South, when a man approached me and asked, "Are you Gary Player's caddie?"

"Yes, I sure am," I replied.

"Do you remember me?" he asked.

"No, we meet a lot of people on the road, but refresh my memory."

"Last year, I asked you to get Gary to speak to my dying father," he said.

"Oh yes, I remember you. How's your dad doing?"

"He passed away," the man said somberly, "but until the day he died, he told anyone who would listen that he had a conversation with his idol, Gary Player," he followed, his voice now happy and upbeat. "Would you tell Gary that he made a dying man's final days really special?" he asked.

"No, I won't do that. I think you should be the one to tell him," I responded. We chatted casually until Gary came walking up.

"Hey, Gary, remember this guy?" I asked.

"No, we meet a lot of people, but refresh my memory."

"You talked to his father last year…"

"Of course, I remember," Gary said, cutting me off. "How is your father?" he asked the man.

"He died a couple of months after I saw you, Mr. Player, but I have to tell you that until the day he died, he told anyone who would listen that he got to speak with his idol. You made a dying man very happy and I just can't begin to thank you enough."

"Don't mention it. It was my pleasure," Gary told him as they carried on a conversation. "Your father is now in heaven, and he is playing the best golf courses that we could ever imagine. He gets to play a course better than Augusta National every day." They finished talking, ending with a handshake, and then the man dissolved into the throng of fans.

This anecdote exemplifies the love, class and compassion that this man not only possesses, but shares with his fellow man. To see someone of his social and athletic stature go out of his way for an average person was anomalous. It was also a daily occurrence, and I never tired of it. I'll admit that at times I pined for the chance to go to work for one of the young guns making his way onto the tour and in the hunt for victory every week, but the greatness that I experienced first-hand with Gary had nothing to do with the number of strokes it took to get around a golf course, and was worth more than tournament wins and big checks. There was no possible way to put a value on it.

Gary is an eloquent man, and coupled with his South African accent, is an excellent raconteur. I loved hearing stories from his past, some about his life and others about interactions with other legends of the game. For instance, Gary was in his mid-teens and was messing around in class when the schoolmaster, fed up with his misbehavior, ordered Gary to stand so he could read him the riot act.

"Player, you're a slacker, going nowhere. What do you plan on doing with your life?"

"Why, I'm going to be one of the best golfers in the world," he replied.

"Don't be ridiculous, Player, you're doing no such thing," the schoolmaster chided.

Several years later, Gary won his first major championship, seizing the Claret Jug in the 1959 British Open. When he returned to South Africa he splurged and spent some of his winnings on a big, shiny convertible, which he happened to be driving one day when he saw a man walking along the road. He pulled over to see if the man wanted a ride and waited as the man walked briskly up to the car. Finally reaching it, Gary asked him, "Can I give you a ride somewhere?" It was Gary's former schoolmaster and once he recognized Gary, he surveyed the luxurious car and replied, "No, thanks. I'll walk."

Gary met his lovely wife Vivienne at a club where he practiced on his way up. She was the daughter of a golf pro herself, and was a formidable player in her own right. They had just married and went to play their inaugural round of golf as husband and wife, Gary telling her on the 1st tee, "You play from the women's tees, I'll play from the back tees, and I'll give you two strokes a side."

Vivienne countered, "I'll play up, you play back, and I'll play you even."

"All right, I like your confidence," he told her, and then proceeded to go out and shoot 1 under par and lost by two shots.

After telling me this story, he asked me, "You know what I did immediately after that? I kept her barefoot and pregnant for the next 10 years. How the hell was I going to win major championships with my wife beating me?"

Even those who don't partake of the game are familiar with the names Arnold Palmer and Jack Nicklaus, for they are icons of their sport and a slice of Americana. What most don't know, and that includes golfers, is how fierce the rivalry was between them, even though they professed to be friends. Arnold was 11 years older than Jack, and is single-handedly credited with propelling the game into the public spotlight. The combination of Arnie, Mark McCormick (the founder of IMG), and television created a volatile mixture that was destined to explode. Arnie's Army was out in full force, and recruiting as if World War III was on the horizon; the public absolutely adored him. Then along came Jack, this chubby kid from Ohio, with his towering length and razor-sharp ability to get it in the hole. He also had the audacious idea that he was going to try on the King's crown, much to the chagrin of the golfing public.

The ultimate golf threesome.

"Larry, they used to call Jack 'Ohio Fats,' and they rooted against him with all their might," Gary would tell me. "I remember seeing a guy standing behind a green with a big sign that read, 'Ohio Fats, hit it here!' with a big arrow pointing down at a bunker. That's how much they hated him for beating Arnold. Eventually, when they realized that he wasn't going away, they gave in and embraced him. How could they not? The man was the best to ever play the game...but I gave him a run for his money!"

It was no secret that The Golden Bear respected Gary for his fierce, competitive nature and how much he had accomplished with the tools bestowed upon him.

I once made the enormous blunder of asking Gary if he thought that he could compete in today's game, given the depth of the talent. Years ago there were no players from Fiji, Sweden or Trinidad and Tobago, and now there are formidable players emerging from all corners of the globe. I wouldn't be a bit surprised to see some new hot shot from Papua New Guinea grab a sliver of the spotlight. "Absolutely," he answered, a glimmer of irritation in his voice, like he couldn't believe I would even ask such a thing. "I believe that I would be more successful today because the cutting edge technologies in the game would benefit me more."

All the stories Gary shared with me were a distant second to those about The Hawk. When Gary talked about Ben Hogan, I was all ears, like a kindergartner during story time. He was very descriptive, and I could paint an exact picture in my mind of what he was portraying to me.

"Larry, I played with Ben Hogan the first two rounds in a major very early in my career, and the man said two words to me in 36 holes...'you're away.'"

Hogan's dour personality was as legendary as his play. He was not a happy-go-lucky guy, rarely spoke to his fellow competitors, and never offered swing tips or advice. It was Hogan lore that a young player once asked him a question about the golf swing, and Hogan cut him off before he could finish and said, "Hit a million balls, boy, you'll figure it out," and walked off. He possessed a flawless golf swing and it was said that Nicklaus used to watch Hogan practice, but Hogan never returned the favor.

After Gary played those first two rounds with Hogan, he was in the locker room changing when someone firmly tapped him on the shoulder. Gary turned, only to find himself staring into those steely blue eyes.

"They didn't call him 'The Hawk' for nothing. Those laser-like eyes of his went right through me," Gary recounted.

"Son, you're going to be one helluva' player someday," Hogan said.

"Thank you, Mr. Hogan," Gary returned.

"Do you like to practice?" Hogan asked him.

"Yes sir," Gary replied.

Then Hogan snapped, "Double it!" and walked away.

Gary went on to remind me that Ben Hogan wasn't a feel-good kinda' guy, and he never offered this type of positive feedback to anyone.

"Larry I felt like someone had just written me a check for 10 million dollars, and that conversation instilled a great boost of confidence in me."

I had once heard a story about Gary and a possible club contract with Hogan, and asked him if it was just tour gossip.

"No, that story is absolutely true. Hogan approached me a short time after the locker room incident and offered me $2,500 to play his equipment. He was just starting the Ben Hogan Golf Club Company and was looking for a young gun to be on staff. It was a nice offer, but I was also offered $10,000 to play First Flight equipment, and seeing as I had eight mouths to feed, I had to go where the money was. They were offering me four times what Hogan was."

A while later, Gary was on the range practicing, and Hogan walked past. He stupidly attempted to ask him a golf swing related question, and Hogan answered with a question. He asked, 'Son, what kind of golf equipment do you play?'

"First Flight,' Gary answered, his tail between his legs.

"Then I suggest you go and ask Mr. First Flight," Hogan quipped.

The predecessor to the Palmer/Nicklaus rivalry was the Snead/Hogan era. Gary told me that someone once approached Snead and said, "Mr. Snead, Mr. Hogan drives the balls so straight that he plays out of his divots from yesterday." Snead replied, "If he's that #$@&in' good, why doesn't he aim to the left or to the right of 'em?"

I derived great pleasure from watching my current employer watch my former boss, Chi Chi Rodriguez, when we were paired together and Chi Chi made a birdie putt, which could only mean one thing; a sword dance was in order. Even though I had witnessed it hundreds of times and Gary, probably thousands, it was still novel to watch, but I enjoyed watching Gary watch Chi Chi, more than the actual routine. He just stood there with the most amused grin on his face, like a kid watching a cartoon. They were friends, and there was a huge mutual respect between them, but Gary leveled with me, telling me that he never remembered Chi Chi even being in the hunt for a Major Championship earlier in their careers. It was no revelation to anyone inside the ropes of professional golf that Chi Chi's putter was the Achilles heel of an otherwise stellar game, and Chi Chi knew it. It was his cross to bear and prohibited him from kissing silver in the big ones.

Even as solid and accomplished as The Black Knight was in the game, I was amazed that The Merry Mex could successfully get in Gary's head, even after all those years. We were paired with Lee at the event in Key Biscayne, Florida, when we got to the tee at the par 3, 12th. Lee had the honor, and was conferring with Mitch about the situation. It was playing to about 175 yards, the flag cut left, with water to the left and a bunker to the right. To confound the problem, a slight breeze was hurting from the right, toward the hazard. It actually set up perfect for Lee, a left-to-right player. He could carve it up into the wind and knock it down. He just had to gear up with enough stick to play to the center of the green.

It was the type of hole that par was a good score; try and go at the flag and a big number was imminent. Lee did just that, landing his ball softly and safely on the green, right of the flag, about 15 feet away. Gary was next to play, and as he and I held a club selection consultation, Lee said to Herman, "Hey, Herm, did you see that fish jump? What kinda' fish you think they got there in that lake?"

Gary was dumbfounded, and said to me anxiously, "What the hell is he doing talking about the lake before I play my shot?"

"You know exactly what he's trying to do to you," I said authoritatively. "Don't let him mess with you. You got this shot."

In truth, it was a more difficult shot for Gary, as he was a natural right-to-left player. With his ball flight and the breeze, he needed to hang it out over the bunker on the right and move it toward the hole, but most players will concur that it's easier to move it away from a hazard than toward it. After choosing the appropriate weapon, Gary teed his ball and fired it directly at the right bunker, but held onto it for dear life. It was clearly a 'you-ain't-going-left' swing. The shot never considered moving left one iota, finishing in the right bunker, which was no trip to Disneyland as it was downhill, downwind and down grain, with the hazard lurking in the distance.

As we walked to the green, Gary bellyached about the upcoming shot and the fact that Lee was instrumental in how it got there, which would have pleased Lee even more. It took all the skill Gary could muster to get it up and down, dodging a Trevino bullet. They're supposed to be friends, but once a hustler, always a hustler. Lee Trevino knew no other way.

I remember walking down the fairway behind Gary and Lee when the conversation turned to J.C. Snead and more specifically, how negative the guy was. I personally don't ever recall hearing him say anything remotely positive. In his mind, the glass wasn't half empty, it was bone freaking dry. Lee showed his hand talking about how he knew how to take J.C. out of the game if he was in a position to win a tournament.

"How do you do that?" Gary inquired.

"It's easy…If I'm paired with him, I just start talking about how bad my hotel room was, and how awful my breakfast was, and what a lousy job the locker room guy did on my shoes all week. Then I just let him go and he'll jump on board and bitch and complain about everything under the sun. Next thing ya' know, he's making bogies."

Later on, Gary expressed his amazement at this ploy and I told him, "Just watch out. He'll try to do the same to you."

One time Herman and I were going back and forth about who was a better caddie. We were both just having a little fun, trying to roust up the other. "I out-caddie you any day a' da' week," he exclaimed. "Herman, you outweigh me and that's about it. You couldn't club a caveman" (borrowing a line from the infamous Silly Billy).

About that time, Lee walked up and caught the tail end of our verbal jousting. "Lemme tell both you jackasses something. Ain't neither one of you worth a shit. I've seen a lot of good jockeys in my time, but I ain't seen one of 'em carry the horse across the finish line. You know what I'm saying?"

I was in my second year with The Black Knight and, as I've already stated, I was surfing a wave that crested a long, long time ago, but there were glimmers of greatness past.

On my second trip to the hallowed grounds of Augusta National, the 58 year old Rock Spider made the cut by the skin of his teeth. He was as nervous as a hooker in church, watching the scoreboard to see if he would play on the weekend. I almost forgot for a minute that the man had won the event three times and finished in the runner-up position as many. One would have thought that he really needed the money. The golf course was a vision of stunning beauty, as the bloom was particularly vibrant that year. By that point in my caddie career, my longevity was beginning to erode and thoughts of retiring crept into my mind at times, but it was a fantastic week, even if we did finish dead last.

Around mid-summer we flew Air Player over the pond for the British and Senior British Opens. I was, once again revisiting my past, as The Open was being held at Royal St. Georges in Sandwich, England. I worked the 1985 Open there, but times and conditions had changed drastically. Needless to say, I wasn't going to be residing in a nylon abode, and I sure as hell wasn't going to have to climb through a window to shower. We missed the cut, but Gary still spent the weekend on the range, as his ball striking was less than satisfactory. To me, this was golf's equivalent of shadow boxing.

It's a short hop over to Blackpool, where we made our way for the Senior British at Royal Lytham and St. Annes. It was really hard to consider this event a Senior Major, due to the fact that most of the premier players didn't even bother to show up for it. I figured we were over there anyway, and it provided me the opportunity to experience a venue where numerous legends had hoisted the Claret Jug, including GP, and most importantly, they were handing out checks at the completion of the tournament.

Senior British Open Royal Lytham & St. Annes 1993.

If I was a big fish in a little pond working on the Senior PGA Tour, then at this tournament I was whale in a fishbowl. The level of caddie ability was underwhelming to say the least. I truly believe some of the golfers dragged people off the street and stuck caddie bibs on them.

Gary was chock full of memories and course knowledge. They say the rough is so thick over there that you can lose a small child in it, and this was verified when Gary hit an errant tee shot during the tournament. I yelled, "FORE!" and everyone ducked for cover, the ball landing right in the midst of 50 spectators. It disappeared in the thick, wispy grass like Amelia Earhart in the Pacific. We looked for the allotted five minutes provided by the rules of the game, but to no avail. A provisional and one-shot penalty followed, and I contemplated whether to alert the spectators if he hit another one sideways.

The Rock Spider fared well at Lytham, but unfortunately got edged out by Bob Charles, finishing tied for second with European Tour stalwart, Tommy Horton.

Toward the end of the '93 season we made our way to one of Gary's favorite locales on the tour. He adored Lexington, Kentucky; the passion wasn't golf-related, but of an equine nature. The man absolutely loves horses, and that part of the world is horse country. I've told many people that if you are fortunate enough to meet Gary, you would probably be inclined to talk golf with him, but if you really want to pique his interest, his passion for the hooved and horseshoed would be the way to do it.

Being there must have done wonders for his spirits, because he was in the thick of it going into the final round, tied for the lead with Dale Douglass. He was as nervous as a 13 year-old leading an AJGA event, but he birdied the first five in a row, coming out of the blocks and shooting a closing 66 to win the one-and-only outing while yours truly was packing for him. I savored the moment, as I was fairly certain I wouldn't be around to experience another tournament win with him. For the year, Gary played in 22 events and had six top 10 finishes, highlighted by the lone victory and the 2nd place finish at the Senior British. A decade earlier, this would have been considered a fantastic season, but I was spoiled by the great runs I had with Crampton and Rodriguez.

The start of the 1994 season kicked off with the Florida swing, and I put my best game face on, hoping that the year would hold some awesome golf and monetary benefits, but in the back of my mind, I knew I was fooling myself. I loved working for an absolute legend of the game, but the Golfing Gods decided that his name was etched on enough silver, and the twilight of a memorable career had arrived. It was a plain and simple fact, and it was non-negotiable. I had tasted the sweetness of tournament victory for so long, and I yearned to be in the hunt, especially since some of my traveling companions were now in the position where I used to be. I also wanted to generate more cash flow. Working for a World Golf Hall of Famer didn't hold any weight when the mortgage was due.

After completion of the west coast swing, Gary invited me to fly with him to the upcoming event in San Antonio. That one didn't take much contemplation. After accepting, he informed me that we were going to make a pleasure stop in Sedona, a destination that he always wanted to investigate, because the red cliffs and western flair appealed to the rancher in him. When I told him that I had arranged to fly commercially with Todd (Dave Stockton's caddie), Gary invited him to tag along.

Gary's son Mark, who runs the Player machine, took the liberty of dipping into the family fortune and had the Hawker 800 dressed to kill, from the multi-colored exterior paint with The Black Knight logo on the tail, to the ultrasuede-wrapped interior. I was personally fond of the 24-karat gold plating that adorned every metal surface in the cabin. The plane was majestic, and while I'm not quite sure exactly where Gary was on the childhood poverty scale in comparison to Chi Chi, it was symbolic of just how far he had come in his life. They definitely shared a parallel in their meager beginnings.

We were airborne before you could say Krugerrand. The flight crew had a scrumptious meal catered, which we savored as we darted across the southern California sky. We laughed and discussed worldly topics, setting the tone for what was to be a memorable day with the Rock Spider. About this time I took my knife and pretended to be sawing on the seat belt strap, which prompted Gary to ask, "What the hell are you doing?" I responded, "I'm trying to hack this flippin' seat belt off, so I can pawn it."

The private airport in Sedona sits on a mesa, and you literally feel like you're landing on a tabletop. Before setting her down, the pilots did a couple of banked 360's around the area, giving us an awesome view of the red clay cliffs beneath us. Gary had his nose pressed to the window, reminding me of a little boy staring through the window of a candy shop, and then he said, "Oh, man, I wish my ranch was here." Gary is South African to the core, but a 5,000 acre ranch in Sedona is worth considerably more than the same on the outskirts of Johannesburg, and when it comes to personal wealth, citizenship is negotiable.

Once on the ground, a guide and a jeep were waiting to take us on a geological tour of the Indian ruins in the surrounding mountains. The guide was an entertaining sort, sharing tidbits of knowledge about the area, its rich history and the indigenous people who called this place home centuries ago. Gary absorbed it all like a 10th grader in a geology class, interjecting questions and comments. After a back-thrashing drive over terrain only suitable for the lifted Jeep we were glad we were in, we finally arrived at our destination. The barely recognizable remains of Indian domiciles were situated in an open semi-circular cave at the base of a humongous rock formation. Standing under millions of tons of granite inclined me to think about gravity; more specifically, the effect of it on the mountain above us. Relief came in the realization that I was there with Gary and he wasn't going like that. No, like Arnold, he is going to die an old man in a bed when he's 100 years old.

Our guide rattled off interesting facts about the ruins, painting a very vivid picture of what it would have been like to be a resident of this mini-metropolis in a bygone era. In typical fashion, Gary transported himself to that place and time.

"Larry, imagine what it was like to live here and wake up looking at these mountains and go out on a hunt for food and then cook it," he wondered with delight and fascination.

It occurred to me that he would have been content and successful no matter when and where he was born. After considerable time at the ruins, the guide announced it was time to head back, as dusk was approaching. Gary was still in full Mr. Rogers mode, soaking up everything he could. I went in search of him and upon finding him announced, "C'mon, Holes-With-A-Wedge, it's time to go."

After the trek back to civilization, the guide dropped us off at a restaurant overlooking the famous rock formation, Teapot Mountain. The perfect end to an awesome day, we dined and drank red wine while the setting sun transformed the colors of the panoramic view by the minute. We discussed all we had learned on our educational tour, and I wouldn't have been surprised if Gary had sprung a pop-quiz on us.

Our stomachs full and feeling no pain from the effects of the vino, we were whisked back to the airport where Air Player was awaiting our arrival. The airport was so primitive that the operators had closed up the terminal and left for the day. They kindly left the runway lights on for us, and there the jet sat, engines whistling and ready for flight. We decided to relieve ourselves before departing, and seeing as the facility was closed, chose the side of the runway as the place to do it. There we stood, me, my friend and traveling companion Todd, and legendary golfer Gary Player, having a whiz with a private jet and open skies awaiting us. I reminisced for a moment about my days on the European Tour when I had to get up in the middle of the night to do the same, and the only luxuries were the smoldering remains of a campfire and a tent.

A couple of months later we found ourselves in rural, rustic Pinehurst, North Carolina for the U. S. Senior Open. I had very realistic expectations about our chances of victory, and was ecstatic about finally getting the opportunity to see this gem of a track. I remember caddying as a kid at North Shore, seeing bag tags from the famed course and knowing nothing about it. Little did I know then that I'd be walking those tree-lined fairways with one of golf's greats.

We were paired with Trevino the first round. About 15 minutes before show time, the head flew off his 7 iron, and, after cart-wheeling down the range, came to rest about 100 yards out. There was clearly not enough time to find a suitable replacement, and even less chance of repairing the severed implement. Lee's a pretty cool cat and didn't let much bother him, but Gary was so frantic you would have thought it was his club. "Lee, what the hell are you going to do?" he asked.

"Aw, no big deal, Gary, I'll just hit a big 8 or a little 6," he answered nonchalantly. He played with 13 clubs in the bag that day and did exactly that.

About this time in my career it was time to face reality. Gary was a ceremonial golfer and was out there only to promote his other business interests. Who could blame him? The revenue generated on the golf course was a spit-in-the-bucket compared to the money he could make from his other businesses. But if Gary was a ceremonial golfer, I was a ceremonial caddie, and the money I was making off the course was diddlysquat. Nobody was willing to pay me shit because I caddied for a famous golfer. Someone once told me that if you're beginning to wonder if it's time to get out, it's time to get out.

Also, my ability to benefit my player wasn't close to what it once was. I really felt like I had lost my edge. Part of this was due to Gary rattling my cage anytime I was asked an opinion and it didn't work out, whether it was a putt or on club selection. Honestly, my confidence was so shaken that I couldn't read a green worth a crap, or pull a club to save my life. The other part of the problem was that my desire to even be out there had diminished to the point where I shouldn't have been out there. I never considered professional caddying to be a job and promised myself that, if that ever happened, I would call it a career and move on. I was really beginning to feel like I had overstayed my welcome, and I needed to find a line of work that was based on my performance. I made the enormous mistake of voicing these feelings to Gary, who took the opportunity to lecture me on how great we had it out there and how much I sounded like his wife. Apparently, she was as burned out as I was, and went so far as to tell him that she was hanging it up when he turned 60. He told me that we lived in a dream world out there and that traveling was in my blood, and that I wouldn't be able to handle not being on the road. I was aware of my inner turmoil, and chalked his opinion up to a classic case of projection. I knew once I made the decision and severed my ties, there would be no looking back.

Like a marathon runner approaching the finish line, I staggered my way through the latter part of that season and made it with about as much energy. Solace came in the form of a several-month respite back at my place in Palm Desert, California. I was due to hook back up with Gary for the Florida swing at the start of the '95 season, and over the course of that winter break, I needed to muster up some enthusiasm or make an enormous and life changing decision to take my life in a new direction.

Winter in the Desert was a welcome respite, and I met Gary in Florida the following February. I really felt my batteries were recharged, but after several weeks of mediocre play, realized there was a short somewhere in the system. I was deflated, and mentally, right back where I was at the end of the last season. Let me put it into perspective for you; I was so burned out, I passed on the chance to work The Masters for the 3rd year in a row. Yeah, I know, I must have been freaking nuts, but by that point, it was just another tournament. In my state of mind, I couldn't get lathered if Bobby Jones miraculously rose from the dead and asked me to caddie for him.

Desert Mountain in Scottsdale had always been one of my favorite tour stops. It takes growing up in the harsh climate of Chicago to really appreciate it, which is why I chose the desert four hours west as my home. Soul searching was still my favorite hobby, but it was early April, and The Tradition was the tournament du jour. Gary was paired with Jack and Arnold the first two rounds, so needless to say, we had half the golfing populace of the greater Phoenix area following us. I had caddied with The Big Three before; it was akin to a politician getting to hang out with Washington, Lincoln and Franklin.

After Jack and Arnold were safely on the green at the 7th (a par 3 of about 170 yards) Gary proceeded to flush a 7 iron right in the hole. Even though I was mentally charred and had witnessed just about everything one could imagine on the golf course, it was still a huge thrill, and the thousands of spectators agreed. Jack grinned at him, throwing him a wink, and Arnold grabbed him by the shoulders with his vice grip-like hands. The whole scene could not have been scripted any better. As we left the tee, Jack asked Gary, "So, how many holes-in-one is that for you?" Gary responded, "Twenty two, but two of them were lucky!" which made Jack chuckle.

The 15th at Desert Mountain is a long par 5 with a water hazard in front, making a layup imminent. Incidentally, the green is a Siamese, shared with the 7th. Gary hit a commercial drive and then asked me what club he needed to lay up with to leave himself 100 yards to the hole; his 56-degree wedge was perfect for that yardage. Course management is what really separates the professionals from amateurs. I calculated what we had left to the hole, backed it off 100 yards and took into account the aiding wind.

"The wind is helping from the right here, Gary. A nice 5 iron up the right side of the fairway should be perfect."

He pulled out the 5 and hit it just the way I envisioned it, starting on the right edge of the fairway and bending a bit left. When we arrived at his ball resting safely in the center of the fairway, I found the nearest sprinkler head and with the aid of my yardage book and the day's pin sheet, figured what we had to the hole.

"Larry, what have we got?" he asked, his hands coupled behind his back and staring at the flagstick.

"Whadja' want?" I countered.

"I told you I wanted 100 yards to the hole," he answered.

That's exactly what you got—100 yards to the hole, Gary."

This didn't occur very frequently, but we could usually get close to our target number, and every so often hit it right on the head.

"The wind's laid down; it should play right at the yardage," I added.

He yanked his 56-degree wedge out of the bag, went through his routine, ended with his patented, right knee-kick swing trigger, and hit his ball crisply at the hole. It landed on line, a couple of yards in front of the hole, and hopped right in. The crowd went nuts. Jack walked across the fairway and bowed down simulating "I'm not worthy" with his arms extended, and then asked Gary, "What the hell did you eat for breakfast this morning?" Arnold came up to him and extended his huge paw, an enormous grin on his weathered face. Gary never putted on that humungous green that day.

On the par 3, 17th, the flag was cut on the front left portion of the green and Gary hit his tee shot right at it. The ball landed on the green and scurried past the hole, narrowly hitting the flagstick on its journey by. It came creepily close to going in, and had he made that second hole-in-one, 3rd holed shot of the round, the tour officials would have asked for a sample of his urine.

We were paired with the Lee Trevino/Herman Mitchell traveling circus the third round of the tournament. An ESPN cameraman was set up on top of a gigantic boulder behind the 13th tee, which afforded him an awesome camera angle looking down on the players as they hit their shots to the green below. When we arrived there, he beckoned us to let us know that there was a huge rattlesnake sunning herself on the ground at the base of the boulder, about 25 feet behind the tee. She showed no signs of hostility, but Herman was totally freaked out by the sight of her. It was Lee's turn to play, but he was having a hard time getting any information out of Herman, who was obsessed with the sunning serpent.

"C'mon, Herman. Forget about that snake. She ain't gonna hurt you, ya' big baby."

"Boss, you don't understand. I hate snakes. I hate 'em!" he declared.

They conferred on the task at hand and Lee proceeded to hit his shot to the green, Herman eyeballing the snake the whole time. After Lee played, Herman went down the side of the elevated tee in an effort to distance himself from the perceived reptilian threat, as Lee threw verbal barbs his way.

"Ya' big pussy. Afraid of a lil' ole snake!"

Herman just glared at him. Then, when Herman was distracted while watching the third player in the group, Lee whispered to me, "Watch this." He grabbed a club from Gary's bag, snuck up behind Herman, and lightly tapped on his ankle with the grip end. Herman let out a yell and somehow got all of his 350 pounds airborne. We howled as Herman went off on a tirade, "WHAT THE #$@&, MAN? Why you always gotta' be messin' with me? Mutha'#$@&a!" which just made us all laugh even more.

The Tradition is considered a Senior Major, making it a four-round event and Gary played steadily through Saturday. The event started memorably, and with the position we were in for the final round, thoughts of victory were seeping into my battle-fatigued mind. This could be the exact prescription needed to jump start my caddie motor and get me moving again.

The flashes of brilliance and aggressive style Gary exhibited the first couple of days were nowhere to be found, and he took a seat on the par train. He was hitting fairways and greens, but couldn't get a putt to drop. Sometimes it's almost better if your man makes a bogey, because it could snap him out of it and start him on a birdie binge. While every amateur golfer would give his first-born to make 18 straight pars, any tour caddie will tell you that it's not going to cut it when your man is vying to win a golf tournament, especially if you're looking at Nicklaus' taillights.

We stepped on to the tee of the par 5, 12th, and nothing had changed. Desperation was setting in and I could feel any chance of Gary winning the tournament slowly slipping away, as Jack was now atop the leader board. The hole was reachable if Gary hit a really good drive, and the pit of my gut told me that our shot at glory hinged on what transpired over the next 10 minutes.

He hit an average drive that left us with 225 yards to the hole, which, with the elevation, would play to around 215 yards. I'm aware that the tour players of today would hit a 6 iron from this yardage, but Gary was nearly 60 years of age, and the equipment wasn't what it is today. He carried a 5 wood in his bag that was the perfect club for this distance. He asked me what we had to the hole and then inquired what we had to lay up. I couldn't believe what I was hearing…talk about two people being on two different pages. As he contemplated what club to lay up with, I piped up and said, "Gary, this is the ideal distance for your 5 wood. It is perfect."

"Oh Larry, I don't know…I'd rather hit it short of the waste area and give myself a chance with the wedge," he replied.

"I understand Gary, but we have to go for it. Jack's walking away with this thing, and with his length off the tee, he'll have no more than a 5 iron in here."

Looking back, this was not a good scene, as Gary was already rich and didn't need the money. I, unfortunately, was not, and did. I should have been the one talking him into playing it safe. After several minutes staring at the green, he beckoned, "Alright, give me that 5 wood."

I couldn't get the head cover off of it quick enough, and after handing it to him, went into a dissertation, doing my best to pump his head full of information and positive thoughts.

"It's 225 playing like 215. You have the perfect club in your hand Gary. Get it up in the air and float it in there. You have room behind the hole. C'mon Gary, positive swing thought here. You got this shot."

After running out of things to say, I pulled the bag back and took a deep breath, like I was going down to save someone in a submerged car. Gary went through the motions and proceeded to make a pitifully scared swing, never releasing the club and blocking it painfully right. It was not the execution I was hoping for, after laying my neck on the chopping block. We walked quietly up the fairway, finally arriving at the approximate location of the ball, where a marshall kindly informed us that it was resting peacefully at the base of a bush. Gary took an unplayable lie, and after wedging it on the green, 3-whacked it for double bogey, making a bad situation even more excruciating. There wasn't a whole hell of a lot of banter going on between us at this point.

Our round ended uneventfully, as victory was now as elusive as a unicorn. Jack, meanwhile, had his way with his nearest pursuers and put another notch in his trophy case.

Gary was extraordinarily quiet as we packed up his gear and made our way out of the luxurious clubhouse. Then the floodgates opened up. "Damn it, man. I should have never gone at that green! That was a bad call and I shouldn't have listened to you, Larry!"

This was not the Congressional Gary I was accustomed to. He didn't address the fact that he held the power to veto my suggestion and make the final call. He was coming at me full bore.

"Look, Gary, I know you were winning Majors when I was in diapers, but there is no way you're going to tell me that we should have laid up there. We had to go for it. It was our last shot and we had to take it. That yardage was a green light. What were we going to lay up with…a 9 iron?" I said, standing my ground, which I was about to find out was shaky at best.

"Oh, man, you are just like my wife. I can't tell you anything!" he responded tersely. Then he followed with, "Look, maybe it's time to make a change. Is there enough time for you to get another bag for PGA Seniors?"

The astonished look on my face must have told him I wasn't ready for that, as he then said, "No, no, no, I haven't given you the proper notice. I'll see you in West Palm Beach."[1]

Instead of heading to Sedona to celebrate the infrequent thrill of victory, my fiancée and I got in the car and headed toward California. We chatted about the chain of events and then she slipped off to sleep, giving me the chance to be alone with the litany of thoughts bouncing around in my head. After hours of deep contemplation, driving in silence, except for the hum of the tires on the pavement, it was crystal clear to me what needed to be done.

Back in California and sleeping in my own bed, I awoke the next morning refreshed and ready to make one of the more difficult phone calls I've ever had to make. I tracked Gary down at the house he rented in Augusta, and diplomatically and respectfully told him that if he

---

1 Just for the record, I checked with Jack's caddie on the club they hit into the 12th hole, and it was a 5 iron.

thought he could do any better with someone else on his bag, that he should have at it, in those exact words. We said our goodbyes, honestly wishing each other the best of luck in our future endeavors. It was a poignant and bittersweet moment. It was painful to think about his absence from my life, and I knew I was going to miss my friend, but I felt a strong sense of emancipation. It was inevitable that this day would eventually come and that I would need to make a clean break from the life I was living.

I began this chapter with the statement that Gary Player taught me valuable lessons about life, not just about golf, so a valid question might be, what is it I really learned from him? Simmered down to its purest essence, I learned that no matter how big you have become, or think you have become, we are all human beings and need to treat each other with kindness and respect. I learned that life is filled with adversity and how we deal with it is the truest measure of a person. Gary always said that it's easy to be a great guy when times are good; it's when life throws a curve that you need to be a gentleman. This lesson is extremely pertinent at this juncture in my life. I learned that you don't have to be large in stature to be a big man. But most importantly, I learned that if you're really fortunate, someone who is extraordinary, might join you on your path of life. Unfortunately, there's no guarantee how long your journey together will last. At some point in time, you will be forced to survive on your memories. It is only then that you will realize how truly fortunate you were.

THE MERRY MEX...
SOMETIMES

"HEY LARRY! WHAT are you doing here?" a familiar voice called to me as I shopped in the Ralph's market in Indian Wells. I turned to see Lee Trevino's wife, Claudia, standing behind me. "Oh, hey, Claudia. I have a place here in Palm Desert."

"Is Gary playing next week in Las Vegas?" she inquired.

"No. He's globetrotting the next month, so I have some time off." Lee's caddie, Herman, was taking a mandatory sabbatical himself. Mitch was grossly obese and was not the picture of health, plagued with an enlarged heart, diabetes and a couple of other issues. Even though Lee abused Mitch like a battered wife at times, deep down, he loved him like a brother and was concerned about his welfare. He forced Herman to get his health in order at Duke University Medical Center, and I knew that meant Lee might be needing a caddie for Vegas and so I asked Claudia, "Who's packing for Lee next week?"

"Nobody," she answered, "He'll pick up a caddie when he gets there."

"I'll work for him," I volunteered.

"You got it Larry! I'll set it up," she replied as she jotted down Lee's phone number for me.

My conversation with Lee was short and to the point. He told me that he would meet me on the range Wednesday morning and that he wouldn't have time to play a practice round. He was unfamiliar with the course and would be relying on me to get him around the track. That meant I needed to really do some thorough course preparation; I surely didn't want to be the whipping boy for the week.

Me, Lee, and Orville Moody.

Lee is a good guy and probably one of the cleverest, most entertaining people you'll ever come across, but he's got an edge about him and will tear your face off if you catch him at the wrong time. He does not suffer idiocy very well, whether real or perceived. I witnessed this firsthand once when a spectator was just trying to be funny and asked him in front of a crowd of people, "Hey, Lee, where's Chi Chi?" It was an innocent question but Lee, for whatever reason, took it the wrong way and jumped down the guy's throat.

"How the #$@& do I know where Chi Chi is? It's not my #$@&ing turn to watch him!"

Another time, he was hitting balls on the range and he hit one off the hosel, half-shanking it. Pro golfers are only human, and they hit it sideways every so often. A woman behind the gallery ropes yelled out, "Lee, that looked like one of mine!" He turned and gave her a dirty look and said, "Lady, about the only thing we might have in common is, you might be right handed."

I need to preface this next portion of my tale with a tidbit of insider information. Lee Trevino and the folks at The Masters did not see eye-to-eye. As a matter of fact, they got along about as well as the CEO of BP and a Louisiana shrimper. I'm not positive where the root of the bad feelings originated, but everyone in the inner sanctum of the game knew about it. I heard that it got so bad toward the end of his PGA Tour days that Lee wouldn't even enter the clubhouse, opting to change his shoes in the parking lot.

I showed up on the driving range Wednesday morning to find Lee already there, hitting balls and holding court with a small group of people.

"Hey, Lar," he said as I walked up, sneaking a peek at me and doing a double-take, as he fired off another shot.

I was wearing a gorgeous jacket that Vivienne Player had bought me from Augusta National. It was multi-colored, a royal blue bottom and the unmistakable Masters logo resting on Augusta green on the top. I absolutely loved that jacket. Lee proceeded to hit another ball and then piped up and said, "Hey Larry, lemme tell you one thing."

"What's that?" I asked innocently, not having any clue what was coming next.

"Don't wear that #$@&ing jacket around me again."

There was a period of uncomfortable silence as all in attendance just stood there, stunned and quiet, including me. I heard someone whisper, "Is he serious?"

"Okay, Lee," I finally answered meekly.

"I'm just kidding," he retorted, easing the tension a bit. He took one more glance in my direction before corralling another range ball and readying it for flight.

I had been around Lee Buck Trevino more than long enough to know that that he was not kidding, so I pulled off the garment, rolled it up in a wad and stuffed it in the zipper pocket of his golf bag. Nice way to start the week, ya' moron, I muttered to myself, wondering how the hell I could have been so flippin' stupid. It was a bit chilly that morning but it didn't matter; I could have been looping in Antarctica. Lee would never see me in that coat again.

I stood there shivering as Lee continued with his warm-up, entertaining all in attendance with his banter on a plethora of subjects. The most unique, or shall I say, peculiar thing about him is that he doesn't even stop yammering when he's playing. He is the only golfer I know of who talks when striking a golf ball. And it wasn't just while he was warming up on the range. He talked while he pulled the trigger on the golf course, even during the Pro-Am.

Lee Trevino would have made a great psychiatrist or spook working for the CIA, because he was a master of mind manipulation. They say golf is a game played on a six-inch course between one's ears. If you were in a battle with Lee, you can bet he was going to find a way to sneak into your cranium.

Years ago, I was caddying for Crampton and we were in a head-to-head duel with Lee, coming down the stretch. Bruce was a still a big gun on the over-50 circuit, and Lee was a relative newcomer. We were on the tee of a long par 3, and Lee and Herman were debating club selection. Lee teed up his ball and then announced, loud enough for all in attendance to hear, "Herman, gimme that 3 iron. I'm gonna break his heart." It's hard to convey in print, the manner in which this little message was delivered. Make no bones about who the intended recipient was. It was Lee's way of telling Bruce that he was the new sheriff in town and he was coming at him guns-a-blazin'.

As we made our way to the first tee, Lee took the opportunity to set the ground rules for the week. Basically, he was putting me in my place, and I wasn't surprised at all by this tactic. I had been around him long enough to know his m.o. I heard when Herman first began working for him he was told, "Herman, lemme tell you one thing. I've never hit a bad golf shot in my life. You know what I'm saying?"

And now he was telling me, "Larry, lemme tell ya' something. I'm gonna do all the talkin' and you're gonna do all the listenin'.'"

"Okay, Lee, I understand."

"And another thing Larry, I can throw these clubs in a shoppin' cart and push it around this golf course, and still win this thing. You understand what I'm saying?"

"I understand Lee."

With the psychological jousting out of the way, we made our way over to meet the Pro-Am participants.

Lee was cordial and really loose with them. He chatted with one about football, who asked him if he ever bet on the games. Lee replied, "Nah. The only thing I know about football is how to raise the pigs they make the balls out of."

At one point, he lifted up his golf shirt, exposing a small scar on his belly.

"What happened? Somebody stab you?" I asked.

He replied, "No, I cut myself on a beer can when I was swimmin' over."

Later in the day he announced, "Some guy stole my wife's credit card."

"Did you report it to the police?" I asked naively.

"Nah," he answered, "He's spending less than she does."

I'm not the brightest bulb in the pack, but I wasn't stupid enough to show up for the first official round of the tournament wearing any article of clothing that had a Masters logo on it. On the practice green, I was watching Lee hit some putts and noticed something very odd. In his pre-putt routine, he would look at the hole and then back at the ball. He'd look at the hole again and then, as his eyes were coming back down the line toward the ball, he'd pull the trigger. By the time his eyes were back on the ball, the putter was at the top of the backswing and was ready to come forward and strike the putt. Being the inquisitive one, I asked, "Lee, what is it you're doing?"

"Well, my theory is that no matter how disciplined you are, if you're set up to a putt, your eyes will automatically be drawn to the moving object, the putter. I start my backswing while my eyes are on their way back to the ball and by the time they get there, the putter is still. Then, all I have to do is hit it."

It was pure genius. Actually, it was pure Lee Trevino. I had heard that one of the putting gurus had picked up on it and was trying to teach it to some of the flat-bellies, but I've never seen anyone actually implementing the technique.

I loved having a front row seat to Trevino's action. His homemade, self-taught swing was not very pretty, but I loved watching him hit it nonetheless. Prior to pulling the trigger, he bounced around and created as much rhythm as Chi Chi did. He picked it up, took it outside and then dropped it inside and held on through impact and then the finish. He went down after it as much as any player I had ever seen, his head dropping drastically at impact. It was a swing that he could duplicate, and one that wouldn't produce a shot going left. He was a master at eliminating one side of the golf course. His epitaph will read, "Here lies Lee Trevino; He talked to a fade, 'cuz he knew a hook wouldn't listen." Lee won eight majors cutting it and made a ton of dinero in the process. For a poor kid from Garland, Texas, he did pretty well for himself.

I was once with Gary at an event where Lee was the defending champion, and in his honor, they adorned the tournament program with a picture of him at the top of his swing. Lee's swing was awkward at any angle, and the picture was shot from one that made it look even worse. Lee himself said his swing was so bad, he looked like a caveman killing his lunch. Gary studied the photo and then said, "Oh my God, man, would you look at that! I think I'm going to be sick."

He had a horrified look on his face, like he had just witnessed a beheading, as he continued, "Look how much he's laying it off at the top. He's the only man in the universe who could get away with that swing, and that's only because he moves his lower body so well."

Gary predicted that Lee would be hampered by physical ailments later in his career because of the mechanics of that move. He was correct, as Lee was plagued with wrist and shoulder problems toward the latter part of his playing days.

After calculating the distance to the hole and choosing the correct weapon on the first fairway, Lee proceeded to hit his approach well past the hole. The same occurred over the course of the next two holes. Lee was befuddled, to say the least. "I know what the problem is," he declared. "Ball ain't climbin' the clubface."

"Sorry, ball isn't what?"

"Ball ain't climbin' the clubface," he reiterated. "I gotta' gear down a club."

I finally figured out what he meant. The fairways at TPC Summerlin were rock-hard underneath, so the club didn't penetrate the earth, but bounced off it. This caused the ball to leap off the face of the club instead of rolling up it before departure, which imparts spin and gives the shot height. When it came to golf, I thought I was fairly knowledgeable, but hanging around Lee made me feel inferior. His mind operated on a different wavelength when it came to the game.

That theory was reinforced the following day when we stepped on the tee of a par 3. Lee was the first to play and asked me what we had.

"Lee, you got 148 yards to the hole, just slightly downhill, and there's a slight breeze helping us here."

"Whaddya' like here, Lar?" he asked.

"A nice 8 iron. You can probably go with a big 9 if you like."

He winked at me and said, "Watch this," as he pulled the 7 iron out of the bag.

I stood there knowing that was way too much club, and pondered what he was up to. He went through his routine and hit it solidly toward the green, the ball landing on the front edge and taking a seat about 12 feet short of the hole. He gave me another wink as he put the club back in the bag. After receiving all the vitals from his caddie, the next player up on the tee asked, "What did Lee just hit here?"

His caddie replied, "7 iron."

"7 iron. Are you sure? I was thinking 9 here," the player retorted.

"I'm positive. He hit 7 iron and it looked like he hit it pretty good, too," the caddie said.

"All right, gimme the 8 iron."

He proceeded to hit a flush shot right at the pin that flew over the green. He scratched his head as he returned the club to the bag. When I had the opportunity, I asked Lee, "What the hell did I just see?"

"That was my rake," he announced proudly.

What I had just witnessed was golf's equivalent of an off-speed pitch in baseball. Lee took extra club, but took his hands out of the swing, basically dead-handing it. The arm speed was still there, which made it look like he hit it pretty hard. It was conniving and deceitful, and his fellow competitor fell for it hook, line and sinker. In a nutshell, it was a thing of beauty.

Over the course of the week with Lee, the conversation shifted to Gary, and more specifically, his eating and workout habits. Lee piped up and said, "That lil' son-of-a-bitch is a phony. I roomed with him at the British Open years ago and I just happened to look in his luggage. You know what I found in there? A case of damn Snickers bars. I'm serious. You ask him about it when you see him."

He also told me about a business venture that Gary talked him in to. Gary's true love was thoroughbred racehorses, and he had a stallion that he believed was a sure thing. He was convinced the horse was invincible, and got Lee to invest in it. So at the start of every month, Lee wrote a hefty check to help defray the cost of upkeep for the future Triple Crown winner. And after accepting each of these checks, Gary would reassure Lee that this horse was going to pay off, big time.

"You know what happened to that #$@&in' horse?" Lee asked me. "He got colic and died. Never ran a race. You ask Gary about that, too."

Lee was still playing pretty well in those days and winning wasn't as elusive as it was for Gary, but he never really got humming that week in Vegas. Truth be told, I was sincerely hoping for a much more productive week. Herman's caddying days were numbered, and Lee was going to need someone steady. As much as I loved packing for Gary, his winning days were a distant memory, and I was in the twilight of my caddie years. What better way to spend them than working for Lee Trevino? Herman did retire, and I threw my name in the hat to be a replacement, but Lee hired someone else. He said that he and Gary were too good of friends for me to come and work for him. I was pretty bummed because he was the Merry Mex...sometimes.

NEVER SAY NEVER

"I WILL NEVER ever caddie for that little son-of-a-bitch again…EVER!"

Just uttering those sentiments was tempting golf fate, and sealed my caddie future. I made the remark several years earlier about Chi Chi Rodriguez when he and I parted ways. Looking back, it was inevitable that I would someday pack for him again. That's just the way the Golfing Gods roll.

Allow me to fill in the blanks. When Gary Player and I split up, I was convinced that I had traversed my last fairway and tended my last pin. I was tearing the band-aid off in one quick motion, and was going to get serious about starting the next chapter of my life. I was going to venture into an alternate business—one that was based on my performance rather than the performance of someone else. What business was that? I didn't have a freakin' clue, but I was going to find it.

I felt my future was in a golf-related endeavor of some sort, because after all, I was Gary Player's and Chi Chi Rodriguez' caddie, for Pete's sake. I had a grandiose notion in my head that there was some easy, high paying position out there for someone with my impressive background that didn't require any education, training or physical labor. To quote Roberto De Vincenzo after he signed an incorrect scorecard at the '68 Masters, "Oh, what a stupid I am!"

Chi Chi in the pine straw.

After too many months of idle days in the desert and no real employment prospects on the horizon, stark reality struck me upside the head like an errant tee shot. I really didn't think this thing out very well. No potential employer gave a crap about who I caddied for; all they were concerned with was my education (or lack thereof), and my job skills (or lack thereof). The longer I went without finding my life's work, the further I sank into the depths of despair. In all my years on the planet, these were not the best of times.

The lifeline that pulled me back from the precipice came in the form of a call from none other than Chi Chi Rodriguez. I had never been happier to hear from a guy that I made disparaging remarks about 18 months earlier.

"Hey, Pards, I hear you're not doing anything right now. Why don't you come over to L.A. and work for me there?" he asked.

"Yeah, sure, Cheech, why not," I replied, trying like hell to mask my desperation. "I'll see you there."

And so it was time to crank up Team Rodriguez once again. The fact that I never thought I'd don a caddie bib again and now would be doing exactly that was a moot point. I was ecstatic to be getting out of the Desert and doing something constructive. The thought of generating some revenue almost made me giddy.

I made my way over to Wilshire Country Club for the Ralph's Senior Classic, and from the moment I stepped foot on the grounds, I had an uneasy feeling. It was as if I had taken a spacecraft to another planet to caddie. Even though I had been off the tour for only a year and a half, I felt totally out of place. I went from being a big fish in a little pond to being a fish out of water. There were a slew of new faces for both players and caddies. The coup de grace was watching a couple of caddies I had never seen before walking the golf course to prep for the tournament. Forget about pacing yardages or even using a yardage wheel. These two had a laser to measure yardage, and were wearing radio headsets to communicate with each other, as one held the laser and the other, the mirrored prism that reflected the beam back to the device. I think I even saw an altimeter hanging on the one's belt. They conversed back and forth as if they were mapping the surface of the moon.

I tried my hardest to get back in the groove over the course of the next couple of days. In the words of the great philosopher Yogi Berra, it was déjà-vu all over again as I, once again in my life, felt like the new kid in the caddie yard. Chi Chi played in the Pro-Am on Wednesday, and I was beginning to get my sea legs, until the morning of the first official round of the tournament when a catastrophic event occurred.

I was reaching into the trunk of my car to grab an empty plastic bag when my back decided to go out. I had never ever had an ounce of back trouble, and in a case of perfect timing, it decided to go on hiatus now. I was in so much pain that just the thought of a sneeze made me wince in agony. In all my years as a caddie, I had gotten it around the track more hung over than a Mexican on the 6th of May, and sicker than someone exposed to Anthrax, but in my current condition, there was absolutely no possible chance of me getting a golf bag five miles around a course.

I called Chi Chi's pilot to let him know there was no way I'd be able to work the first round. He told me not to worry about it and that Chi Chi could find someone to work for him, which I did not like the sound of. I feared that if he went out and played well with another caddie, it might get him to thinking, what the hell do I need Larry for? My fiancée whisked me to a chiropractor, who performed a series of adjustments and alignments on me. I had always thought of chiropractors as quacks that had aspirations of becoming MDs but couldn't make the grade and settled on being DCs. I thought of them as the mini-tour players of the medical world. However, I desisted from sharing my beliefs with the large gentleman who was bending me into a pretzel and then resting two-thirds of his 270-pound frame on me as I lay on the padded table.

In the midst of my treatment I gave Chi Chi's pilot a call to see who substituted for me and what Chi Chi shot. David informed me that Chi Chi's friend Hank, a local FBI agent who had no caddie experience, worked the day for him and more importantly, that Chi Chi fired a smooth opening round of 67 and was one shot off the lead. Hank was about as helpful as sunscreen at midnight when it came to caddying, and the fact that Chi Chi shot what he did led me to rethink my level of importance in the whole scoring equation. David asked me how I was faring, and after hearing the news he had just given me, I assured him I was going to be in working condition for the second round. This was an absolute exaggeration, as I had no idea if this alleged doctor's hocus pocus was going to do any good at all or if I would be able to get it around the following day. The fact of the matter was, after going through the previous 18 months of pathetic revenue generation, you could have hacked both my feet off with a dull saw and I still would have attempted to work the second round.

As soon as I hung up with David I told the chiropractor, "Doc, do everything you can to make me better, because I need to work tomorrow."

"Will do," he said. "How about acupuncture? It's been known to work wonders on back ailments."

"Sounds great," (even though it didn't sound great at all). "If you think it may work, give it a go!" I was so desperate, if he had told me castration would help I would have done it. I was getting married, so I knew it was going to happen sooner or later.

Testing the stability of my back the following morning reminded me of walking across a lake on very thin ice. I moved very timidly as I tried to assess if it was going to support me. Luckily, all the treatment I endured the previous day did some good, as I was going to be able to work the second round, even though I was extremely sore and tender. I hobbled gingerly around the course that day, and Chi Chi obliged me by bettering his first round by a shot. He was leading by one and in a good position to hoist the trophy the following day.

I was now feeling absolutely fabulous about the situation I was in, mostly because the previous 18 months of hell seemed to be coming to an end, and because Chi Chi hadn't been doing anything stellar on the golf course as of late. His best finish occurred at the PGA Seniors back in April when he finished tied for 4th. A strong Sunday finale would put me in excellent standing with him and his management team, and more importantly, line my pockets with some much-needed moolah.

Sunday, Chi Chi was in the day's final pairing with his old adversary Jim Colbert, who trailed by one but could cause some trouble if he got hot with the flat stick. They were neck-and-neck, along with Senior Tour newcomer Gil Morgan, who had just passed the half-century mark 11 days earlier.

The greens at Wilshire were suspect to begin with, and a week's worth of play had taken a serious toll on them. By late Sunday afternoon, as we were coming down the stretch, they were riddled with spike marks the size of speed bumps. Needless to say, for a man who putted as poorly as Chi Chi did on pure surfaces, this was not advantageous to our position. Then again, the thought occurred to me that this just might level the playing field and neutralize the good putters. This is the way a caddie is forced to think (or wish) when his man is shaky with the blade.

Chi Chi hung tough and stayed in contention right down to the wire. The trophy was going to have the name Rodriguez, Colbert or

Morgan engraved on it. Dr. Gil was in the group in front of us and posted the clubhouse lead at -11. Chi Chi was at -11 playing the last; a birdie would give us a win, and a par would put us in a playoff. I didn't want to consider any other option beyond those.

He hit a solid drive down the pipe, giving him a good look at the green with about 180 yards to go. I did my best to slow him down and discuss the elements affecting the shot. With a hint of a breeze hurting us, and a slight uphill elevation, we agreed that a nice 5 iron was in order. Chi Chi took dead aim and rifled it at the hole as I held my breath. The ball sailed through the air like a cruise missile, hit just short of the cup and then, instead of checking, took a leap like it landed on a runway. It eventually came to rest in some cabbage over the green, leaving us a slick downhill chip onto a green that was looking rougher than Charlie Sheen the morning after a bachelor party. Surprisingly, Chi Chi didn't gripe about the predicament, nor did I catch any flack about the club selection. To this day, I can't tell how that shot went as far as it did, but I knew one thing for certain... it had ugly written all over it.

Knowing him as well as I did, I seized the opportunity to inject my two cents. "Cheech, this is gonna be lightning fast coming down that hill. Just cozy it down there and we'll take care of this guy in a playoff. Don't be a hero with this thing."

I had barely finished my dissertation when he turned into Tom Watson behind the 17th green at Pebble in the '82 Open. "Pards...I'm gonna hole it."

Like I said, knowing the man as well as I did, this statement did not surprise me. God bless him, he played to win, and didn't give a hoot about finishing in second position. I stood back and watched nervously as he raced the chip past the hole, leaving a six-footer coming back up the hill through a minefield of the most treacherous spike marks I had ever seen. The fact that he left himself an uphill putt was the only saving grace. If someone had to make a six-footer to save your life, he's not the one you would want hitting it.

I tried in vain to pump his head full of positive thoughts, but he proceeded to put the tomahawk on it and never came close to sniffing the hole. It was pretty pathetic. Gil Morgan won his first in a long line of victories on the Senior PGA Tour, and I left another event thinking we should have won the damn thing. In retrospect, it's amazing how rapidly perspectives can change. If you had offered me a second place finish an hour before Chi Chi's life-saving phone call two weeks prior, I would have traded my first-born child just for the chance. Now, I was pissed off and dejected. The tempting whiff of victory will do that to you.

I was engaged to be married in early April of the next year, and my fiancée Lynne was traveling with me at the time. She's half Mexican and half Canadian, which makes her my little frozen burrito (she doesn't think it's all that funny either). Trevino used to razz me about her being Mexican. "Don't marry that Mexican broad, Larry. No sirree, it'll be O.J. in reverse. She'll cut ya'."

"Lee, we're getting married next year. The date is set," I responded.

"Well, alright, suit yourself. But remember one thing: if you get in an argument with her, do not go to sleep!"

Lynne and I had dated for quite some time, and now she was going to be out on the road with me to see the other side of the coin. We made our way from L.A. up to Napa for the tournament sponsored by Transamerica at Silverado Country Club. When I saw Chi Chi up north, he asked me where I was staying and I told him "some 'no tell motel' down the road." I never really cared much about where I stayed, as long as it was reasonably clean and had a bed, shower and a television. You have to remember, I was a Sod Hog in a past life, living in a tent on a driving range. Now that my better half was with me, I needed to scrutinize more thoroughly when choosing suitable digs. Chi Chi felt the same way and let me know as much. "Pards, you're with me and I don't want you and your future wife staying in no ratty hotels."

From then on, he had his pilot book a room for us where they were staying when making travel arrangements. There was no argument from me or Lynne. Chi Chi also made it clear that all our expenses were to be reimbursed by his office. I never tired of his generosity and was grateful that he was accepting Lynne as part of our traveling family.

Chi Chi never really got in the groove in Napa, but still had a respectable top 10 finish, which prompted one of the players to approach me and say, "Larry, you do an excellent job for Chi Chi. He needs you on his bag." I countered, "Thank you. Now would you go and tell him that?"

Next tour stop was El Dorado Hills outside of Sacramento for the Raley's Senior Gold Rush. The tournament had been played at Rancho Murrieta Country Club every year that I had been on the Senior Tour, but was now moved to Serrano Country Club. This was a bummer. It was to a seasoned tour caddie's benefit to have an event stay at one venue year after year. The course knowledge gained over time was invaluable, and gave you an edge over the other loopers who hadn't been there as many times or even better, at all. The pain endured from a miscue one year, could be a hard and valuable lesson learned for the next. For example, your man's in contention on Sunday and you're in perfect position on the 16th fairway. The flag is cut at the back of the green and there's a breeze coming from the right and helping just a bit. You're between clubs and you remember that last year, this hole played a little shorter than the distance and your man blew it over the green into rough nastier than a flattened porcupine and had Bob Hope's brother, No Hope, of getting it up and down. He didn't, and you heard about it all the way up until you put the clubs in the trunk of the car and he drove away. You wisely advise your man to go with less club.

Another plus to revisiting a tournament locale was that it reduced the amount of prep time needed prior to the tournament. If a venue was the same one we played the last five years, I'd rip around the course faster than Mario Andretti just to see if any changes had been made to it. I was also wise enough to keep my topographic drawings of all the greens, just in case Chi Chi started that crap again. Wizzie was renowned for doing his course preparation looking from the window in the bar of the clubhouse.

When I'm talking golf with someone and I tell them my background in the game, many inquire why I chose to leave the profession. It's apparently hard for some to fathom why one would leave such a unique and exciting way to make a living. While I fully understand how they could assume that it's an absolute dream job, the fact is that I left because I pined for family life. There was one instance that put everything into stark perspective and began my exodus from professional caddying. I guess you could call it the straw that broke the caddie's back.

Chi Chi and I were standing on the 11th tee of Serrano Country Club discussing club selection during the first round of the tournament. He was the first to play and the guinea pig of the group, as the other two golfers he was paired with were afforded the luxury of seeing what he hit and where the shot finished. This information is worth its weight in gold, which is why Chi Chi always harped about outdriving his playing partners. He wanted to know what they hit into the green, even if it meant walking across the fairway and looking into the other player's bag. If I was out with one of my friends, they saved me the trip by flashing me a hand signal of what their man was hitting. Under the rules of golf, I must admit that this was an infraction, as players and caddies are not allowed to ask for, or offer any information to another player or caddie. Only through observation is a player or caddie allowed to glean information from another, but I always figured, what's the difference if I go and look or my buddy saves me the trip and tells me? Just call it our 'don't ask, just tell' policy.

The 11th at Serrano is a par 3 of about 180 yards with a healthy elevation drop of around 100 feet to a green that is guarded in the front by a creek and a bunker behind. The flag this day was cut front right, really bringing the hazard into play. I went into my normal pre-shot banter, "Cheech, we got 162 yards to the right front edge, 169 to the hole and 182 to the back edge. There's a little breeze hurtin' from the right. There's plenty of room behind the hole."

The last statement was a very important one and you must understand the psychology of the verbiage used. Working for Chi Chi, I couldn't just come out and say, "We can't be short here. That flag is cut close to that hazard." That is a very negative statement and if he happened to hit it in that hazard, I would be on the hook for it, whether he hit the shot properly or not. I'd catch an ear full of, "Pards, that was a really negative statement. You brought that hazard to my attention." I'd been down that road before, and after years of getting my hand burned, knew enough not to touch that hot stove.

Chi Chi stood looking down at the green with his hand on one of the irons in the bag. "Pards, whadda' you like here, 8 iron?"

Funny, I had been with him so long, I knew he was going to like 8 iron. Making sure to avoid the dreaded vapor lock, I chimed right in, "I like 7 here, Cheech."

"Pards, I think I can get 8 there," he retorted.

"I think you can get 8 there too, but it doesn't leave much margin for error. There's plenty of room behind the hole," referring back to the basic premise that the one place you didn't want to visit was Shortsville.

"I really think I can get 8 there, Pards," he stated once again.

"Cheech, your name is on the golf bag. It's your call," I said, and then quickly followed with, "The wind is hurting from the right, Cheech. Carve a little 7 iron up into it. C'mon, sauté it in there."

There was a brief period of uncomfortable silence as he stood looking down at the green, his hand still clutching the head of the 8 iron. Then he quickly grabbed the head of the 7 iron and pulled it from the bag and announced, "Okay, Pards, you win. I'll sauté the 7 in there."

About this time I was engulfed in the horrible reality that I had just put my ass on the line on a shot being played on a golf course that I barely knew. If at any point in this book I told you that I never pulled the wrong club, I apologize, because I was lying through my teeth. In fact, once, I not only talked Chi Chi into hitting the wrong club, I apologized afterward, to which he quickly replied, "Don't worry about it, Pards. It hurts you more than it hurts me. I don't need the money; I'm already rich! You're not."

I had a sickening feeling in the pit of my stomach as I looked around at the throng of people around the tee box. If this didn't work out, I was going to get torn a new one in front of thousands of strangers. Chi Chi put a good swing on it and executed the shot just the way I envisioned it. The ball reached its apex in the sky and began its descent to the green. I was mumbling under my breath, "Get down. C'mon baby, get the #$@& down." I prepared myself for the incoming verbal barrage if this shot landed in the back bunker. The ball finally completed its journey, hitting just past the pin and then screwed back, right in the jar. Chi Chi had just made the fourth hole-in-one of his professional career! The crowd erupted into a thunderous roar, and Chi Chi, playing off them, started one of his patented dance routines. I let out a sigh of relief that would have powered every wind turbine off the coast of Scandinavia.

The fanfare eventually simmered down. Chi Chi put the club back in the bag and didn't say a word to me about what just transpired. No "good call," or "way to pull the right club Pards," or "that's what I pay you for." Nothing. I had been a professional tour caddie long enough to know that he wasn't going to make a public proclamation to the spectators that I was the one who talked him into hitting 7 iron, and that if I hadn't, they would have been deprived of witnessing one of the biggest spectacles in the game. I also knew that some golfers decline from giving positive feedback to their caddies because they're afraid our egos will become so overinflated that our heads will explode. I certainly wasn't expecting Chi Chi to get down on bended knee and kiss my ring, but a pat on the head and an 'atta boy' wouldn't have killed him.

A couple of holes later, Chi Chi had a long putt from 35 feet away, below the hole. Now, just for a moment, I need you to refer back to my dissertation about new tournament venues and how much of a drag they were because the learning curve started anew. This course was set in some foothills, and the greens were a bit on the tricky side to read. It was difficult to obtain an accurate lay of the land, and in some cases, it was what Chi Chi referred to as an 'optical disillusion.' A surface that appeared to be sloping one way was actually sloping the other.

I made my way around the green, stalking Chi Chi's line like a prowler casing his next victim. I always found that looking at a putt from as many angles as possible was the best way to decipher which way a putt was going. After making my way back to Chi Chi's ball, where he was crouched behind it, I took the standard caddie position behind him and started my oral thesis. "Cheech," I instructed. "You're going uphill most of the way here, until that ridge about five feet short of the hole where it levels off. The green is sloping left at the hole and the grain is into you and to the left. I like this about two and a half feet outside right. It's gonna be slow up to the top of the ridge. Give it enough speed to get it up there, where it will make a left hand turn to the hole."

I proceeded to the flagstick, where I took my stance two and a half feet right of the hole. I always tried to stand on the intended target line if possible, to give Chi Chi a good visual image of his line. He addressed his putt and took a pretty healthy swipe at it, the ball beginning its trek directly toward me. Line and speed appeared to be right as it approached the top of the ridge. Now all the ball needed to do was die gently to the left as it lost its speed. We'd have our two putts and be on to the next hole. Unfortunately, it made absolutely no attempt to move left, and actually started drifting a tad to the right, eventually coming to rest about four and a half feet from the hole. This was far from the length of putt he wanted to be left with, and I was fairly certain I was going to hear about it.

"Godammit, Pards, NICE READ!" he bellowed sarcastically across the green for me and 10,000 spectators to hear.

Word spread like wildfire around the course that he made ace at the 11th, so we had even more people watching than normal.

"YOU'RE READING THESE GREENS LIKE RAY CHARLES!" he followed.

I had heard this line before and it really didn't bother me all that much, even though I could see people whispering in the gallery, and knew the topic of that whispering was my agronomical miscalculation. But then came a little beauty that I hadn't heard before. "HEY, PARDS, YOU FORGOT TO BRING YOUR DOG," insinuating that I needed a seeing-eye dog. To this day, I cannot tell you why this frosted my ass so much, but it did. The fact that I heard spectators snickering about my faux pas pissed me off even more.

Chi Chi made the putt he was left with, literally by a stroke of luck. About this time, I was madder than a Bernie Madoff investor as I tore the head cover from the driver and handed it to him. I needed to get as far away from him as possible, so I decided to forecaddie down the par 5, 14th. Lynne walked beside me outside the gallery ropes as I vented, "Can you believe this little son-of-a-bitch? I talk him out of hitting the wrong club two holes ago and the prick makes an ace AND HE NEVER SAYS A #$@&ING WORD TO ME, and then I misread a green and he belittles me in front of half of Sacramento. I gotta' tell ya', I don't know how much more of this shit I can take."

Chi Chi never made a serious run at the top of the leader board that week, but still had a respectable top 10 finish.

It was coming to the latter part of the season, and Lynne and I made our way back to the Desert for some down time, even though I had only worked three events. The drive to southern California gave me some time to contemplate all that had occurred over the course of the past couple of weeks, and I came to the conclusion that there was light at the end of the tunnel, and it wasn't a guy holding a flashlight. Christmas was coming up and I had some money coming for the events I had just worked, and my fiancée was welcomed into our itinerant clan. The drive also provided me with some time to replay the hole-in-one story over and over and over…

After a restful and enjoyable holiday season, I began to prep for the upcoming year on the road. First up was a tournament in my back yard, and one that was a complete surprise. Arnold Palmer was a close friend of Bob Hope, and even though Bob was no longer of this world, Arnold continued to play in Hope's event for ceremonial purposes. Unfortunately, The King was diagnosed with prostate cancer sometime in late 1996 and wasn't going to be able to play, so Chi Chi was asked to substitute.

I had no illusions about the outcome of the week. It was going to be fun, as Chi Chi was in the celebrity group, which meant he'd be playing with the athletes and movie stars, but I had more chance of dating Cindy Crawford than he had of making the cut. He was asked to participate in the Tuesday afternoon shoot-out where they start out with 10 players and eliminate one per hole over the course of nine holes.

Two things became very apparent to me during this golf extravaganza. First, Chi Chi could still hold his own playing with the round-bellies, but it wasn't feasible for him to compete with the younger guys (the flat bellies). Lastly, he had more personality than all the other nine golfers combined. He was funnier than hell and gave the gallery their money's worth. It didn't hurt that Gary McCord emceed the thing; the two of them together were like Rowan and Martin. A couple of the younger guys tried to jump on board the good humor band wagon, but they say you can't fix stupid, and you can't be funny, if you're not funny.

As I expected, Chi Chi whiffed the cut and I had the weekend free, but luckily, didn't have to travel too far to get home. The week really put into perspective how fortunate I was to be embedded in the Senior Tour during a very special era of its history. Sure, I could have been making a lot more money packing for a flat-belly, but it was priceless hanging out with the cast of characters on the Senior Tour. I had a revelation after working the Hope that week and came to one conclusion about the PGA Tour. It's like watching Pamela Anderson on television; you can mute the volume and derive just as much pleasure.

A couple of weeks later we made our way to the east coast for the Florida swing. The ether had worn off from my triumphant return of late last season, and Chi Chi and I settled back into our routine. We were right back to acting like a married couple. His play was not exactly stellar, and there was always an excuse to blame it on me.

In Naples, the golf course maintenance crew drove the mowers down the right half of the fairway toward the green, made a semi-circle at the green and came back toward the tee on the left. This meant that half the fairway was down grain and the other half was into it. Chi Chi kept driving down the left side and would get no roll off the tee shot. A couple of times it actually came backward a foot. He was getting out-driven by a player he normally flew it by, except the other player kept driving down the right side of the fairway and getting an extra 90 yards of roll. Chi Chi got so pissed off about it that after the round he tersely instructed me to go tell the greens keeper to have the crew cross cut the fairways, which takes considerably more time. I pretended like I was going and went and had a beer in the clubhouse.

The next week he left a putt hanging on the lip of the cup, and claimed it was because the grounds crew wasn't using the heavy metal ring when cutting the hole in the green. He sternly instructed me to go and tell the greens keeper to make sure the crew uses the heavy metal ring when cutting the holes. I pretended like I was going and went and had a beer in the clubhouse.

He also belly-ached continuously about what he perceived as a run of very bad luck. He claimed that the wind was always in his face.

"Can you believe the wind is in my face again? It was in my face the last hole, too. Pards, my luck is so bad, the only time I'm downwind is when someone's got bad breath." I laughed without letting him see me.

I was also catching more than my fair share of crap for stuff that didn't have anything to do with me. Normally, I could just let it roll off my back, but as I said previously, I was getting married in April and my fiancée was traveling with me. So instead of getting off the golf course and letting off steam in my usual way, I was forced to listen to wedding songs and pick out doilies. A couple of times I was so close to losing it that I would have eaten a cyanide capsule if I had one.

A couple of weeks later we were back in Scottsdale for The Tradition, one of the Majors on the Senior Tour. One morning while eating breakfast, Chi Chi told Lynne and me to meet him and his pilot, David, in the hotel lobby afterward.

We got in the car and started on a journey somewhere, the final destination a secret. After a lengthy drive, we finally pulled into an RV dealership.

"Cheech, you thinking about buying a motorhome?" I asked.

"Don't worry about it, Pards," he answered.

A man in a tie approached us, and after introducing himself, brought us over to a gorgeous coach that was equipped with slide-outs and all the bells and whistles. He promptly began his canned speech on all the features of the vehicle, and was directing his pitch at me. At one point I noticed a $260,000 price tag. The tour completed, Chi Chi asked, "Well, Pards, what do you think?"

"About what?" I asked.

"About this motor home!" he shot back.

"It's beautiful Cheech, but why do you need a motor home? You've got a jet."

"It's not for me, Pards. It's for you. I'll buy this, and you and Lynne can travel in it. I'll get you a gas card to cover the fuel expense," he finished.

I had been with Chi Chi long enough to have a pretty good idea what he was going to say in most situations, but I surely wasn't expecting this.

"Well, whaddya' think?" he asked.

I'm usually not at a loss for words, but I was caught flat-footed, and I was speechless. Lynne and I canvassed the vehicle like we were touring a luxury condo, and in a quiet moment away from the others, had a brief conversation.

"Well, what do you think? Do you want to travel the country in this thing?"

"I don't know," she replied. "I mean, it is gorgeous. Do you?" About now, you're probably thinking we were nuts not to jump at this chance, but you need to consider a few key factors. First, I had done more than my fair share of driving across the country, and the novelty of being on the open road had long worn off. When we flew commercially, Chi Chi covered the cost, or we flew on his jet. If I had to be in Florida by Wednesday, I could fly out from the west coast on Tuesday. Driving the same route meant I would have to leave a week earlier. Also, driving across the massive state of Texas would be a real trip to Disneyland, seeing as I would be piloting a land yacht and the wind blows so hard in The Lone Star State that the birds choose to walk. Lastly and most importantly, Mrs. Rodriguez had a little bit of a shopping problem, and when I saw the cargo hold underneath this coach, I was absolutely certain that thing would turn into a rolling Costco. Chi Chi's jet could accommodate up to 12 passengers comfortably and I remember flying on it several times when it barely sat three of us, it was so packed to the gills with stuff. I tread on thin ice once when I compared her to Imelda Marcos, and thankfully she took it as a compliment.

We left the RV dealership and I refrained from approaching the subject, but my mind was made up. When we got back to the hotel, I took David off to the side and told him it was a nice offer but I wasn't interested. He assured me he would smooth it over and get Chi Chi off the idea. David was a bit bummed because he held an ulterior motive. He knew he'd be able to buy the thing cheap from Chi Chi a couple of years down the road. It must be nice to be wealthy and have that kind of money burning a hole in your pocket, because David succeeded in getting Cheech to forget about buying that motor home. Instead, he wound up buying a $350,000 boat that he used twice and ended up selling at a loss. When I asked Chi Chi why he got rid of it, he told me he didn't want to end up like Amelia Earhart. I was tempted to tell him that, if that was a big concern, he should sell his plane and not his boat, but I just let it go.

Tommy Aaron has always had a hair up his ass about me, and I'm not quite sure why. Whatever the reason, the man really loathed me, and I derived some sick pleasure from the fact that he did.

We were paired with him at The Tradition and playing the 18th hole, a reachable par 5. Chi Chi hit a lousy drive and was forced to lay up, while Tommy waited for the green to clear before he went for it. I decided to make my way up toward the green so I could get a jump on calculating Chi Chi's yardage to the hole. This entailed crossing the fairway about 200 yards ahead of Tommy, but George Archer was putting out in the group ahead of us. As I crossed, I heard someone yelling behind me and figured out Tommy was the culprit. He was screaming like a banshee, his arms flailing wildly. I muttered under my breath, "What the #$@& is his problem?" as I walked.

After we completed the round and I was exiting the scoring tent, he confronted me. "Don't you ever get in my way when I'm playing. Do you hear me? EVER!"

"Tommy, George Archer was still putting out. You had to wait!" I shot back. The altercation over, Tommy stormed off. Chi Chi came over and asked what the problem was and, after hearing the story, instructed me, "Pards, go knock him out! I want you to go and drop him like a turd from a tall horse!"

As close as I was to the end of my tenure as a professional tour caddie, I gave it strong consideration. I'm no Chuck Norris, and there were a couple of players on the Senior Tour I wouldn't want to mix it up with, even at their age, but I was fairly certain I could kick Tommy's skinny ass.

The Legends of Golf was relocated to the Desert and played at the infamous PGA West Stadium Course for a couple of years in the mid-90s. Chi Chi was paired with big hitter, Jim Dent in 1997. I received a call from David on Friday night instructing me to meet Chi Chi on the back of the range at 6:30 a.m.

"David, we don't tee off until 12:40 p.m. tomorrow. Why the hell would I need to meet him on the back of the range that early?" I asked. "

Because Sam's giving him a lesson," he replied.

"I'll be there!" was my response, knowing which Sam he was referring to.

Chi Chi was not hitting it anywhere, especially off the tee. He was getting up there in years but with the aid of technology, he could still pump it out there when he wanted to, usually. For some reason, he lost that ability and asked Sam "The Slammer" Snead for a little help. I'd happily empty a latrine to spend some time around this living legend of the game, so getting up a tad early was no big deal. I also informed my new wife that her attendance was required for photographic purposes. I wanted her to get some shots of us, knowing as old as Sam was, it might be our last chance to do so.

We showed up as the sun rose, and Chi Chi and Sam were already there. I said good morning to Sam, but he looked right through me to stare at Lynne. He had always been renowned as being pretty smooth with the opposite sex, and didn't mind one bit being introduced to her. She was wearing a tight-fitting sweater that I bought her at Augusta, which showcased her voluptuous figure. He eyeballed her pretty good with a nasty smirk on his face. I wasn't sure if he was happy to see The Masters logo or the large breast that was underneath it.

They got down to the business at hand, with Chi Chi doing a quick warm-up and then pulling out his driver. Sam watched quietly, his arms folded in front of him, as Chi Chi popped a couple off. It didn't take Sam very long to decipher where the problem was. He talked to Chi Chi about grip pressure, getting him to loosen up and get the club behind him more. It helped immensely, as Chi Chi started to hit it harder with more carry on it.

Me & Sam Snead at PGA West.

The lesson complete, we packed up our gear. "Mr. Snead, can I get a couple of pictures, please?" I asked.

"Sure," he responded.

Sam, Chi Chi and I mugged for the camera while Lynne snapped a few pictures. Once done, Sam started to walk away when I asked, "Uh, Mr. Snead, can I get a shot of you and my wife?"

Not surprisingly, he answered, "Why, sure," that crooked smile adorning his face. He pulled her in tight with his arm as they assumed a pose. This was before the days of digital photography, so it was taking a bit of time as I manipulated the 35mm lens. I could tell Sam didn't mind at all and decided to have some fun with it. Dropping the camera from in front of my face, I said, "Don't worry, Mr. Snead. I'll take my time."

Without any hesitation and an ear-to-ear grin, he shot back in a diabolical tone, "Don't take too long!" Chi Chi broke into laughter and blurted out, "Pards, you better listen to him. You take too long and she'll be his!"

Air Rodriguez was chock full leaving the Desert, as Chi Chi invited Sam, his nephew J.C., X, my old boss Orville Moody, and Bob Goalby to join us. After completion of the tournament, we all made our way to the Palm Springs airport to wait for the arrival of the jet. As we waited, Sam entertained us with jokes and stories that were fairly clean to begin with, but got progressively worse. He'd start to tell one, look at Lynne with inhibitions about continuing, and then throw caution to the wind and carry on. I heard more sheep jokes in that 60 minutes than I heard in my whole life.

Question: Where does a professional tour caddie take his new bride on a honeymoon? Answer: A golf tournament. Where else?

I am embarrassed to admit I took Lynne to West Palm Beach, Florida, for the PGA Seniors *on our honeymoon.* Now you might say there are worse places to go than West Palm Beach for a honeymoon, and you'd be correct, but understand that I was still going to work a golf tournament. Let me put it into perspective for you. I went to Maui approximately 12 times over the years to work the event there, but all I ever saw was the airport, the golf course, my digs for the week and some bars and restaurants. When I returned several years later on a proper vacation, I was sipping a cocktail in a restaurant in Lahaina after a day of sunbathing and snorkeling, and my wife asked, "Why do you have that goofy smile on your face?" I replied, "I just realized that this is a damn nice place to visit!"

I promised Lynne that someday I would take her to some romantic locale like Paris or Venice for a real honeymoon, but you know the adage; life is what happens when you're busy making other plans, and now, one child and two grandchildren later, I still haven't taken her to these places.

Flying 35,000 feet above the west en route to West Palm Beach, I rested comfortably in the knowledge that if I had opted for the motorhome, I'd be three days into a journey aboard the U.S.S. Winnebago, hating life and wondering what the hell I was thinking.

A couple of weeks later we were in the hospitable city of Birmingham, Alabama for the Bruno's Memorial Classic, paired with football quarterback legends Bart Starr and Brett Favre in the Pro-Am. When Favre caught a glimpse of my new wife, he took the opportunity to sidle up to me and say, "Son, you married way up." I recently asked her if she received any text messages or pictures from him.

Another event occurred that week that was well beyond anything I would have ever expected to happen, especially at that point in time. I've painted a very thorough picture of how a player/caddie relationship ebbs and flows over time, just like any other union. There are good times and bad, wins and losses, and eventually the relationships end. It's also no secret that I was dangling precariously at the end of my caddying rope and that I yearned to make a break from the nomadic lifestyle of a pro jock.

My relationship with Chi Chi had run its course and was tenuous at best, and I knew it was only a matter of time before we parted ways once again. That being said, as I was setting Chi Chi up on the driving range that week and I spilled the balls out on the tee, out of nowhere he said to me, "Pards, I know I give you a lot of shit for stuff that has nothing to do with you. I just want you to know that you're my friend and I love you."

My first thought was to ask, "Who are you and what have you done with the *real* Chi Chi Rodriguez?"

This came out of left field, and over the course of all the time I worked for him, he never expressed that type of emotion. It was as if all the hell and anxiety he put me through over the four years I worked for him was forgiven and forgotten with that one statement. It also told me that, deep down, he cared about me and was sorry for treating me poorly. "I love you too," I replied. "It's been a privilege and an honor to work for you."

We were at The Country Club of the South outside Atlanta for the Nationwide event about a month later, and Chi Chi was back to his old tricks. The shit was rolling downhill and I was at base camp. I was pissed at myself for not recording his speech to me in Birmingham so I could play it back whenever I needed a spiritual pick-me-up. It got so bad on the course that after one of the rounds, a friend of Chi Chi's said to me, "Larry, I like Chi Chi and he's my friend, but I wouldn't take that shit from any golfer." I found this statement amusing because he was outside the ropes and the blast zone. I was inclined to tell him, "Oh yeah, then you wouldn't be a professional caddie for very long."

They say death and taxes are the only absolutes in life, but they're wrong. The fact that I was going to get the axe was just as certain. Things got so rough at the Senior Open that I was almost goading Chi Chi into firing me. It worked, because after completion of the tournament, Chi Chi met me in front of the clubhouse and announced, "Pards, I got some bad news and I got some good news."

"Okay, I noticed I'm getting the bad news first. What is it?" I asked.

"Stick a fork in you—you're finished. I'm puttin' you out to pasture," he declared.

Well, that was no huge revelation. "And the good news?"

"The good news is I got you a job selling cars. You're going to work at Desert Lexus." He was friends with the owner and had it set up.

And so my time as a professional tour caddie came to an abrupt end. I never hauled a professional golfer's bag around a golf course again. Incidentally, I worked at Desert Lexus for the next six years and made a comfortable living there. Chi Chi Rodriguez himself came in and bought two cars from me valued at around $120,000, and he needed more cars about as much as Tiger needed more mistresses.

Life is funny, because my wife always said she didn't want to marry a caddie, but she did. And she certainly never wanted to marry a car salesman, but she did that too. Once I told her I was considering getting into politics and she said very definitively, "That's where I draw the line. I will be down the road!"

The 1979 Coca-Cola commercial featuring Mean Joe Green is considered one of the best commercials ever made. If you've ever seen it, you know how heartwarming it is. If I had to choose one commercial to symbolize what is was like to caddie for Juan "Chi Chi" Rodriguez, that's the one I'd pick. Caddying for him was like living that scenario on a weekly and sometimes daily basis. Chi Chi was not only an ambassador of golf, but an ambassador of goodwill, and the wonderful things he did for people, and more specifically for children, are etched in my memory for eternity. I know that I painted a bleak picture at some points, especially toward the end, but you have to understand that a lot happens in the heat of battle when you're in the pressure cooker of professional golf. To be fair, the Coke commercial would symbolize 95% of my time on his bag; the other 5% would be a Rolaids commercial.

I did have my hands full with him on the golf course at times, but that's part of the package when caddying for him, and the positives dwarfed the negatives. I bear part of the responsibility, as I probably over-stayed my welcome. The fact remains that I was unbelievably fortunate to have a front row seat to one of the most skilled shot-makers and genuine showmen to ever play the game. I loved that he wanted to give something back to the thousands of people who came to watch him, and he did that, not only with his skill, but with his wit, and with his love.

TOP TEN CADDIE
BLUNDERS

I want to mix it up a bit and give you a list of The Top Ten Caddie Blunders (as I see them). Some will be new to you, as they occurred on the European circuit, others are quite familiar and received a lot of press. I've ranked them in order of magnitude, starting with the most benign.

10

Number 10 is from the European tour and involves Wizzie, my partner in crime. He was working for a dashing stud from Italy named Baldovino Dassu. In those days the money wasn't nearly what it is today, and it was very possible that if your horse just barely made the cut, you'd have to work the weekend for a mere pittance. If the tournament venue was a good locale, a cost/benefit analysis made it clear that it wasn't in your best interest to just barely make the cut. Your time would be better spent hitting the local hot spots. I am inclined to tell you that this was a caddie's perspective, not a pro's. Wizzie's man was teetering on the brink coming down the stretch. It could go either way, but the bottom line was, if he made the cut, it would be by the skin of his nose.

Standing on the 18th fairway, Dassu was right on the cut line. Wiz took matters into his own hands; an Agatha was in order. It was the perfect time for a mystery yardage. Wiz told Bal that he had 165 to the pin when actually he was 151 yards away. He pulled his 6 iron out of the bag and proceeded to flush it, dead at the flag. He held his pose as the shot soared through the air. The ball airmailed the green, nailed a woman in the breast and then caromed back onto the green, three feet from the hole. Meanwhile, Dassu paced the yardage to the hole and was well aware of the mistake. Wiz was going to hear about that. To make matters worse, he holed the putt, allowing him to make the cut by one shot. Had Wiz just given him the correct yardage, he most probably would have hit it 20 from feet from the hole, 2 putted for par and missed the cut by one. The Golfing Gods really have a sense of humor.

9

The rules of golf allow a player to carry a maximum of 14 clubs in his bag. The penalty for violation of this rule is two shots per hole, with a maximum of four. Duncan was a caddie on the European tour who let his man tee off with 15 clubs in the bag, not once, but twice, in consecutive rounds. We promptly nicknamed him, what else, but '15 Club Duncan.' Not really the kind of label you want if you're a professional tour caddie. "Have you seen "Wrong Ball Larry?" Or how about "Where's Incorrect Scorecard Malestic?"

8

Scotty Gilmour, the man responsible for my becoming a pro jock, is the recipient of the number eight spot. Hooking up with a good bag is a lot like surfing. You want to search for that perfect wave, get on it, ride that baby as long as you can, and avoid the dreaded wipeout. Hopefully, you'll pick one that's about to crest and stay away from those that already have. Scotty wasn't a very good surfer. He had the knack of bailing out at the wrong time. He left Nick Price (who went on to become a superstar) to work for Greg Norman. He then split up with Norman (who went on to become the world's #1 player for 300+ weeks). He prematurely left Paul Lawrie (British Open Champion), Jean Van De Velde (should have been the British Open Champion), Wayne Grady (PGA Champion), and most recently, Michael Campbell (yes, the one with his name engraved on the U.S. Open trophy). I once told Scotty that a sure-fire way to succeed in this business was to pick up the bags that he left behind.

7

Back to Europe. Rick the Rattler was so named because he was always rattling on about something. He had a trailer that he lived in while following the tour. He was caddying for Wayne Westner, a crazy South African, and had brought his clubs and shoes back to his trailer overnight for security purposes. The following morning, while the Rattler was enjoying a cup of tea in his trailer, Wayne Westner was standing on the 1st tee wondering where Rick was, and more importantly, his golf clubs and shoes. Apparently, Rick wasn't very adept at reading a pairings sheet and thought they were off later. Thank God Westie took his putter back to his room with him that night. When it was evident that Rick wasn't showing and risking disqualification, Westner played the 1st hole with his putter, wearing street shoes, and made a par 4. Rick showed up the next hole, needless to say, it was his last week on Westie's bag.

6

I'm staking a personal claim to the sixth biggest caddie blunder. What did I do? I got out of the business too early. Don't get me wrong. I love my life and I don't miss the packing, the travel and the restaurant food, but when I see the money that some of these guys are making out there, I'm sick to my stomach. You can caddie for a no-name on the Uruguayan Tour and make 200 large per year.

5

Stevie Williams, you are the winner of space number five. The blunder? Dropping Tiger's 9 iron in the lake at the Ryder Cup several years ago. I am aware that shit happens, but I couldn't believe *that* shit. The only thing more amazing than the event itself was Tiger's reaction. He laughed! I got bitched out by Crampton years ago for whistling on the golf course. If I would've lost one of his implements, my ass would have been down the road. I'm not saying that I was the best club puller in the history of professional caddying, but when it came to holding on to them, I was most definitely in the top 10.

4

The fourth on this prestigious list is most probably the hardest to believe. If someone were to tell you that two professional golfers, (and their caddies!) played the wrong hole in the 3rd round of a tour event, you'd say, "No way! Can't happen!" But it did.

Kent Kluba and Rafael Alarcon were paired together for Saturday's round of a European tour event being held just outside Paris. There was a set of train tracks that dissected the golf course, which had to be crossed to get from the 11th green to the 12th tee. Somehow, all four of these brainiacs ended up crossing the tracks and going to the 14th tee, a hole that ran parallel to 12th. It wasn't until they hit their shots to the green that they realized their mistake. A kid named Andy, one of our crew, was one of the two loopers in the group. Previously known as 'Big Ears' due to his unusually large auditory organs, he was immediately re-nicknamed 'Gazumba', which was derived from an off-color joke about a 'wrong hole' (use your imagination).

3

If your man is fiddling around with drivers or wedges looking for that perfect one, you need to be all-the-more careful. This next blunder is one of the 'too many weapons' variety. Ian Woosnam teed off at The Open with an extra club in his bag. Woosie is a pretty cool guy, and I remember him taking the heat off his caddie by saying that it was his fault. I totally disagree. If you want to become a professional tour caddie, remember these five basic rules and you'll do fine:

1. Show up on time.
2. Never miss a great opportunity to shut up.
3. Make sure your man hits the right ball.
4. Make sure your man signs a correct scorecard.
5. Make absolutely sure there are only 14 clubs in the bag.

As I stated, Woosie is one of the cooler players, so he didn't sack his caddie, even though he was disqualified from the British Open. The axe came down on him the following week when he arrived late to the course. Even Woosie had his limits.

2

Number two is, without a doubt, one of the toughest golf-related events I've ever witnessed. I was literally screaming at the television. Watching Jean Van De Velde play the last hole of The Open as his 3 shot lead vanished like a fart in the wind was as excruciating to watch as Chi Chi over a four-footer for par, or a Colin Montgomerie interview. I've never felt so helpless. I asked Scotty Gilmour what he would have done if he was still on Van De Velde's bag and they were playing that 18th hole. He told me he would have started snapping the heads off the clubs, starting with the driver, all the way down to the 5 iron. I can still hear him saying, "For #$@&s sake! He coulda' hit 3, 6 irons on that #$@&ing green and 3 whacked it and still won the #$@&ing thing!" Too bad he wasn't on the bag.

1

And now, the moment you've all been waiting for (drum roll, please). Actually, the biggest blunder in caddie history, as I see it, is the mother of all no-brainers.

Mike 'Fluff' Cowan getting canned by Tiger Woods was golf's equivalent of the Kennedy assassination. Everyone remembers where they were when Fluff bit the big one. I knew he was done 30 days before it happened. One of my old compadres was a club rep on the PGA Tour, and he was a very reliable inside source. He called me out of the blue and said, "You're NOT going to believe this one!" I couldn't wait to sink my teeth into some juicy caddie gossip.

"Fluff is history." he said. Then he went on tell me about how Tiger was sick of having to wait on the 1st tee, ready to play a practice round, while Fluff was somewhere signing autographs, or doing a TV interview. He was popping out of suitcases on T.V. commercials and doing radio ads. I think I saw him modeling underwear on a billboard.

Fluff violated the #1 rule when caddying for a big name player. It's not your show. You are just along for the ride. Don't start believing your own press. As someone snidely once told me, "You caddies shouldn't take yourselves so goddamn seriously. After all, you're just a bunch of glorified skycaps."

Fluff may be telling people that he likes where he's at and that he has a great gig with Jim Furyk, and that may be so, but I'd bet the farm that losing the best seat on the Tiger Train was more painful than a scorching case of herpes. I mean, how hard can it be to caddie for Tiger? Apparently, you can jettison equipment at will, just to amuse him. The only one more devastated than Fluff when he got whacked must have been his wife, followed very closely by his banker.

And there you have it, my list of the biggest shanks in caddie history. I have one final thought…I sure hope that I don't occupy another spot on this list by writing this book.

ODDS AND ENDS

THANK GOD FOR the First Amendment. It affords me the platform to address some personal observations and conclusions I have come to, as well as share some iniquities that I have had the displeasure of experiencing.

A Gripe about Grips

It bugs me when the topic of conversation turns to golf and the person I'm speaking with demonstrates a golf swing with a fist cup grip. You know, the one where they make a fist with one hand and then wrap the other around it. I know this is a little thing, but I have never seen anyone actually play the game with that grip, and frankly, I don't think it would be possible. I once watched a man play cross-handed, and really well at that. Charlie Owens was a fine player on the Senior Tour back in the 80s, and he played the game left hand over right. That being said, if someone were to do an air golf swing with a cross-handed grip I might be inclined to give them the benefit of the doubt, but the moment someone mimics a golf swing with a fist cup grip, I know he or she can't play a lick. The same is true for the exact opposite. If you ask a golfer to see his grip, even without a club, and you know the game at all, you can get a pretty good idea if the person has any game whatsoever. I had the pleasure of meeting LPGA Hall of Famer Marlene Hagge recently, and in a quiet moment I said, "Marlene, let's have a look at your grip." She put her weathered hands together to form one of the prettiest sights I have ever seen.

Caddy Shacks

Why is it always called a caddie shack? You could be at a golf course in B.F. Egypt and the place where the loopers congregate would still be called the caddie shack, even in a non-English speaking country. My beef with this verbiage is that shacks are synonymous with bums and transients. Shacks are what you find next to railroad tracks, or in pitiful third-world villages. I've seen shantytowns before; maybe I should be grateful it's not called the caddie shanty.

So, this is what I am proposing. With the caddie industry gaining respectability at every level, I motion that the designated looper area, now be referred to as a caddie haven, caddie emporium, or my favorite, the caddie palace.

Caddies Consciousness

I hate it when someone introduces me and then throws in, "Larry used to be a golf caddie." It's not the caddie part of it that irritates me; I wear that label proudly. It's the term *golf caddie*. It makes us sound like butlers or something, as if the golfers have little bells they ring and their caddie comes a runnin'. The proper terminology is professional tour caddie, but through experience, I realized that the term caddie held a negative connotation. This became truly evident to me when I left the industry and got a "real" job. After getting to know my co-workers, they leveled with me and admitted that when they heard a former caddie was coming to join them, they hid all of their valuables. One of them even said she was surprised that I had a full set of teeth.

While still out on the road, I discovered that the term was counterproductive when I was in need of something, whether it be access to a clubhouse, parking lot, or extra badges to the tournament. Even when I was caddying for a big name like Chi Chi Rodriguez, I was still a caddie. Therefore, if I walked into an event office I learned to say say, "Hello. I *work for* Chi Chi Rodriguez" instead of "I'm Chi Chi's caddie." I figured they didn't need to know my full job description. Let them think I was his pilot or part of his management team. This being said, my distinguished colleagues and I spent countless hours concocting attractive and exotic, substitute denominations. Here are a few favorites:

1. Professional Yardage Technician
2. Certified Distance Calculator
3. Agronomy Cryptologist

Caddie Q & A

I fully understand that human beings are curious by nature, but getting hit with a barrage of the same questions got really old after a few years in the business. I gave serious consideration to having the following printed on some shirts; then when someone asked me one of the questions, I could just point to the correlating answer. They are so mundane that you don't even need to know the questions:

▶ Base pay and a percentage of what the pro makes.
▶ I met a tour caddie who took me under his wing.
▶ We make our own way there, usually.

- ▶ Yes, they're that good.
- ▶ It depends on who you're working for. Some want a lot of help, others just want you to get the clubs around the course.
- ▶ No, we don't get to play the courses.
- ▶ No, I do not miss it.

Aces

When I hear someone say, "He hit a hole in one," I know the person speaking doesn't know much about the game, and even less about playing it well. Here's a little bit of information to help you at least sound like a golf aficionado. If you are referring to the situation where someone deposits the golf ball into the receptacle on his first shot, say that "he holed it," or "he aced it," or "he stuffed it" or "he canned it," or even better, say that "he flew it in the jar." But under no circumstances say that he hit a hole in one. You will be exhibiting your golf ignorance.

Caddie Commercialism

I am extremely offended that every useless, trivial gadget ever invented is referred to as a caddie. The Clothes Caddie keeps your garments organized. The Shower Caddie holds your bathing condiments. The Kitchen Caddie assures that your pots won't be mingling with each other. The Office Caddie provides a tidy desk. My favorite, The Poop Caddie, assists in the retrieval of your animal's excrement. Do you see what I'm getting at here? Inventions named after other professions perform a glut of useful services. The Rug Doctor deep cleans your carpets and upholstery. The Video Professor teaches you how to use your computer to its fullest potential. The Sky Caddie is the least offensive example. It is a computerized device that provides a golfer with information like the distance to the hole and layout of the green. While this is a useful gadget, for it to be truly worthy of the label caddie, it should be able to take verbal abuse and get the clubs around the course hung over.

Golf Lingo

Did you ever notice that when a professional golfer gets interviewed after a round, how generic it sounds? If he had a low round he'll say:

- ▶ I struck the ball well today.
- ▶ I knocked it close a few times.
- ▶ I made some putts.

If he didn't score well, he'll say:

- ▶ I didn't strike the ball well today.
- ▶ I missed a lot of greens.
- ▶ I couldn't make a putt.

I realize that they're limited in how much they can say to describe a round of golf, but give us something we can sink our teeth into like, "I played like shit today because I stayed up late drinkin' and then my buddies and I went to a strip club and…"

Or, how about, "Man, I scored like dog crap because I didn't sleep well. My wife and I got in a knock-down, drag-out because she accused me of ogling a gorgeous brunette in the gallery yesterday, and while I do admit to taking a look-see, I did not ogle."

Skins Format

Stick a freaking fork in The Skins Game. It's done. The format is more worn out than a hooker after an insurance salesman convention. It was getting a little tired when they had personalities like Trevino, Zoeller and Stewart playing in it. With the guys they stick in there now, it's a real flat liner. They need to put it to rest already.

Caddies Need Gatekeepers Too

As a professional tour caddie, I got more than sick of spectators beckoning to me from outside the gallery ropes, in an attempt to have a question and answer session with me. They thought I was a mobile information kiosk whose sole purpose was to satisfy their trivial curiosities about the game and its participants. Even worse were those that wanted to tell me about a shot that they *think* they saw Chi Chi hit in '64. You knew they just drove the Cadillac down to Florida from Jersey and they'd stand there yelling, "Caddie! Caddie! Could you come over here please?" Sometimes, I'd go over there for shits-and-giggles if the time was right.

"Tell Chi Chi I saw him hit a hole in one at Doral in 1964. I was wearing blue pants and a yellow sweater. Ask him if he remembers me," they'd say.

As I wandered back to the fairway, Chi Chi would ask me, "What the hell did he want?"

"Nothing. He says he saw you make an ace at Doral in '64."

I'd barely finish my answer and he'd counter, "I didn't play Doral in '64."

I know people want to know about the inner workings of the game, and they like to share golf minutia, but during the round was not the time or place. The golf course was my office, and contrary to their beliefs, caddying was not a hobby. It was the way I made my living. Had they approached me after the round, I would have answered their inquiries until the sun went down. I might have made them buy me a beer.

Does This Really Matter?

I'm sick and tired of hearing about the Tour Qualifying School being referred to as the 5th Major… and how important it is. They always build it up like the players are going to be executed by lethal injection if they don't qualify. While I understand how important it is to *them,* in the grand scheme of things, it's really *only* important to them. I wonder what one of these guys would say if I were caddying for them and they were in a position to earn their card and before the final round, and I said to them, "Go out there and play as well as you can and let the chips fall where they may. Worst case scenario, you won't qualify and you'll just have to suck it up and get a real job like the rest of the civilized world. It may not be that bad; you might find a job you don't absolutely loathe."

Miller Time…NOT!

Is it just me, or was Johnny Miller's whiny voice more irritating than nails on a chalkboard? I know he bugged the crap out of tour players, but that's because he always managed to make inflammatory remarks that got under their skin. Oddly enough, that's what I liked about him. Just when I thought he'd made the most idiotic statement, he pleasantly surprised me. I almost miss him in the booth.

Caddie Class Wars

After being out there as long as I had been, nothing wore on me more than being treated like a second-class citizen. People looked down their noses at me because I was a caddie, like I was one rung below a used car salesman on the respectability ladder, never mind that I was making six figures a year and flying privately.

I was dating one of the golfer's daughters and I heard through the tour grapevine that one of the other player's wives made the statement, "I would *never* let my daughter date a caddie!" I cannot begin to tell you how close I was to telling her, "Oh yeah, well your daughter fell out of the ugly tree, and hit every branch on the way down! It's a bridge I don't think you'll ever have to cross!"

As a professional tour caddie, we got crap from everyone. Once, the crew and I went out for a night on the town and bumped into a couple of the journeymen players in a nightclub. They treated us like we had bad breath. We ended up chatting with a couple of girls later, who told us (after they found out we were caddies), that those golfers had told them that they weren't allowed to associate with caddies. I guess those geezers forgot that they were 50 years old, sporting pot bellies and wearing hideous polyester golf attire. The only chance they had of scoring *was* to hang out with us. Once again, I bit my tongue to keep from going over to them and saying, "I'm aware that we're not at the course, but lemme give you some caddie advice. If either of you clowns has any shot of getting laid, you'd better lose the Sans-a-Belts!"

Whose Course is it Anyway?

A huge misconception everyone has is that as tour caddies, we got to play the tournament course. Nothing could be further from the truth. If we were seen hitting a putt, or a ball on the range, we would be taking a six-week sabbatical without pay, per the Senior PGA Tour official that witnessed the infraction. That's right, you're down the road for a month and a half, just for hitting one little putt on the practice green.

The Senior PGA Tour wanted nothing to do with us when we needed something. "You're independent contractors," was the standard line used to brush us off. But the minute they saw us doing something they deemed a rules violation, it was "You're outta' here!" unless you were related to a VIP and above the law.

I fully understand that if the caddies were left to do as they pleased, it would turn into the swimming pool scene from Caddyshack, but if there were rules governing caddies, they should apply to *all* caddies, regardless of familial relationships. I can't tell you how many times I watched a pro's kid hit balls on the range and then caught hell from an official because I was in the locker room on some errand for my player.

One year, at the Senior TPC in Dearborn, Michigan, play was halted due to inclement weather. My colleagues and I were corralled like steer under a flimsy tent while the heavens unleashed a deluge. It was so flooded, I saw Noah float by in the ark and thought we were going to need a rescue chopper to get out. They did provide stale donuts for us, which was more than we got at other events. As I was trying to stay warm and dry, I just happened to peer over at the clubhouse and noticed in one of the windows, one of the pro's kids (who was caddying for his daddy) eating a steak sandwich and sucking down a cold one. When he finished, he hopped onto one of the free MCI phones that were provided for the pros to use. He looked genuinely satisfied and comfortable, God Bless him. I would have been torn a new one just for stepping foot in that locker room.

At the tournament in Atlanta, Chi Chi told me to have his golf spikes replaced by the locker room attendant, which would require going behind enemy lines. I entered the locker room, did the task, and promptly left. No harm, no foul, right? Wrong.

When I returned to the driving range with the shoes, the ever-pleasant Mike Hill gave me a rash of shit. "You were in the locker room for so long, I thought you were one of the pros." he said snidely.

"Mike, I was doing what my player asked of me!" I said in an attempt to stick up for myself.

"I don't #$@&ing care, you're not supposed to be in there for any reason." he shot back.

Chi Chi caught wind of what was going on. "What was he saying to you?" he asked.

I tried to downplay it, "Nothing, he was just giving me flack for being in the locker room."

Chi Chi became really agitated and said, "Pards, here's what I want you to do. I want you to go over there and knock 'em out!"

"What?" I returned, "You want me to do what?"

"Go down there and drop him like a bag a' dirt! Go ahead. Do it!"

"Yeah, right. I'd never work on any tour ever again." I said.

Then he really got excited, "Let 'em ban you. We'll sue 'em, and if we have to, we'll take 'em all the way to the Supreme Court."

Incidentally, Mike's son, Mike Jr., worked for his dad on a regular basis and was a fixture in the locker rooms and the pros' dining areas. And I wish I had a dollar for every ball I saw him hit on the driving ranges.

Probably the biggest regret that I have is that I didn't stand up for myself when I should have. My philosophy at the time was, don't rock the boat; just take the money and run. Looking back, I would've done things a lot differently. I guess I made a lousy Rosa Parks.

12

THEN AND NOW

CHI CHI RODRIQUEZ once quipped, "Times have really changed. I was on an airplane the other day, in first class, and there was two guys sittin' next to me kissing. I couldn't do a damn thing about it...and I couldn't smoke! What the hell is this world comin' to?"

He's right in assuming that times really have changed, and it's blatantly apparent in the world of golf.

At the grass-roots level, country club caddying is becoming a thing of the past, which is sad, because golf carts have invaded the game. It's unfortunate, because my Caddyshack days provided me with wonderful memories that I'll take to my grave. It amazes me that I live in a resort area with over 100 golf courses and there are only a handful of caddie programs in existence here. What's even more amazing is that even though everyone is riding a cart, a round of golf can take anywhere from five to six hours. It doesn't make any rational sense. The sad fact is that with caddie programs dwindling nationally, we run the risk of missing the next Hogan, Snead, Nelson or Ballesteros. Caddying was their conduit to the game.

Caddying at the professional level has evolved at a rapid pace. As you've already read, I witnessed a fair portion of this evolution during my somewhat brief tenure as a pro-jock. Bear in mind that many years prior to my entrance into the profession, caddies didn't even calculate yardage. The full extent of the club pulling process was "I like a big 6." or "Just feather a little 4 in there." I was watching a PGA Tour event recently and I could hear a caddie barking a myriad of instructions at his player, and I'm almost positive I heard him say something about dew point and barometric pressure. After regurgitating all that information, he gave the guy a golf lesson right there on the 71st hole of the tournament. I was waiting for him to pull off his caddie bib and hit the shot.

There is no doubting that just the way the golfers of today have become more proficient at playing the game, professional caddies have evolved right along with them. Any top-notch player will concur that a great caddie is worth his weight in gold, literally.

It's no big secret that the game of golf has morphed into an almost science-like sport. First, the technological advances in the equipment are absolutely staggering, from the golf ball (which allows the players of today to control launch angles and spin rates), to club metallurgy (which allows manufacturers to design and build a driver out of an alloy where the head is the size of a swollen foot and yet, lighter than a slice of bread).

The advances in agronomy have vastly altered the face of the game. The tees of today were the greens of yesterday. Watch the old Bobby Jones instructional tapes and you'll hear him talk about releasing the putter on longer putts. That was the only way to get it to the hole on a green that resembled shag carpeting.

The mode of transportation for professional golfers has also changed significantly. Chi Chi reminisced about traveling the tour in a '64 Pontiac Bonneville, and that meant sleeping in it too. But nowadays, any player in the top 125 of the PGA Tour is probably flying privately. The strides made in jet technology have made the globe a significantly smaller sphere. Gary told me that it took 48 hours of flight time to travel from the U.S. to South Africa aboard a turbo-prop years ago (not counting layovers). I shudder to think what he could have accomplished in the game if he had access to the aircraft of today.

The manner in which the players approach the game today has changed as dramatically as any other aspect. The forerunners of golf didn't work on their physical fitness one iota. As a matter of fact, they purposely deferred from any type of workout routine, believing it would cause loss of flexibility and muscle-boundness. My former employer, Gary Player, went against the grain by working out like an Olympian and becoming the first to openly stress the importance of physical fitness. The tour players of today not only work out like madmen, but their personal trainers are part of their entourages, which also might include a personal chef, flexibility expert and masseuse. These entourages also consist of swing coaches, sport psychologists and putting gurus. Having trouble with the short putts? Just give the putting master Dave Pelz a call and he'll fix you up right quick. The great Ben Hogan actually had a putting coach…his wife. I heard he was battling the yips later in his career and was griping to her about missing three-footers. You know what she told him? "If you're having trouble getting it in the hole from three feet, then I suggest you knock it closer to the hole!"

And then there's the money.

Just like every other sport, big money has contaminated the game. Let me put it into perspective for you. A while back, Fuzzy Zoeller made more money winning two Skins Games than Sam Snead made winning 84 PGA Tour events over the course of his career. Here's another one…

Jim Furyk won The Tour Championship and The FedEx Cup a couple of years ago, and the combined $11,350,000 was more than the total purse for The Senior Tour in 1988. Funny thing is, he didn't even look all that excited about it. I would have been charged with a couple of misdemeanors after I stripped naked and did laps around the 18th green if I ever saw a payday like that. I've heard the younger players of today practice with iPods stuck in their ears so they don't have to talk to each other. There's just too much money on the line these days, and golf is not a team sport. It's every man for himself. Hell, even Trevino got quiet when there was big money on the table.

Some things remain the same as my daughter is now 19 years of age and is blossoming into a gorgeous young woman. Now, more than ever, I wouldn't let her go anywhere near a caddie. I believe today's PGA Tour players are a bunch of over-indulged prima donnas who should be paying Jack Nicklaus, Gary Player and the estates of Arnold Palmer and Mark McCormick a percentage of everything they win, like the way gangsters pay 'tribute money' to the mob bosses when they pull off a score in the mafia movies. They have absolutely no concept of the sacrifice the forefathers of the game endured so they could play for the obscene amount of money they do on a weekly basis.

Throughout this book I have referred to nicknames. For whatever reason, they seem to play a prominent part in the golf industry at every level. More specifically, I talked about how appealing it was to have a good one and how detrimental it was to get shellacked with one that you wished everyone forgot. The infamous Wiz, my former partner in crime, is still walking green miles on the Champion's Tour. He's been out there for so long that he is now referred to as *The Was,* which he doesn't mind one bit. He said his former nickname always made it sound like he had a bladder problem.

Former Senior Tour player Harold Henning had the absolute preeminent and most coveted nom de guerre ever laid on any man. His alias was Horse, and no, it wasn't because he possessed a deep affinity for the four-legged animal.

Things have changed so much on the Senior Tour that when I went to an event after several years removed from caddying, I said hello to Gil Morgan's caddie Shitty, and he scolded me. He told me that no one called him by that name any more. I apologized and walked away thinking, *I'll call you whatever you like, but you'll always be Shitty.*

And finally, I am more than 20 years removed from my life as a professional tour caddie. I might be persuaded to don a caddie bib once again if I could go back to the old days of the European Tour, when the money was as lean as our needs and there was an unrivaled cast of characters, or the glory days of the Senior Tour when the pairing sheet was a Who's Who of men who poured the foundation of the sport. Oddly enough, I still have recurring dreams that I'm caddying for Chi Chi, or Gary, and they're so life-like, it's unbelievable. In one, I'm on the tee without the clubs and it's the worst feeling you can imagine. I search frantically for them, but they are nowhere to be found. I gather this is the caddie equivalent of the naked dream where you're naked in front of strangers.

I had someone ask me years ago what one becomes after being a tour caddie, and the jury is still out on that one. I am currently employed in the real estate industry, and I am so very thankful to be able to make a solid living, and provide for my family. But now, more than ever, I question my decision to leave the world of professional caddying, or not working more diligently toward getting a college degree.

Or getting in Player's will.

13

FINAL THOUGHTS

THE GLIB LEE Trevino once stated that pressure is playing for five bucks when you only have two in your pocket, and while that may be true, it's only partially true. If you lose on that bet and can't pay up, you risk losing your reputation and possibly a couple of teeth. But since leaving the world of professional caddying, I've learned that genuine pressure is trying to provide for your family at a job you absolutely despise, but are still thankful to have because it's better than joining the ranks of the unemployed. True pressure is working at a 100% commission job with nothing out for the month, knowing that the mortgage is due and your lienholder could give a flying leap about the state of the economy, or who you caddied for.

I've been on both sides of the equation, and I know what it's like to live and die with every shot. I was once brainwashed into thinking that if the game were abolished, the earth would cease to rotate, but after years away, I have come to realize what wise and balanced people already know. The grand old game of golf is in fact, just a game. Professional golfers aren't finding cures for terrible diseases or putting heinous child molesters behind bars. They are entertainers, which is a good thing, because we all need to be entertained at times. Over the last decade I have been given a perspective adjustment. My wife is an oncology nurse, and through her, I experience vicariously, the hell of the war on cancer. When she shares her day with me, I am reminded that life is short and that you have to live every day like it's your last, because someday it will be. I've also come to realize that if you're even remotely interested in golf, it's a great time to witness his prowess with club in hand, but in the grand scheme of things, it doesn't really matter if Tiger Woods wins 19 Majors.

My father passed away a few years ago, and I was very fortunate to have one last visit with him to say all the things I never had the chance, or the inclination to say. It's an opportunity many are not afforded. He was a rabid sports fan and, more specifically, a Chicago sports fan. He would have been a perfect fit for the *Saturday Night Live* skit where all the Chicago Bo hunks are sitting around yammering on about Da' Bears, Da' Bulls and Da' Cubs.

One of my sisters decorated Dad's hospital room with newspaper clippings commemorating some of the highlights of Chicago sports. There was one of Michael Jordan affectionately hugging the NBA championship trophy with tears streaming down his face, another of the Bears after they won the Super Bowl in '85, and another from the day after the White Sox clinched the World Series a handful of years ago. And then there was one that I never knew existed. It was a front-page picture from The Chicago Tribune showing Jack Nicklaus shaking hands with Chi Chi Rodriguez, taken in 1991 at The U.S. Senior Open played at Oakland Hills Country Club outside of nearby Detroit. In the background is the blurred image of yours truly. But the thing that really grabbed my attention and warmed my heart wasn't the fact that my father had kept the picture all these years. It was something he wrote underneath it. There, in my Dad's chicken-scratch writing were the words, *The three biggest names in golf: Nicklaus, Rodriguez…and Malestic.* My father never played the game, but he did follow my good fortune caddying professionally and that picture was a stark and poignant symbol of his pride.

I'll man up and admit it. At my professional zenith, I thought I was pretty cool and my ego got so big I had to avoid sharp objects. I can clearly see that now. My close friends called me on it after I left the tour. They told me I was a cocky asshole and that the only time they ever heard from me was when I was on someone's private jet, eating caviar, en route to Switzerland, or on the golf course with the Queen of England.

I'm here to tell you that times change, and the Good Lord has a constructive way of humbling us all. In the past two decades I've consumed more than my fair share of humble pie, and I have a belly full of it. But it's okay, because it's rumored that what doesn't kill you makes you stronger and I'm still kicking. I'm 59 years old and life is truly good. I am in a word, Blessed.

So there you have it. That's my story and I'm sticking to it. I was uber-fortunate to see the world and have a blast in the process. I witnessed spectacles in the game that most couldn't even fathom, and I experienced more than the 15 minutes of fame that Mr. Warhol allotted each one of us. I rubbed elbows with the true legends of the game at a time when it was about the love of the game, before it was contaminated by money. People always refer to the Golfing Gods, and while I sometimes feel like I sold my soul to the Golfing Devil, naively trading a college degree and a solid profession for a slew of unbelievable memories, there's no turning back the clock. I'll never play in The Masters, much less win it, but as a wise one once said,

"We all can't be in the parade. Someone has to line the route." I've been enlightened, and realize that my daughter Lauren is *my* Green Jacket, and my wife Lynne is *my* Claret Jug, and they complete me.

Looking back, golf always has, and always will be a part of my life, and rightfully so. I lived on Golf Road.

Printed in Great Britain
by Amazon

15269006R00192